AF386995

Erecting the Pulpit

Erecting the Pulpit

Muscular Christianity from Teddy Roosevelt to Donald Trump

Amy Laura Hall

BLOOMSBURY ACADEMIC

NEW YORK · LONDON · OXFORD · NEW DELHI · SYDNEY

BLOOMSBURY ACADEMIC
Bloomsbury Publishing Inc, 1359 Broadway, New York, NY 10018, USA
Bloomsbury Publishing Plc, 50 Bedford Square, London, WC1B 3DP, UK
Bloomsbury Publishing Ireland, 29 Earlsfort Terrace, Dublin 2, D02 AY28, Ireland

BLOOMSBURY, BLOOMSBURY ACADEMIC and the Diana logo
are trademarks of Bloomsbury Publishing Plc

First published in the United States of America 2026

Cover design by Jen Huppert
Front cover images: "Keeping Fit" / Social Welfare History Archives, University of
Minnesota Libraries and © iStoc_.com / hanohi_i

Library of Congress Cataloging-in-Publication Data

Names: Hall, Amy Laura author
Title: Erecting the pulpit : muscular Christianity from Teddy Roosevelt to
Donald Trump / Amy Laura Hall.
Description: New York : Bloomsbury Academic, 2026. | Includes
bibliographical references.
Identifiers: LCCN 2025047739 (print) | LCCN 2025047740 (ebook) | ISBN
9798216383475 HB | ISBN 9798216383499 ePDF | ISBN 9798216383482 eBook
Subjects: LCSH: Nationalism–Religious aspects–Christianity |
Nationalism–United States–History | Masculinity–Religious
aspects–Christianity | Masculinity–United States–History |
Christianity and politics–United States–History |
Evangelicalism–United States–History
Classification: LCC BR517 .H33 2026 (print) | LCC BR517 (ebook)
LC record available at https://lccn.loc.gov/2025047739
LC ebook record available at https://lccn.loc.gov/2025047740

ISBN: HB: 979-8-216-38347-5
       ePDF: 979-8-216-38349-9
      eBook: 979-8-216-38348-2

Typeset by Integra Software Services Pvt. Ltd.
Printed and bound in the United States of America

For product safety related questions contact productsafety@bloomsbury.com.

To find out more about our authors and books visit www.bloomsbury.com
and sign up for our newsletters.

The church is blamed for its indifference and praised for minding its own business, commended as an agent of social salvation and denounced as a haven for meddlers, acclaimed as a guarantor of social stability and cursed as an insidious peddler of dope.

—Yale Professor Listen Pope, *Millhands & Preachers: A Study of Gastonia* (North Carolina) (1942)

If you look at the architects of this language that leads us to "one nation under God" and "in God we trust," in their public speeches and their private correspondence, the state power that they're worried most about is not the Soviet regime in Moscow, but rather The New Deal and Fair Deal administrations in Washington, D.C.

—Historian Kevin Michael Kruse, on NPR's *Fresh Air* with Terry Gross (2015)

Carol Tisdale Hall completed her B.A. working overtime at Sears in Abilene, Texas. She completed her M.A. on Bertolt Brecht while stitching our clothes on her Singer in Denton, Texas. She followed wherever a Methodist Bishop sent my father. From Graham, Commerce, Boyd, Kyle, Austin, San Angelo, Victoria, she managed everything. She took any teaching post available within a 30-mile radius. Our family needed her income, and she loved to teach. French, American History, World History, Theater, English, she taught them all. Her favorite grade was 7th because they needed someone to help them find their locker, discover their writing skills, hone their adolescent way in the world, and stand up to bullies. On Sundays, she was a regular visitor to the older men's Sunday School class. Having worked all week beneath the regional aristocracy of petrochemical potentates, come Sunday she sought the conversations of older men she trusted. This is the book she taught me to write.

Contents

Preface

This book examines a powerful yet overlooked form of Christian Nationalism—one that fuses faith, masculinity, capitalism, and political power under the guise of moral leadership. I trace the conceit of faithful and fit male leadership through figures like Billy Graham and cultural institutions like political prayer breakfasts and modern mega-churches, noting how religious rhetoric has been wielded to sanctify power and divide communities. Drawing on firsthand experiences—from Cowboy Churches to NASCAR chaplaincies and storefront churches with folding chairs—I examine the cultural and political forces that have made evangelicalism "ambient" (Daniel Vaca's term) while consolidating wealth and influence. At a time when politicians are expected to pray in public and religious themes shape public policy, I offer a lived exploration of how faith has been strategically repackaged to sustain political and economic hierarchies.

This book began decades ago, in 1999, as my younger students at Duke asked me to understand their upbringing. Students referred to Young Life, Campus Crusade for Christ, InterVarsity, and Navigators, but I had scant interest in any of these intertwined ministries at the beginning of this research. I came to realize that some of the students aware of this network of evangelicalism had a sense of urgency about the stakes of their success (or lack of) as evaluated by people assessing them from within Duke, from peers at the school to some administrators hooked into the parachurch network. There were academic grades, of course, and various student awards, but there was also an unwritten, subterranean set of evaluations for "fitness," as some administrators put it. I knew that denominational bodies in American Protestantism could be exacting and opaque, but the rule books and the history of most denominations represented at Duke Divinity were sufficiently staid to have basic procedures for equity and accountability to which they were ostensibly held accountable. I had to learn more about these parachurch forms of mainstream evangelicalism to understand how even within mainstream Methodist churches in the Southeast and Midwest (in particular) there were, as journalist Lawrence Wright words it, pressures to bend in certain ways and to perform specific forms of piety. This was fueled in part by funding. I explain how fears about the loss of influence in mainline denominations, and a focus on the dearth of young, white men entering the mainline ministry led to steeple envy. Anxiety about institutional relevance gave entry to conservative donors eager to shift mainline Protestant seminaries to the right. I was also increasingly disturbed by the concomitant rise of neo-Calvinism and a gospel of austerity.

I begin with some basics. The term "Muscular Christianity" was coined to describe Charles Kingsley, the Anglican clergyman charged with advising Queen Victoria. In his sermons, treatises, and books for boys and young men, Kingsley wrote a version of Christianity to baptize a social form of Darwinism. I focus throughout on mainstream forms of Muscular Christianity. What do I mean by mainstream evangelicalism? Outré forms of white Protestantism—from Antlers Man at the insurrection on January 6, 2021, to the paid provocateurs at anti-mask rallies, to showcased prosperity televangelists—function as a circus side show. I do not focus on white men behaving strangely. I instead focus on the forms of evangelicalism welcome at the National Cathedral. Common to these forms of acceptable evangelicalism is a commitment to order and an endorsement of authorities in business as usual. The "gospel" in these forms of evangelicalism is masculine and muscular, but also orderly. The overall economic thrust is against labor agitation, the message for which media magnate William Randolph Hurst told his presses in 1949 to "puff Graham."

As I was completing the final edit of this book, Kevin Michael Kruse responded to yet another devastating Supreme Court ruling by posting on the social media outlet Bluesky. On July 14, 2025, at 4:07 pm Kruse wrote: "At this point, I wouldn't be surprised if the MAGA majority on the Supreme Court didn't issue a ruling that was just 'go fuck yourselves, peasants!'" This is the toxicity I am most determined to explain. Duke Chapel and Riverside Church precede the current U.S. Supreme Court by almost a century. The history of erected pulpits, bully pulpits, and oligarchs paying people to sell a version of Christianity congenial to men with power—this is a thread that connects Victoria's Anglican advisor not only to myths about the holy husbandmen of the frontier, but to the realities of "go fuck yourselves, peasants" during the Great Depression.

My position as a pro-labor, feminist, Christian scholar at a mainstream, evangelical seminary for twenty-six years allows me a unique, bridging role. I did not grow up evangelical. While thoroughly churched, I take nothing about "ambient evangelicalism" as normal. I am the only daughter of a Texas Methodist minister and his beloved. I was born in Graham, Texas in 1968. The patriarch of that church called my mother "the little hereford" when asking my father about his pregnant wife. The notion that humans are akin to grazing mammals does not strike me as odd. I was taught to judge people by how they treat farm animals and one another. The conceit that some men are suited to sort people, to determine the fitness of human "stock"—that form of hubris offends me at my core. In other words, cowboys do not bother me. Men who engage in cowboy capitalism and cowboy diplomacy, treating people supposedly beneath them, and one another, as if machinery—that form of Christianity is the villain of this story.

Acknowledgments

The *Oxford English Dictionary* (the *OED*) is the ever-expanding Periodic Table for words published in English.[1] I am grateful for the editors who continue that project. I could neither teach nor write without their help. In *Mine Eyes Have Seen the Glory*, Randall Balmer describes his book on evangelicalism as "a kind of travelogue," noting that "what began as an exploration of the variegated forms of American evangelicalism quickly turned into a personal odyssey of sorts." Balmer is not only a "student of American religious history" but also "a product of the evangelical subculture." Balmer says he "abandoned the detached and dispassionate analysis" he "had originally envisioned."[2] I am *not* "a product of the evangelical subculture." I became immersed in evangelicalism teaching at Duke. To use Balmer's imagery, this research became "a kind of travelogue" involving the institution in which I have been embedded since 1999. Thank you, evangelical people, for trusting me with your questions and insights. Your predicaments led to my decidedly attached and passionate analysis. A retired colleague in American religious history used to say, with a mixture of rue and defiance, that someone needed to write a book about the Eli Lilly Foundation's effect on theological education. He would add "and it will be the last book they publish." I am grateful for his candor. This effort follows in his wake. Early on, I was accused of writing "journalism" rather than scholarship. I am honored. True journalists are so menacing to the powers-that-be that their outlets have been gutted. Without journalists, librarians, and archivists, the truth withers. No wonder they have been underfunded and are now blatantly under attack. May the forces that erase memory, who seek to occlude the truth, diminish. May public school teachers, librarians, and journalists flourish. I am grateful for your assistance and your valor. We each matter. There are many different ways to be brave.

Introduction

What Is Muscular Christianity?

Historians attribute the term "Muscular Christianity" to an 1857 reviewer for the English periodical *Saturday Review,* who used the phrase to epitomize Victorian churchman Charles Kingsley:

> We all know by this time what is the task that Mr. Kingsley has made specially his own … fostering the love of a muscular Christianity. His ideal is a man who fears God and can walk a thousand miles in a thousand hours … breathes God's free air on God's rich earth, and at the same time can hit a woodcock, doctor a horse, and twist a poker round his fingers.[1]

The *OED* includes a reference to this term: " … concerned with or devoted to good works and social issues, as opposed to asceticism; (more generally) setting store by the moral benefits of physical exercise; energetic and outgoing … associated with the ideal of robust religious character and Christian life supposedly expressed in the writings of Charles Kingsley."[2] I first encountered Kingsley's writing referenced in eugenic tracts from the U.S. in the early twentieth century, in sermons attesting that the fittest men shall and should inherit the earth.

Why a Pulpit?

How did "Muscular Christianity" become a recipe distributed across mainstream evangelicalism? How does a phrase carry through to the U.S. in eugenics tracts, into the mid-twentieth century, to be used today as a summons?

A key ingredient is "the pulpit." Mainstream evangelicalism relies on the erecting of pulpits. The *OED* has as the first definition of the word pulpit, from 1387–1683: "A stage or platform used for public speeches … " The second definition, related to "Christian Church," begins in 1390, "A raised, enclosed platform in a church or chapel … from which (in some denominations) the officiating minister conducts the service."[3] The third definition reads, "Any of various structures which give the occupant a conspicuous or elevated position, or enable him or her to direct or address others." The pulpit involves the elevation of a preacher to speak with authority to "direct" those beneath.

The term "Bully Pulpit" combines all three. The *OED* notes the first use as in "U.S. Politics" in 1909: "A public office or position of authority that provides its occupant with the opportunity to speak out and be listened to on any issue." First known usage "by United States President Theodore Roosevelt to explain his personal view of the presidency." "He … swung round in his swivel chair, and said: 'I suppose my critics will call that preaching, but I have got such a bully pulpit!'"[4] "Muscular Christianity" involves the placement of a man in such a position that, whether a politician or a preacher, he is given the power to "preach." The "burden" of Roosevelt's speeches, as Lyman Abbott described it, is "national righteousness." Abbott wrote about Roosevelt: "His influence as a moral reformer will ever remain in the higher civic ideals and the quickened patriotic life of a great people." And regarding the "bully" part? "He is accused of being noisy … When eighty millions of people are asleep, and corruption, like the fable vampire, is fanning them into a deeper somnolence that it may suck their life blood, it requires a shout to wake them up."

What Is Mainstream Evangelicalism?

Daniel Silliman published a clarifying title in 2021: "An Evangelical is Anyone who Likes Billy Graham: Defining Evangelicalism with Carl Henry and Networks of Trust."[5] Evangelicalism "exists in networks, associations, and flows of conversations, in mailing lists, magazine subscriptions, and book distribution systems." Before I became embedded in a mainstream evangelical institution, I would have defined evangelicalism as a form of Christianity that emphasizes beliefs related to Jesus, heaven, and hell. I could have told you "Campus Crusade for Christ," a parachurch organization to recruit teenagers and college students, was evangelical from the name. "Young Life," a parachurch organization to recruit teenagers and college students, is another brand of the same effort. The words "Young" and "Life" themselves connote youth and living, not a crusade on campus. I learned their overlap through, as Silliman explains, "the networks" and "associations" of people who "like Billy Graham." Silliman elaborates: "The identity is imagined through theological claims, genealogical narratives, and common enemies, but it is organized and structured by the material realities of social connection and communication."

Kingsley served as Victoria's official religious advisor. Billy Graham became the unofficial, religious advisor to scores of U.S. leaders at the White House, crafted by money to become a symbol of manly leadership and influence, initially becoming a household name through the efforts of newspaper publisher William Randolph Hearst. A 1997 *Los Angeles Times* piece about Graham's memoir *Just as I Am* describes the publishing magnate's influence: "Evangelist Billy Graham recalls in his new book the pivotal point in his young ministry when, during a 1949 Los Angeles crusade, a two-word directive from publisher William Randolph Hearst to 'puff Graham' made him an instant celebrity nationwide." The description continues, "the sudden front-page coverage showered on Graham by Hearst newspapers in mid-October (after three weeks of little notice) was quickly matched by other newspapers and newsmagazines—literally a media circus descending on his rallies under a big tent."[6] As Elliot Berger notes, Hearst saw in Graham a tool for crushing forms of labor organizing threatening monopolies like Hearst's.[7] To "like" Billy Graham as a symbol of manly Christian leadership relates to a crusade to win capitalism for Jesus, and vice versa.

A mainstream evangelical is someone who does *not* like Jeremiah Wright, another preacher who briefly became an evangelical household name in relation to the White House. On March 13, 2008, in the middle of the primary battle between Barack Obama and Hillary Clinton for the Democratic nominee for president, ABC News reported "Obama's Pastor: God Damn America, U.S. to Blame for 9/11" with the headline: "Even Obama campaign aides concede Rev. Wright's rhetoric is 'inflammatory.'"[8] ABC News reported that they had commenced a "review of dozens of Rev. Wright's sermons, offered for sale by the church, [and] found repeated denunciations of the U.S. based on what he described as his reading of the Gospels and the treatment of black Americans." Their crew came up with this stick of dynamite: "The government gives them the drugs, builds bigger prisons, passes a three-strike law and then wants us to sing 'God Bless America.' No, no, no, God damn America, that's in the Bible for killing innocent people," he said in a 2003 sermon. "God damn America for treating our citizens as less than human. God damn America for as long as she acts like she is God and she is supreme." The ABC report continued, "In addition to damning America, he told his congregation on the Sunday after September 11, 2001 that the United States had brought on al Qaeda's attacks because of its own terrorism." They quoted from Wright's sermon on September 16, 2001: "We bombed Hiroshima, we bombed Nagasaki, and we nuked far more than the thousands in New York and the Pentagon, and we never batted an eye." The ABC report concluded by quoting Wright: "America's chickens are coming home to roost."

Jeremiah Wright had been the senior minister of Trinity United Church of Christ, the largest congregation of that mainstream denomination for decades. The church is in the Washington Heights neighborhood of Chicago, and Barack and Michelle Obama had attended the church regularly. Mainstream evangelicals do *not* like Jeremiah Wright. Wright insisted that America and God are distinguishable, that God could plausibly be on the side of people who end up in jail for taking drugs, and that God could plausibly punish the United States on behalf of people from another country. During this close primary race, Clinton strategists brilliantly linked this preacher to a Black aspirant to the White House. The preacher who was clearly the appointed chaplain to U.S. Presidents was Billy Graham, a respectable white man whose smile and *gravitas* linked Christian faith and political leadership. If elected, the news story implied, Barack Obama's chaplain would be this unpatriotic firebrand.

Consider another juxtaposition. The contrast between Billy Graham as someone mainstream evangelicals like and Jeremiah Wright as someone that mainstream evangelicals decidedly do not like also allows for a comparison between non-mainstream evangelicalism and mainstream evangelicalism.

Pat Robertson and Jerry Falwell suggested on September 13, 2001 that 9/11 was brought on by God to punish the United States for being too accepting of gay people, abortion, and the American Civil Liberties Union. They are, while evangelical, not *mainstream* evangelical. They are too weird to be mainstream. As the *Guardian* reported September 19, 2001: "What Mr. Falwell said on Thursday on The 700 Club, while chatting with the programme's host, Mr. Robertson, was this: 'What we saw on Tuesday, as terrible as it is, could be minuscule if, in fact, God continues to lift the curtain and allow the enemies of America to give us probably what we deserve.'" Pat Robertson replied: "Jerry, that's my feeling. I think we've just seen the antechamber to terror. We haven't even begun to see what they can do to the major population." Later in the segment, Fallwell elaborated, going into more detail about which groups of people were to blame for God's ire: "The abortionists have got to bear some burden for this because God will not be mocked. And when we destroy 40 million little innocent babies, we make God mad." Fallwell went on, "I really believe that the pagans, and the abortionists, and the feminists, and the gays and the lesbians who are actively trying to make that an alternative lifestyle, the ACLU, People for the American Way, all of them who have tried to secularise America, I point the finger in their face and say, 'You helped this happen.'" To which Mr. Robertson said: "I totally concur, and the problem is we have adopted that agenda at the highest levels of our government."[9]

Their conversation is instructive. They consider the possibility that 9/11 was God's wrath, but keep the core conviction that the people to blame are those who distinguish church and state—who separate God and America—"all of them who have tried to secularise America." The third definition of the word "secularise" in the *OED* connects: "To dissociate or separate from religious or spiritual concerns, to convert to material and temporal purposes; to turn (a person, his or her mind, etc.) from a religious or spiritual state to worldliness."[10] The villains are "alternative" to what Jerry Falwell and Pat Robertson assume to be mainstream, and binding these "alternative" people and organizations is the effort to separate the United States from religion, specifically white, evangelical Protestantism.

These contrasts are important to understand the difference between mainstream and culturally marginal forms of white evangelicalism, a distinction that narrows the focus onto forms of Christianity and nationalism that are fit for polite company, and the White House. Billy Graham would never have made such a televised blunder. Graham had no need to appear on Pat Robertson's "700 Club." That venue is beneath the circles of influence on which his boosters had set their sights. The *Guardian* article notes that Jerry Fallwell was brought to heel for his remarks the very next day. Fallwell apologized and recanted, retaining his invitation from the Bush administration to a presidential service held at the (Episcopal) National Cathedral in Washington D.C. Billy Graham preached.[11]

Mainstream evangelicals "like Billy Graham," dislike Jeremiah Wright, and consider Fallwell and Robertson to be gauche. And, mainstream evangelicals accept the propriety of a National Cathedral. Mainstream evangelicals grant that a "National" "Cathedral" is a reasonable place to gather representatives from across all religions and none. Construction of the Cathedral involved the placing of the cornerstone in 1907 with the blessing of President Teddy Roosevelt. The National Cathedral has hosted presidential funerals and worship services after presidential inaugurations. The Cathedral hosted a prayer service following President Donald Trump's inauguration on January 21, 2017. By presidential instruction, no one preached.[12] Billy Graham was at that point in his late 90s. The next year, after Graham's death, ABC News reported, "President Trump and First Lady Melania will travel with Vice President Mike Pence and Second Lady Karen Pence to Charlotte, North Carolina for [Billy] Graham's funeral. Trump will be the only living president to attend."[13]

Silliman explains, "Evangelicalism is given shape by who *likes* whom, who *trusts* whom, who *talks* to whom, and how people are connected. Evangelicalism is only real when people are connected. Evangelicalism is ultimately an imagined community."[14] He describes how mainstream evangelicalism in the U.S. was set up from the get-go as a network of who likes whom, who trusts whom, who is willing to talk to whom—with connections across the U.S. Regarding the founding of *Christianity Today*, in 1955, Silliman reports the effort began with two men who trusted one another. The creators "sought to create an alternative, updated form of the [fundamentalist] movement. Something more serious, more organized, and, most of all, more respectable. They branded themselves evangelical.

The word was useful because it was familiar but did not specifically name anything. Nobody was using it for anything particular." Silliman relates that L. Nelson Bell "wrote a list on the back of a prescription pad. He started with the name of the man he thought could fund the enterprise. On the top of the page, in blue ballpoint, he wrote 'Howard Pew.'" He continues "Pew was a Presbyterian and president of Sun Oil Company. Bell and Pew had begun a correspondence in 1953, sharing concerns about the liberals ruining American Presbyterianism." How to counter the "liberals ruining" mainstream Calvinism in the U.S? "Bell knew Pew had deep pockets and funded a lot of conservative causes," Silliman explains. "Bell then wrote down the name of his son-in-law, Billy Graham. Graham was, of course, too busy with his crusades to oversee a magazine, but he would serve as the face or figurehead of evangelicalism, much as [Dwight L.] Moody had embodied fundamentalism."[15]

In his 2014 article "*Christianity Today*, J. Howard Pew, and the Business of Conservative Evangelicalism" Darren E. Grem includes an image indicative of how money shapes, as Silliman puts it, ways "people are connected." In 1965, Bell wrote one of many letters to Pew. Bell tried to keep their focus on their "common enemy," the National Council of Churches, whose "support of civil rights activism, the union movement, or the welfare state" gave them common cause against the National Council of Churches. Grem describes this moment in the correspondence between supplicant (Bell) and donor (Pew): "'This letter is to be read with the above in mind,' Bell wrote on a small scrap of attached stationary. On it, Bell had sketched two stick figures, one as himself, the other as Pew." Along with the trusting and liking, there was bowing and scraping. "The Pew figure, seated with his head turned slightly up, hands on his lap, and posture stiff, overshadowed the Bell figure, who bowed prostrate, arms outstretched on the floor," Grem writes, "trying to convey a sense of respect that bordered on reverence."[16]

There is obvious overlap of mainstream Protestantism and mainstream evangelicalism in the U.S. Mainstream Protestantism has largely accepted the ideas of mainstream evangelicalism, shifting to the center, away from the priorities of the National Council of Churches in the 1960s, efforts disturbing to J. Howard Pew, L. Nelson Bell, and other people who "like Billy Graham." In this way, the architects of *Christianity Today* have succeeded in constructing "Christianity" "Today."

Mainstream Protestants have also been taught to assume church and state intertwine, and that the intertwining is salutary. People disrupting the orderly working of the state or federal government suffer the burden of proof that their activity is inspired or godly rather than delusional and dangerous. To question the propriety of a National Cathedral, this mix of church and state erected with dignity (and Indiana limestone) by the Episcopal Church, in accordance with an act of the U.S. Congress, blessed by Teddy Roosevelt and Donald Trump alike—to question this erected pulpit is to be unpatriotic and anti-Christian. The National Cathedral represents a form of Christianity and nationalism on which mainstream Protestants, whether "evangelical" or "progressive," agree. I do not.

Deciders

Another aspect of mainstream evangelicalism is a presumption of decision making and divine providence. When back on his heels from growing criticism of his Secretary of Defense Donald Rumsfeld, then President George W. Bush announced in 2006, "I'm the Decider."[17] A working assumption from within the forms of mainstream evangelicalism I cover in this book is: God works through "Deciders." Consider a 1958 cover of *Together: The Midmonth Magazine for Methodist Families.* The cover showed a white family with father at the wheel of a motorboat, cowboy hat on, mom, daughter, son, and an American flag waving behind them. A title ran: "Who Should Own the Moon?" Under that title read "In Color: The Christian Family." Part of mainstream evangelicalism in the U.S. then and now is the idea that men driving a motorboat with "the Christian Family" ought to have a say about the ownership of the moon.

There was dissent. Soon after Methodist deciders decided to produce *Together*, the *Nation* ran a review of the effort. "Slick Paper Christianity" appeared in the January 19, 1957 issue and contrasts now to the liking, trusting, and connecting that established *Christianity Today*.[18] Dan Wakefield's review does not sneer from outside but comments from within:

In the forward-looking eyes of contemporary religion … the greatest of sins is to be "out of date." … In an age accelerated by the miracle of the mass media, the most "successful" of the modern religious leaders have adopted the old slogan, "If you can't beat 'em, join 'em." … this current industrialization of Christianity has now reached another milestone with publication of a new Methodist magazine—*Together*.

Wakefield describes how *Together* depicts Christianity through one featured illustration of "Jesus." Reproducing a series of images of Jesus through the centuries, the editors of *Together* then offer one for contemporary readers. Wakefield elaborates: "finally we come to the current Christ, a curly haired, smiling fellow, who is pink of cheek and shorn of scars and sorrows … the most happy fella imaginable—and more handsome than any man who ever played the role in a Cecil B. DeMille production." In 1957, the U.S. had committed the wholesale bombing of the people of Japan twelve years earlier. Wakefield has as the last detailed examination of *Together* what he describes as "the most serious, and also the most gruesome" feature in the early issues. In "a piece, called The Hiroshima Maidens Go Home … [*Together*] tells the story of how twenty-five girls who were badly disfigured in the atomic bomb blast at Hiroshima, were taken to America by a group including Methodist Church members and given free treatment." He continues, "If that is presented to warm the hearts of Methodists, or anyone else, then the immorality of our times is so grotesque that we had all better weep for our souls."

Wakefield's review entered the world of mainstream Methodism to reveal to readers the absurdity, the grotesquery, going on. If mainstream Protestantism was marked in the U.S. in the mid-twentieth century as a people well-suited to decide who should own the moon, then those same people were also a people responsible for the decision to bomb two Japanese cities. Wakefield concluded his review calling out the hail-fellow-well-metness of Methodism, reminding people inside the Protestant sect that they were failing at the task to which they were called as "leaders":

Too many religious leaders have sought to be together with their era, and become shabby followers and imitators … they have dressed Jesus Christ in a gray flannel suit and smothered his spirit in the folds of conformity. The new slick page Christianity cheerily rises in the midst of a world, seeking answers to survival and offers an All-Methodist football team.

"Dynamite or Gospel"

Thirty years prior, the Moody Bible Institute in Chicago offered an all-evangelical anti-labor team. To explain that story requires backing up to 1885. The Moody Institute's *Record of Christian Work*, ran on the first two pages an appeal to donors with a contrast "Dynamite or Gospel."[19] The effort was built around Massachusetts-based evangelist Dwight L. Moody. Moody became as much a sensation across the U.S. and the United Kingdom as evangelist Billy Graham eventually became in the 1950s. Quoting "one of the Chicago daily papers," the *Record of Christian Work* warns readers in 1885, "we are living in a time when men are stricken down, and the assassin escapes, or if caught, not unlikely through some technicality of the law, he escapes, or his case is continued, until the cost of his trial is doubled or trebled." With donations to the Moody missions from people reading the missive, potentially "hundreds of such workers could be sent out every year into all this land, but more especially into our cities, and they could be helpers to pastors, workers and missions, street preachers, house to house visitors, and lay evangelists."

The answer to "What can we do?" leads to the decision: "Dynamite or Gospel." The authors explain that it is not merely a "sentiment, in these times" to ask the question "How shall we reach the masses?" The problem, the piece explains, is that "some of the unreached are restless." Noting a recent "parade" of Socialists in Chicago, and quoting "one speaker" who "openly proclaimed that they were the 'cut-throats of society,'" the piece goes on to name signs held by participants. "Lawlessness means equality for all." "Down with government, God and gold." "Capital represents stolen labor." Another contrast continues the appeal. Donors must consider the contrast between money lost by destruction of property during a "riot" to the cost of a "training school for Christian workers." Through "the introduction of these restless elements," "the times" called for a "strong, skillful, and wisely directed effort."[20] Parading socialists called for strong measures.

Reading Timothy E.W. Gloege's 2015 book *Guaranteed Pure: The Moody Bible Institute, Business, and the Making of Modern Evangelicalism*, I was struck by a poster he includes. It is a visual representation of the textual appeal in the 1885 *Record of Christian Work*. The version reprinted here is from the May 1920 issue of the Moody Bible Institute of Chicago Bulletin.

The poster begins "The Moody Bible Institute of Chicago Bulletin" and announces in all capital letters: "THE ANSWER TO LABOR UNREST." Gloege explains that the Bulletin was a request to donors for the Institute, appealing to their interest in such forms of missionizing as described by the writers for the "Dynamite or Gospel" warning/appeal in the *Record of Christian Work*. The viewer is advised: "Study this picture of representatives of different nationalities in the student body of the Moody Bible Institute of Chicago."[21] At the bottom of the poster runs a continuation of the plea in bold lettering: "Labor unions have their paid agitators constantly busy among the workers. We appeal for your support in our work of training 'agitators' for righteousness." The image features twenty-six men standing on the steps of the entrance to the Moody Bible Institute lecture hall and business offices. The men are numbered one through twenty-six. Underneath the photograph runs this description: "Out of this real American 'melting pot' come 'walking delegates' who are 'agitators' for the gospel of Jesus Christ, which makes men of whatever class or nationality upright, industrious, and peaceable, whether educated or uneducated." These men are presented as the answer to the question "Dynamite or Gospel." They are the answer to divisions of every kind. They are in the pot through which differences are melted. And, as delegates walking around the greater Chicago area, and soon the world, they offer a solvent, using their specific qualifications to render inhabitants as hard working and "peaceable."

The term "melting pot" had only been recently coined and popularized.[22] The *OED* gives origination from 1909 to Israel Zangwill (1864–1926) who wrote a play first produced in 1908 in the U.S. entitled "The Melting Pot." A 2017 production of the play runs the same quotation: "God's Crucible, the great Melting Pot where all the races of Europe are melting and reforming!"[23] In putting this phrase at the beginning of their description of the effort, the creators of the 1920 poster connect words made popular through the production of the play and press coverage during the beginning of the twentieth century.

The Moody Bible Institute of Chicago Bulletin

THE ANSWER TO LABOR UNREST

Study this picture of representatives of different nationalities in the student body of THE MOODY BIBLE INSTITUTE OF CHICAGO

OUT of this real American "Melting Pot" come "walking delegates" who are "agitators" for the gospel of Jesus Christ, which makes men of whatever class or nationality upright, industrious and peaceable, whether educated or uneducated. Men and women of many nations, and of nearly all religious denominations, are fused into one spirit and aim in The Moody Bible Institute. The Day Classes are held in the forenoons chiefly. Afternoons, week nights and Sundays the students evangelize by teaching, preaching, house to house and hospital visitation, shop meetings, open air meetings, etc., (save as employed in working their way). Note the brief significant facts concerning the men in the picture, given below:

1. PORTO RICAN

F. B. Colon, age 25. Preaches Sunday afternoons to Mexican track and round-house men on South-West side, employed by the Santa Fe Railway Co., and does house-to-house visitation in their homes; also holds a class in English for them Friday evenings. Is training for work among Spanish-speaking people.

2. IRISH

S. G. McGuigan, 42. For many years an infidel, radical agitator among workmen of Pacific Coast cities. Now soundly converted, preaches in the missions, and is training to evangelize men of his class.

3. AMERICAN-BOHEMIAN

Frank R. Filek, 20. Deceased, April 11, 1920.

4. SWEDISH

Harold L. Lundquist, 25. University of Minnesota graduate. Abandoned law practice in Minneapolis to train for the ministry. Preaches in jails, missions and churches.

5. ENGLISH

Harry G. Briault, 29. In U. S. secret service during the war. Visits jails and hospitals and teaches Bible class at Mayfair.

6. CZECHO-SLOVAK BOHEMIAN

Frank J. Bedlik, 23. Superintends Sunday School of First Bohemian Baptist Church, teaches Sunday School class and holds open-air meetings. Preparing for life work among Bohemians.

7. SCOTCH

L. D. Ballingall, 39. Has been dry goods buyer for foremost department stores of Montreal, Toronto and Detroit. Is training for the ministry. Preaches in Christ Congregational Church, teaches a Bible class and also a teacher training class.

8. ASSYRIAN

P. O. Daniels, 26. Attended Presbyterian Mission College in Urumia, Persia. Preaches at Carter Memorial Assyrian Chapel; leads their young people's meetings and Saturday afternoon choir; teaches Sunday School class and does visitation work. Was in the army.

9. SOUTH AFRICAN

Alfred P. Gibbs (English descent), 30. Preached in spare time for six years at Johannesburg to natives employed in the mines; also to South African troops during the war. Teaches two Bible classes, conducts gospel meetings and gives stereopticon lectures on Bunyan's "Pilgrim's Progress." Preparing for the ministry.

10. RUSSIAN JEW

Moses Gitlin, 24, from near Odessa. Speaks Russian, Hebrew, Yiddish and English. Holds class in English for Russians at Marcy Center five nights a week, and a gospel service Saturday evenings. Preaches to Jews on West Side Sunday nights; speaks and sings at Russian service, West Division Institute, Sunday afternoons. Training for work among Russians.

11. ITALIAN

Michael Maletta, 22. Does open-air gospel work among Italians in "Little Hell"; teaches a large class of Italian young people in Moody Italian Mission, of which he is assistant superintendent. Also superintends Italian Sunday School of the Trinity Reformed Church. Training for work among Italians.

12. CANADIAN

J. R. Stephenson, 29. Fifth of his family to train in the Institute. Does visitation, evangelistic and Sunday School work. Preparing for ministry.

13. DUTCH

Bert Sprik, 29. Owns a farm in Michigan and has worked in lumber woods. Conducts mission and a Sunday School in West Side Italian district, and does house-to-house visitation. Training for work in rural districts or lumber camps.

14. CANADIAN

Norman W. Taylor, 25. College man, lieutenant and then captain in Canadian Air Service in France during the war. Dubbed "Horseshoe Taylor" by comrades because of many narrow escapes. On one occasion, after encounter with enemy squadron, returned unhurt, with his pilot, with seventy-two bullet holes through plane and their clothing. Shot down three times, landed safely and got away. Teaches Bible class, superintends a Sunday School and leads an evangelistic group. Preparing for ministry.

15. RUSSIAN

Stephen Shepul, 28, from Grodno, six years in America. Working among Russians. Opened a mission in Argo, Ill., in which eleven Russians were converted. Preaches to Russians Sunday afternoons at West Division Institute, Sunday nights at Russian Evangelical Mission, Fourteenth and Halsted Sts., and Saturday nights at Marcy Center. Visits house-to-house among Russians nearly every night and distributes tracts for Chicago Tract Society. His family was recently re-united in Grodno. One brother returned from German prison camp totally incapacitated for work; a sister returned from Austria where she had been imprisoned for two years; another sister returned from Siberia, where she had fled to escape the Germans, and another brother had just returned from service under General Yudenitch.

16 and 17. NORWEGIAN

Oscar S. Waltzin, 22. Evangelizing in jails and churches and by tract distribution. Preparing for foreign missionary work.

Bernhart Ram, 28. In U. S. 10 years. Serving as pastor of Emmaus Evangelical Free Church (Norwegian). Preaches Sunday night, superintends the Sunday School, leads young people's meetings, and does house-to-house visitation. Is preparing for the ministry.

18. FRENCH

S. E. Bernhardt, 20. Converted under Paul Rader. Does house-to-house visitation, conducts young people's meetings, distributes tracts, etc.

19. AMERICAN NEGRO

Tuliver Chinam, 42. Had a grocery at Memphis. Training for work among negroes. Now assistant pastor at Calvary Baptist Church; also holds open air meetings.

20. SYRIAN

Albert C. Hakim, 26, from Homs, a day's journey from Damascus. Attended mission school in Homs. Converted through Salvation Army in New York. Gave up large business prospects for Christian work. Preaches in churches, open-air and factory meetings and missions. Training to be an evangelist.

21. JAPANESE

K. Hirakawa, 52. In Seattle about twenty-seven years. Converted fifteen years ago. Taught ten years in Japanese Sunday School. Preparing for work as pastor of Japanese church on Coast.

22. FINNISH

Yrjo Nummi, 31. Had four and one-half years in Helsingfors University. High school teacher. Worked seven years as assistant pastor of Finnish Seamen's Mission, New York City. Preaches Thursday and Sunday nights to Finnish congregation on North Side, visits from house to house, and holds neighborhood meetings for Finnish families. Preparing for foreign missionary work.

23. ARMENIAN

Louis J. Yelanjian, 23. Joined his father in America shortly before the war. His grandparents, mother, two brothers and a sister were deported by the Turks from Angora to Aleppo, seventy days on foot, and all perished from abuse, starvation and disease. Preaches and sings in missions, and at U. S. Machine Shop noon meetings. Preparing for foreign missionary work.

24. GERMAN-BOHEMIAN

A. Stury, 25. German high school education, also took agricultural course at University of Wisconsin. Visits jails and factories, plays violin in orchestral group, and distributes tracts. Preparing for foreign missionary work.

25. GERMAN

J. J. Berner, 30. In U. S. fifteen years, served in army medical corps overseas, and taught Bible classes in the army. Works in Chicago Hebrew Mission, in jail meetings and in hospitals. Preparing to return to Germany to preach the gospel.

26. AMERICAN

Toward Laraine, 24. Clerk in Navy Yard at Philadelphia during the war. Preparing for foreign missionary work.

Labor unions have their paid agitators constantly busy among the workers. We appeal for your support in our work of training "agitators" for righteousness.

The Moody Bible Institute of Chicago Bulletin is published monthly by The Moody Bible Institute, at 153 Institute Place, Chicago, Ill. This is the May issue, 1920, Volume 6, Number 5. Entered January 30, 1915, as second class matter at the Post Office at Chicago, Ill. under Act of August 24, 1912. Acceptance for mailing at the special rate of postage provided for in section 1103, Act of October 3, 1917, authorized on June 18, 1918.

Figure 0.1 *May 1920 issue of the Moody Bible Institute of Chicago Bulletin. Credit: Moody Bible Institute Archives. Used with permission.*

Teddy Roosevelt had attended the opening night in Washington, D.C.[24] This connection to a smash hit play about "God's Crucible" is brilliant marketing. "The gospel" is the most effective liquefier to render each particular man, in his own race and ethnicity, useful for an effort to counter "agitators" for "labor unions."

The details included continue this message:

"Porto Rican [sic], F. B. Colon, age 25. Preaches Sunday afternoons to Mexican track and round-house men on South-West side employed by the Santa Fe railway company, and does house to house visitation in their homes; also holds a class in English for them Friday evenings. Is training for work among Spanish speaking people."[25]

"South African, Alfred P. Gibbs, English dissent, 30. Preached in spare time for six years at Johannesburg to natives employed in the mines; also to South African troops during the war. Teaches two Bible classes, conducts, gospel meetings, and gives stereopticon lectures on Bunyan's *Pilgrims Progress*."

"Russian Jew, Moses Gitlin, 24 from near Odessa. Speaks Russian, Hebrew, Yiddish, and English. Holds class in English for Russians at Marcy Center five nights a week, and a gospel service Saturday evenings. Preaches to Jews on West Side Sunday night; speaks and sings at Russian service, West Division Institute, Sunday afternoons. Training for work among Russians."

Also listed are men labeled: "English," "Czecho-Slovak Bohemian," "Scotch," "Italian," "Canadian Dutch," "Canadian Russian," 2 "Norwegian" men ages 22 and 28, "French," "American Negro," "Japanese," "Finnish," "Armenian," "German Bohemian," "Syrian," and, finally, at number twenty-six "American."

Mr. Gibbs worked in South Africa with "natives employed in the mines." This reads as a subtle suggestion that he has worked before with men who were, on another continent, contending for their rights. The specification that one of the twenty-six men is a "Russian Jew" who is fluent in "Russian, Hebrew, Yiddish, and English" and "preaches to Jews" reads as reassurance every base is covered, including that of converting Jewish people to "the gospel."

The labor movement was in full swing during these decades. Railroad industry workers had begun the Pullman strike in the Chicago area in 1894. The effort crossed between labor sectors, with men and women, boys and girls, working on machines and working on transported textiles. The conditions of work in "Pullman" were bleak—a town built by the owners of the factory and ruled with no semblance of democracy. The 1894 strike spread across the country, even to "cowboy" country. In *Capitalism on the Frontier: Billings and the Yellowstone Valley in the Nineteenth Century*, Carroll Van West draws on primary documents from Billings, Montana, showing how support for the strike divided along predictable lines. "Stock raisers were especially antistrike, whereas the small farmers … supported the union." West reports "on the first Sunday of the strike, the local Methodist minister and union supporter J. W. Jennings compared the Pullman boycott to the Boston Tea Party of the American Revolution." Pastor Jennings "chastised both the state and the national Democratic party for abandoning 'the faith of the Jacksonian fathers.'" Rather than defending "the rights of the people against aggression and oppressive corporations," "party leaders were 'the pliant tools of the codfish monied aristocracy who seek to dominate this country.'"[26]

The marketing of a peaceable "gospel," bringing order to educated and non-educated, connects with later efforts. "Conservative Christianity" as some might call it, is often better interpreted using the term "reactionary." If a mainstream evangelical is someone who "likes Billy Graham," again to borrow Daniel Silliman's title, it is true that many efforts now considered "conservative" Christian were, in context, not conserving something traditional but reacting to disruption in a temporary and/or recently established status quo. This poster, cowboy mythologies about the "West," the faux traditional grandeur of Duke Chapel and Riverside Church, the use of "Aristotle" and "Virtue" at a Tyson Chicken plant in 2010—all of these are part of efforts to link "the gospel" in the U.S. to structures of power. In industrial era Chicago, the effort was bluntly to "conserve" the configuration of power and money that was only a minute old in the scope of things. The city of Chicago was formally named a city in 1837.

The *Encyclopedia of Chicago*, an effort of the Chicago History Museum, the Newberry Library, and Northwestern University gives readers this summary of the period during which the idea of "Dynamite or Gospel" is spread. Labor historian James R. Barrett narrates that "[t]he 'Great Upheaval' of the mid-1880s brought a dramatic expansion of unionism among virtually all occupations, including craftsmen." The effort crossed gender, language, and political lines, Barrett explains, "[w]orking together, the radical Central Labor Union's German and Bohemian socialists and anarcho-syndicalists, the immigrant and native-born craftsmen in the mainstream Trades and Labor Assembly, and the Knights created perhaps the strongest and most radical movement in the United States."[27] The form of "the gospel" to be disseminated by the men in the poster was not an inevitability. Some people, when looking at a document like this poster, will say "consider the time." Yes. Consider the time. The context offers stories of otherwise, including Pastor J.W. Jennings in Billings, Montana. In another detail on the poster, patrons are told: "Irish, S. G. McGuigan, 42 For many years an infidel, radical agitator among workmen of Pacific coast cities. Now soundly converted, preaches in the missions, and is training to evangelize men of his class." These men, touted as foot-soldiers for the Moody training efforts, may not have been as unidirectional in their ministry as advertised. The same complexity of immigration history that could lead Pastor McGuigan to leave his work as a "radical agitator" renders it open to imagination that some would be privy to and persuaded by the work of radical solidarity going on in labor efforts across cities in the U.S.

Where Am I?

Billy Graham was born and raised in Charlotte, North Carolina. When it came time to designate a church to which he would attach his official membership in 1950, Graham designated First Baptist Church in Dallas, Texas.[28] I had no idea where Billy Graham was from or where he had attached his church membership when I started this research two decades ago. But Dallas makes sense. Money, God, Oil. These were in a movie my mother made sure I watched when it came on Channel 11 out of the Texas Metroplex. The 1956 movie *Giant* is a film adaptation of Edna Ferber's 1952 novel. As Rock Hudson drives Elizabeth Taylor west of the 98th, Taylor looks with increasing distress out on the red, flat terrain. My mother always commented, "She's thinking, how did I land on Mars."

I did not know where I was going when I signed my Duke contract. My first year teaching I made an inadvertent, instructive blunder. I said something along the lines of "if you grow up white in America, you grow up racist." It was a "that thing we all know" comment. Some of the white students were incensed, and I was confounded. A student who had grown up in the South told me: "You just told all of them that they are trailer trash. Only *poor* white people in the South are racist." Relating this to Lauren Winner, a North Carolinian, she recommended I read a 1949 series of essays called *Killers of the Dream* by Lillian Smith. MaryBe McMillan, another North Carolinian and leader in the AFL-CIO, recommended I read Liston Pope's Yale dissertation and 1942 book *Millhands and Preachers: A Study of Gastonia* (North Carolina).[29] Both North Carolinian women helped me understand the land of brand Billy Graham.

Liston Pope's study of the form of preaching in the mill town of Gastonia is a microhistory of one county, noting the precipitous rise of industrial mills in the region and the financing of churches on mill town property by mill owners. Pope documents a shift from churches to which mill workers would travel outside their immediate vicinity to churches where the congregations were economically homogenous—meaning, they all worked as or were somehow related to laborers at the mill. *Millhands and Preachers* could have been titled: "Millowners and their Hired Preachers." Pope explains that around the turn of the twentieth century, "emerging social stratification began to become manifest in the building of separate churches for the industrial workers." Specifying a difference among three categories of churches in the county, mill churches were different than "rural" churches not on mill property, and uptown churches in Gastonia proper. "Twice as many mill churches were organized in the first decade of this century as between 1880 and 1900, while the number of new rural and uptown churches declined sharply."[30]

It had only been a decade before Pope's book went to press, in 1929, that Ella May Wiggins had been shot and killed for her leadership of the Loray Mill Strike in Gastonia. Patrick Huber, writing for the journal *Southern Cultures* in 2009, puts it bluntly. Ella May Wiggins "was silenced by a mill thug's bullet on September 14, 1929." He also notes: "Unlike the other white millhands at the plant in which she worked, she chose to live in a wooden shack in Stumptown, an African American hamlet on the outskirts of Bessemer City, rather than rent a company-owned house in the mill village."[31] The history about the history says much. One detail often reported to this day is that the Loray Mill was a "Yankee" mill, financed in 1900 by money outside of the South by investors eager to exploit out-of-work farmers and sharecroppers, and people from Appalachia desperate for money to feed their families. All of this is true.[32] Union organizing at this mill, the National Textile Workers Union, was also Communist, as in, actually Communist. Communist periodicals at the time showcased the strike as a crucial test for organizing in the South. This allowed for a narrative at the time, and one that continues, blaming "outside agitators" for the courageous uprising for labor rights that crisscrossed gender lines and scandalized the church ladies and gentlemen. Such a lack of civility and of proper amiability could only be caused by Yankees and Communists![33] Liston Pope's chapter "Expulsion of the Communists" details the coverage of arrests: "The reign of terror continued in Gaston County for about ten days. Freedom of assemblage was suppressed." Besides Wiggins, "another organizer was kidnapped and taken into South Carolina, where he was beaten and warned not to return to Gaston County … Not until September 20, when the union suspended all activities in the county, did the wave of violence end."[34]

Union organizers from North Carolina relate that this period continues to reverberate in communities whose relatives were part of such efforts. The story of the 1929 uprising and the "wave of violence" that followed serves as a warning, a form of shame on shame. People had been brave together, and then they had been subject to brutal retaliation. Then there was a passing on, a refusal to face what had happened between good church people of one class and church-going people of a lower class. In the case of Wiggins alone, as Pope explains: "Though the murder had been committed in daylight, with at least fifty persons present, no conviction was ever secured."

The second of the three sections of Pope's book is entitled: "Modes of Control," with quotations from mill town pastors and preachers and Pope's interpretation of their negotiation as industry embedded chaplains.[35] He explains in summary form a set of ideas and emphases shared by many of the mill town preachers: "There is much emphasis on the saving power of 'the blood of Jesus,' and continual admonition to follow the 'Jesus way.'" This, Pope suggests, leaves material conditions unaddressed. "There is almost never any direct application of these admonitions to practical problems of economic life; when it is made, references to such virtues as kindliness, forgiveness, and honesty comprise the net result."[36]

Lillian Smith explained race, sex, and labor disorganizing in her 1949 essay for *Killers of the Dream*, "Two Men and a Bargain." Her analysis of the South highlights the obvious, because these things are blatantly intertwined here. John C. Inscoe begins his entry on Lillian Smith's *Killers of the Dream*, for *The New Georgia Encyclopedia*: "No southerner was more outspoken in expressing moral indignation about the region's injustices and inequities during the pre–civil rights era than the writer Lillian Smith." "First published in 1949, and revised and expanded in 1961," Inscoe calls the book "the most influential and enduring of the many writings this self-described 'tortured southern liberal' produced over her three-decade career."[37] "Two Men and a Bargain" is a "parable," a grim fairy tale explaining "the lessons" of the South. Inscoe states: "she illustrates the conscious conspiracy between Mr. Rich White and Mr. Poor White to subjugate Blacks economically by shutting them out of lowly employment opportunities, thus allowing a fuller exploitation of a poor white labor force—who were grateful not to have to compete with Blacks for jobs."[38] "Once upon a time, down South, Mr. Rich White made a bargain with Mr. Poor White," Smith writes.

> He studied about it a long time before he made it, for it had to be a bargain Mr. Poor White would want to keep forever. It's not easy to make a bargain another man will want to keep forever, and Mr. Rich White knew this. So he looked around for something to put in it that Mr. Poor White would never want to take out.

She explains how white men who owned land and factories in the South made a bargain with white men who worked on land and, in a town like Gastonia, in factories, reinforcing compliance through anxiety about their capacity to provide for their families, using segregation and the threat of terror if they crossed over to organize with African American men. Through shame about the arrangement, industrialists silenced dissent. Preachers in mill towns preached "the gospel" of hard work and, to use Pope's summary, "kindliness, forgiveness, and honesty" to stymie solidarity and agitation for justice.

Fathers Know Best?

There is a strand of mainstream evangelical culture that has extended the logic of the 1965 Moynihan Report to all families in the U.S. President Lyndon B. Johnson's administration determined to take on the problem of poverty in African American communities across the country. "The Negro Family: The Case For National Action," written by then Assistant Secretary of Labor Daniel Patrick Moynihan made the news and served as a quick and handy explanation for the fact that African American men were far more likely to be incarcerated than white men, that African American men made far less for identical jobs than white men, and a myriad of other glaring disparities. The report's "finding" was nifty, in that "the problem" diagnosed was in fact about race, and about the original sin of slavery, but not about a system of dehumanizing exploitation at the workplace. The solution involved shoring up the nuclear family and reinforcing a norm of "Father Knows Best." Poverty in African American neighborhoods was due to emasculating women, the explanation went. That was the serviceable, bumper-sticker version of the report.

Muscular Christianity within evangelicalism—mainline to hard right—has had key words in common: "crisis," "leadership," "gravitas," "brotherhood," "measure," "fight," "passivity," "impact," and "feminized." When I began this project, I had no idea we were headed again toward a decade of "Make America Great Again" and that *Atlantic* magazine would be waxing nostalgic for Ronald Reagan. When students first brought me John Eldredge's *Wild at Heart* (2001) an evangelical call to restore the fundamental distinction between what is manly and what is womanly, I tried to reckon the book's mind-blowing popularity. At the turn of the twenty-first century, traditionally male jobs in North Carolina were being shipped elsewhere. Many jobs that remained were in an underpaid service sector or in marketing firms. With a high-school degree, you might find work at Arby's; a college degree might secure you a job crunching data on women's scent preferences for Procter and Gamble. A few months after *Wild at Heart* came out, thought-leaders began to use 9/11 as a summons to restore the nation's virility. As Susan Faludi writes in her 2007 book *The Terror Dream: Fear and Fantasy in Post-9/11 America,* mainstream commentators in the months after 9/11 churned out stories of men and women "cocooning" (her term) and surrounded the viewing public with images of uncomplicated, heroic "manhood" and vulnerable "womanhood," a mix of princess movies and Eisenhower-era automobile advertisements.[39] Eldredge's webpage today reads: "Wild at Heart. Love God. Live Free," with options "Real Men," "Captivating Women," "Jesus Really," "The Larger Story," and "Prayer that Works." His brand's schtick goes that boys are inherently wild, mostly in a good way, but need taming by a woman sufficiently "captivating" such to entice him to stay closer to home—Jesus plus Walt Disney's 1955 *Lady and the Tramp*.

Billy Mauldin is the President and CEO of Motor Racing Outreach, a ministry connected to racing, from motorcycles to motorboats to NASCAR. Pastor Mauldin asked me in the middle of a long day at their headquarters in Charlotte, North Carolina, to recommend a Christian book for single dads. He explained that there is a need in the communities served by their chaplains for resources about how to raise children well in a household without a mother. It was an "Aha!" moment for us both. I could not think of one single Christian author or speaker who had addressed single fatherhood as a viable endeavor. Period. I ended up recommending a situation comedy that ran on ABC from 1987–1995, about a widower and his daughters: *Full House*.[40] The idea that a Christian man could parent children alone, and do so well, blurs lines of work and manliness. A wholesome single father is an oxymoron within evangelical publishing. This is the flip side of the notion that a man's worth is defined by his wage-earning work to provide for his wife and their children.

1

Fitness

The cattle range is represented as a Social Darwinian laboratory, perfect for testing hypotheses about human nature. The lawlessness and opportunities for gain offered by the Frontier are invitations to all sorts of ambition, both industrious and criminal.

RICHARD SLOTKIN IN *GUNFIGHTER NATION: THE MYTH OF THE FRONTIER IN TWENTIETH-CENTURY AMERICA* (1998)[1]

"It Is the BRITISH WAY!"

A scene from the 1992 film *The Muppet Christmas Carol* has sustained every edit of this chapter. How do I explain why a Victorian churchman helps to explain both Teddy Roosevelt and Donald Trump? The version of Charles Dickens's ghost story that my grown daughters know best was created by the Henson family, directed by Brian Henson, son of puppeteers Jane and Jim Henson. The relevant scene reads:

Sam the Eagle to Young Scrooge: "Tomorrow, you become a man of business!"

Young Scrooge to Sam the Eagle: "I'm looking forward to it, Headmaster."

Sam the Eagle: "Mm, you will love business. It is the AMERICAN WAY!"

Gonzo to Sam the Eagle: "Uh, Sam?" [He whispers in Sam's ear]

Gonzo, whispering: "It's just that the story takes place in *England*."

Sam the Eagle: "Oh … It is the BRITISH WAY!"

Young Scrooge: "Yes, Headmaster."[2]

Charles Dickens's *A Christmas Carol* traveled across the ocean, carrying a message contrary to ruthless business for profit. Charles Kingsley's writings also traveled from England to the U.S. The "BRITISH WAY" became the "AMERICAN WAY" in the appraisal of all things both manly and business, and Christian.

My first acquaintance with Charles Kingsley, Church of England Canon and friend of Charles Darwin, emerged from research on the eugenics movement in the U.S. When I explained to people involved in ministries about which I was writing that "Muscular Christianity" is a term created to describe Kingsley, most people nodded politely while walking away. The descriptors—Eugenics, England, Queen Victoria, Darwin, Fitter Men—seemed arcane and inapplicable. There were exceptions. At a Motor Racing Outreach event in Charlotte, North Carolina, a woman who had listened to this history explained as standard practice catheterization before racing a stint that would require stamina (hydration) and wheels on the ground (no toilet breaks). She stressed that the muscle car industry could also be intimately emasculating.

In *Westerns: A Women's History*, Victoria Lamont notes the difference between roles played by characters in "Western" fiction who worked hands-on with livestock and characters representing people who provided the money. In myths about "the West," as early as Emma Ghent Curtis's *The Administratrix* (1889) and Owen Wister's *The Virginian* (1902) struggles over ownership of cows, access to water, where fences were allowed, who paid whom for what, and who had the authority to hang whom and how (and how quickly) were up front and basic. Teddy Roosevelt's Harvard schoolmate is credited with the first "Western" or "Cowboy" novel. Few know Emma Ghent Curtis, the populist-agrarian suffragette who wrote about a woman dressing in her husband's clothes to save their land. This says much about the stakes in Americana regarding the power and allure in these myths of fitness on the frontier. Lamont writes: "In cowboy fiction, the western cattle range became a mythic space in which ideological struggle between labor and capital played out, its outcome carrying the weight of natural law."[3]

Richard Slotkin's words about the West as laboratory, and "the weight of natural law," both involve Social Darwinism. The *OED* gives the earliest usage as 1877, around the time when "Muscular Christianity" was the British/American

Way of Business: "The theory that societies, classes, and races are subject to and a product of Darwinian laws of natural selection. Often used to justify political conservatism, imperialism, and racism."[4] When Protestant preachers sought to win sermon contests organized by the American Eugenics Society in the first decades of the twentieth century, they turned to a combination of Social Darwinism and a reading of the bible to describe the divinely planned triumph of men achieving success.[5] A Protestant ethic of work, a sense that the good of a man is his worldly success, and the idea that the best men come out on top is integral to Muscular Christianity.

How the West was actually "won" was brutally. An obvious, initial question within Muscular Christianity is: Why not nihilism? Why not violent nihilism? Given Social Darwinism and the actual history of Western expansion in the U.S. why not commend two Western genre films that came out the same year—*No Country for Old Men* and *There Will Be Blood*? Why not create a Sunday School series about those men? Both films were released in 2007, in the middle of two U.S. wars. Both storylines follow men in no-holds-barred fights for their own survival in 1980 southwest Texas drug wars (*No Country for Old Men*) and in early twentieth-century southern California oil wars (*There Will Be Blood*). Given the realism of each film's chaotic, anomic violence in each region and period, why not take on the perspective offered by the compelling character of Anton Chigurh from *No Country for Old Men*, who, caught as a mercenary in a feud over millions, tosses a coin to determine life or death? I put this question in the extreme to emphasize the strangeness of mixing Christianity and the "Social Darwinian laboratory" of the West. The watered down, simplified "Darwinian" idea that a species thrives on competition makes "love one another" seem unnatural. When combined with the genocidal reality that was "the West," the mixture is macabre.

No Country for Old Men is based on Cormac McCarthy's 2005 novel of the same name. When Cormac McCarthy died in 2023, the allure of nihilism came back up in tributes. The *New York Times* ran his obituary as "Cormac McCarthy, Novelist of a Darker America, Is Dead at 89." The author notes that McCarthy's novels wrote a "bleak world of violence and outsiders."[6] Greg Grandin wrote an extended close reading of McCarthy's words for the *Nation* under the title "Cormac McCarthy's Unforgiving Parables of American

Empire."[7] Grandin concludes his review: "McCarthy demonstrated how the frontier wasn't an incubator of democratic equality but a place of unrelenting pain, cruelty, and suffering. He rubbed away the veneer of Manifest Destiny, revealing US nationalism and empire to be nothing but the right of conquest updated for the democratic age."

Grandin then answers the question inside of the reality of "the West" with a rare (for Grandin) appeal to the "we" of his readership: "We should … resist McCarthy's punishing gnostic nihilism, and a pessimism that can only result in moral idiocy, in circle dances that go nowhere … where existence is original sin and the racial terror inherent in empire building, and the land grubbing that comes with it, is but part of the sublime." What Grandin means by "punishing gnostic nihilism" is the notion that there is a special form of knowledge, or *gnosis*, that comes from experiencing life, or "existence" as violently absurd. By "sublime," Grandin addresses the idea that, through knowledge wrought from killing, a person may be elevated or levitated psychically elsewhere than merely here, and touch that which is to be revered.[8] Grandin's words sound as practical wisdom, and a caution.

In an essay entitled "Giopiety," for the collection *West of 98: Living and Writing in the New American West*, Jim Harrison wrote a statement to read alongside Grandin's appeal. Harrison is best known as the author of the stories on which the 1994 movie *Legends of the Fall* was based. Harrison offers a way out of the "punishing gnostic nihilism," the "circle dances that go nowhere" with a call for "honest reparations": "the dominant responsibility of the West would be to finally totally admit what we did to our first citizens as a rag-tag invading army of soldiers and settlers." He calls this "the true ghost in our immense closet" and tells readers that "reparations are in order to honor the long nightmare of millions who did not ask to be born on the routes of our conquest." The volume is about writing embedded in "The New American West," and Harrison warns that, without this reckoning, there is little "justifiable sense of belonging where we are."[9]

This question of fitness and a form of "the gospel" that refuses brutality as sublime is part of the story of manliness and American mainstream evangelicalism. This was the worry over the closing of the West as a space for wild, manly experimentation and testing of will at the turn of the nineteenth to the twentieth century during the days of Teddy Roosevelt. As Social Darwinism became the basic, common sense understanding of how nature itself worked, how could a Christian justify solidarity, equality, charity? These are some of the fissures within Christian progressivism in the early twentieth century, and they continue in churches and parachurch organizations into the era of Donald Trump.

"Keeping Fit"

About the time that actual cowboys on the Western frontier were trying to find factory work in Chicago or a spot mining in California, the Young Men's Christian Association intended to secure a future for young white men in the U.S. so the industrializing nation could progress. A YMCA poster series from the early twentieth century promoted fitness using photographs of children disfigured by venereal disease and warnings against gambling bookies, along with lessons about fit reproduction for the sake of "the race." The cover of this book features the image on the opening poster of the 1919 series.

The series "Keeping Fit," is part of the Social Welfare History Archives, "a 48-poster series produced by the U.S. Public Health Service and the YMCA in 1919 … designed to educate teenage boys and young men about the dangers of sexual promiscuity [urging] them to embrace moral and physical fitness." The cover of my book on proper domesticity, race, and science in magazine advertising is a Norman Rockwell drawing for the series. It features a man, woman, and child assembled around an armchair adorned with a bouquet of flowers. The couple is looking at architectural plans while the toddler sits with building blocks, looking up at them. It is one of the rare Rockwell drawings with a halo around the image, and the drawing explains with one image that eugenics is as American as Apple Pie. The poster series for women prescribes: "Build your home upon a partnership. Partners, fit and congenial: radiate happiness; maintain personal health; transmit their fitness for a finer race; share joys, sorrows, and responsibilities in the spirit of mutual love."[10] Another poster in the series advises: "To both boy and girl, sex gives a new joy in living, a desire for a career, a longing to do great things for a race. It inspires the arts, the sciences, and the culture of civilization." The language of race runs through both series, with practical advice about exercise and nutrition, alongside cautions concerning the choice of mate to contribute the right qualities to advance one's own family and civilization itself. In a poster entitled "What kind of children?" the writers for the series suggest that, when choosing a human mammal with which to reproduce, one must consider not only the individual, but members of his family: "Children get their basic qualities by inheritance. If they are to be strong, keen, efficient, and great, there must be good blood back of them. If you want your children to be well-born, choose your husband because of fine qualities in his family as well as in himself."[11] A background element is the movement of young adults to industrial centers, away from regions where they would know one another's "blood" and who was born of whom.

There is also a strand through both poster series reinforcing what it means to be a proper "girl" and what it means to be a proper "boy." A poster for men in "Keeping Fit," "The Spirited Horse and the Sex Impulse" has a man astride a large horse rearing up in full height, the text reading: "A spirited horse is a great prize. It is a joy to ride him to feel his strength and boundless energy under one's control. The sex instinct, when directed, is the source of power and of a richer, fuller life."[12] This split of "charm of manner" and "power" "strength" and "energy" is characteristic of a mainstream concern at this time about the virility of white men as they moved inside factories and offices.

The feminist historians behind the "Dig History" podcast write their words for schoolteachers, with sources linked for further study. Their pedagogically attentive explanation of this dynamic in "National Parks in America: Health, Manhood, and Wilderness" (2018) references Teddy Roosevelt's 1899 speech "The Strenuous Life."[13] Sarah Handley-Cousins connects an emphasis on "the willingness to work hard with your hands, fight for what is right, do your duty in the world as a white American man." Quoting from the speech, Handley-Cousins lists the traits not in line with the ideal: "the timid man, the lazy man, the man who distrusts his country, the over-civilized man, who has lost the great fighting, masterful virtues, the ignorant man, the man of dull mind." Co-host Elizabeth Garner Masarik continues with an entertaining, accurate summary: "you can't be a true American man sitting behind your desk in the city pushing paper—you need to get out and camp and kill buffalo and experience life!" She continues, "when men started being diagnosed with neurasthenia … In order to be healthy, you needed to be more masculine by being out in nature—just like women needed to be more feminine by being inside in bed."

The *OED* explains neurasthenia as "chiefly historical." Beginning in 1833, the term referred to "A disorder characterized by feelings of fatigue and lassitude … originally attributed to weakness or exhaustion of the nerves and later considered a form of neurotic disorder."[14] In "The Nervous Origins of the American Western," Barbara Will explains fears about fitness regarding white working men in the U.S. through the contrast of two fictional stories related to the grandfather of neurasthenia, physician/novelist Silas Weir Mitchell: Charlotte Perkins Gilman's "The Yellow Wallpaper" and *The Virginian*, by Owen Wister. She explains: "*The Virginian* articulated a new and urgent literary vision of masculine potency and conquest in the face of perceived cultural 'effeminacy.'" "Gilman's story," Will explains, "speaks to the damage incurred by neurasthenic women on Rest Cures," while "Wister's novel, narrated from the semi-autobiographical perspective of an Eastern neurasthenic 'tenderfoot,' adheres closely to Mitchell's core ideas about the use and value of the West for nervous men … " *The Virginian*, she explains, is "a tribute to Mitchell and his West Cure, and was amply rewarded by the continued support and good favor of the doctor, who paved the way for Wister's first Western 'sketches' to be published in *Harper's*."[15] Wister presented a useful fiction that connected aspirations at the national level, using "the West" as an arena for middle-class men to be rejuvenated in manliness while also involving themselves in the expansion of wealth into newly decimated Indian country. "Wister imagined the potency and sex appeal of the Western hero, whom he saw as the direct descendent of the Anglo-Saxon knight, to emerge from the moments in which he strives to 'master' his Western environment," Will writes, and "these efforts to 'master' the West … underwrite not only the ethos of American national expansion but the originary fantasy of the American pioneer … "[16]

Teddy Roosevelt and Owen Wister go back to the relation of Muscular Christianity and Social Darwinism. Did these men succeed in the struggle for the fittest? Did the natural law of the West produce more virile men? And, again, what kinds of mental gymnastics were required to make this somehow relate to "the gospel"? Barbara Will notes that "[the] West Cure, after all, was intended to simulate the mythic vitality of rustic outdoorsmen, not to experience firsthand its actual and emerging realities, which included interracial tensions, labor disputes, and vigilante 'justice.'"[17] This brings back into view the class conflicts represented in the celebration of *The Virginian* as the first novel in the genre. Owen Wister (like Teddy Roosevelt) had in mind a particular stock fit best to populate the land West of the 98th meridian. Quoting from Wister's essay of 1895 called "The Evolution of the Cow-Puncher," Will explains that Wister calls recent immigrants "encroaching alien vermin" who "degrade our commonwealth from a nation not something half pawn-shop, half broker's office."[18] This vision is about "Anglo-Saxon civilization." The conceit of "The Strenuous Life" rests on a providentially chosen race of men, men chosen to master the terrain on which other "vermin" are to fall into line. G. Edward White traces the relationships of these figures to particular schools and institutions in "the Establishment" such as it was in the northeast at the time.[19] He explains "Frederic Remington, Theodore Roosevelt, and Owen Wister were born within three years of each other in the decade of the Civil War, products of an East whose accelerating economic situation paralleled their own growth to maturity." Their status as men briefly related to "the West" bolstered their careers after their return: "In later life each man became identified with powerful and prestigious elements in eastern society but retained his reputation as an exponent of western life."[20]

The culmination of the 1919 YMCA "Keeping Fit" poster series is a set of three posters each with the image of one man as a paragon of masculine fitness. "Robert Falcon Scott, England's South Pole hero. With brave companions he struggled thru snow, ice, and storm 923 miles to the pole." "Abraham Lincoln was prepared for the great service he rendered because he kept himself fit in body and mind." And, looking intently at the viewer through spectacles and with his signature mustache, "Sickly and frail when a boy, Roosevelt by faithful training achieved the vigor of manhood."[21]

Teddy Roosevelt had not won by the basic metrics of cattle or money while on "the Frontier" but still served as a story of national, manly victory over the elements. It did not matter that his cows had either frozen to death or died of starvation during what is known as "the Big Die-Up" during the winters of 1885–1887. The myths of the men of the frontier still travel through museums and syndicated television. New York City's American Museum of Natural History website offers as Theodore Roosevelt's "timeline": "Theodore Roosevelt first traveled west in 1883 to pursue his boyhood dreams of frontier life. When he returned to New York in 1886, he began to lobby for conservation and his presidency would mark a turning point for the nation's wilderness and wildlife."[22] This is true, and mythical.

Holy Husbandry

Lawrence Goodwyn's *The Populist Moment: A Short History of the Agrarian Revolt in America* is a 1978 abridged version of his 1976 *Democratic Promise: The Populist Moment in America*. Both books were timely, as the U.S. celebrated "The Bicentennial!" I was eight years old when the patriotism of 1976 swept through. We were living in the unremarkable land of small-town Texas. But I was properly dressed in a handmade version of Laura Ingalls Wilder's dress and bonnet from *Little House on the Prairie*, a television series that ran from 1974–1983. My mother, teaching in the Hays Texas County School system, stitched costumes based on characters from the show. The television series is set in Minnesota at the time of the Agrarian Revolt, and it offered a successful television recipe for the post-Watergate era.

Historian Rachel F. Seidman wrote about her attachment to the books in "This Little House of Mine" with candor: "I'm not sure how I made it this far without realizing that I would find Wilder's books on the fiction shelf." She gives as summary: "There are eight in the series, written by Wilder in the 1930s, when she was in her sixties." "The books follow the late-nineteenth-century Ingalls family from their home in the 'Big Woods' of western Wisconsin, to Kansas, Minnesota, and finally South Dakota." Seidman explains that, "the straightforward, realistic style … seduced generations of readers with their apparently true rendition of the Ingalls's pioneering life."[23] She discovers that Wilder wrote her stories during the Great Depression, and that she had been "an officer in the Missouri Home Development Association, which sought to bring a degree of scientific and professional expertise to farm women's work." She also recounts the "politics" of the books: "After I described my project to an acquaintance, she replied that she believed much of Wilder's emphasis on self-sufficiency and independence was a rebuttal to Franklin Roosevelt's New Deal. My heart sank … it had never occurred to me to think of the *Little House* books in the context of the Depression." With these revelations about her own process of historiography Seidman explains which fictionalized stories become so true as to be a touchstone.

"Pa" is a man engaged in holy husbandry. He is both "settling the West" and building a house for his family with his bare hands. The television series ran through the Gerald Ford administration (1974–1977), the Jimmy Carter administration (1977–1981) and into the Reagan administration. In *The Way We Never Were: American Families and the Nostalgia Trap*, Stephanie Coontz details the nostalgia that the storylines provided for readers and viewers: "Our image of the self-reliant pioneer family has been bequeathed to us by the *Little House on the Prairie* books and television series, which almost every American has read or seen."[24] In a 2017 retrospective in *Smithsonian Magazine*, Kat Eschner notes: "The third book, which has the same name as the series, takes place when the Ingalls family settled on the Osage Diminished Reserve from 1869 to 1870."[25] The creation of this powerful myth of the homesteading family, headed up by a man able to withstand drought, a plague of locusts, fire, and even make friends with the local Indians (yes, that is in the series) intersects with worries about husbandry and manliness during the Great Depression and Roosevelt's New Deal, running through to the American bicentennial in 1976, to the Make America's City on the Hill Great Again that was the election of a Hollywood actor and conservative reactionary.

In his introduction to his 1978 book *The Populist Moment*, Goodwyn connects his own time with the time about which he is writing—the time in which the *Little House* books are set. He makes this link in the last pages of his introduction. Goodwyn gives a "final prefatory comment" reminding readers that "the Populist moment … came before the global twentieth-century struggle between the East and the West." Goodwyn summarizes the ramifications of that bifurcation. The choice had become by 1978, "man is either a competitive being or a cooperative being." Capitalism and Marxism have given people "few conceptual options through which to assert believable political aspirations to the mass of the world's peoples." Going back to this period allows Goodwyn to think before this binary and all the "supporting linguistic accoutrements" of each. "The Populists did not know that the Russian Revolution, the Chinese Revolution, and the ascendancy of the multi-national corporation were to be the coercive and competitive products of the industrial age." Goodwyn recommends the collaborative complexity of the "populist moment" as having "their own unique brand of rustic relevance," inviting his readers to consider that "out of their cooperative struggle" emerged "a new democratic community." The agrarian movement gave people "what Martin Luther King would later call 'a sense of somebodiness.'" In their own way, "the Populists attempted to insulate themselves against being intimidated by the enormous political, economic, and social pressures that accompanied the emergence of corporate America."[26] This history offers not a grand strategy but an example of otherwise. This is another good news, a grounded "gospel" of people being brave, together. Goodwyn reminds readers that there is a way of thinking about small d democracy that does not require a vow of allegiance to any particular system—any particular set of "linguistic accoutrements".

In the question "why not nihilism," or why not embrace the amoral swirling into glorified violence in defense of oneself and one's kin, there are respectable answers available in mainstream, white American culture. One is to adapt "the gospel" as a corporate aesthetic. This is available as a pre-packaged, market-tested version of manliness available at your local megamart. John Eldredge and HGTV's Chip Gaines, both *Christianity Today* approved, offer individual manly success alongside wife and children. With attractive homes and media empires, they succeed in passing on their genes *and* their brands. They offer a version of Pa Ingalls if Pa Ingalls moved to Colorado Springs (Eldredge) or Waco, Texas (Gaines) and used his Pa-appeal to assist in recrafting a region economically and politically. In both cases, their brand's success involves connections of influence with other men willing to sell a form of "the gospel" to sell other things and solidify a mainstream evangelical vision of family.

I will return to Goodwyn's history and Cowboy myths in the next chapter. I now explain the importance of the wedding of Social Darwinism, proper boyhood, and holy husbandry in the writings of Charles Kingsley, who made the match of "science" and "the gospel" during the reign of Queen Victoria. Kingsley's writings smoothed the way toward the Muscular Christianity of today.

"Westward Ho!"

The full title of Kingsley's 1855 book is no less than *Westward Ho! Or The Voyages and Adventures of Sir Amyas Leigh, Knight of Burrough, in the County of Devon, in the reign of Her Most Glorious Majesty, Queen Elizabeth, Rendered into Modern English.*[27] Most of Kingsley's books for and about boys and young men are historical fiction. He connected to historical events to conjure a mythical past of English chivalry in boats and on land across the colonial era. The stories served a purpose similar to that of cowboy novels published a half-century later in New England. It was after a 2013 lecture on Kingsley that a student sent me a lament about lost boyhood from the Witherspoon Institute.

April 23, 2013, the Witherspoon Institute ran an essay by Anthony Esolen "A Boy's Life with Unisex Scouts," with the headline: "The Boy Scouts are *en route* to holding that there is nothing to being a boy, and nothing to the boy's becoming a man … " The essay is about the inclusion of uncloseted gay boys.[28] Esolen writes a refrain, contrasting a "healthy time," a time prior to the current "wasteland" wherein the concept "to quit oneself as a man" has splintered a boy's moral compass.[29] Esolen begins, "I see a boy [who] has the boy's body that shadows forth the body of a man. He will have sturdy shoulders, and the swelling in his throat suggests the timbre of the man's voice. He is going to be taller than the average woman." The boy, Esolen calls him "Luke," is not perfect: "Fallen creature that he is, Luke stretches to the limit of what his parents allow, but already he is taking into his heart the Rules his mother represents, Rules that make for decent life among other people from day to day, and the Law his father represents." "He is a boy: *vir futurus*, a going-to-be man [who] will join other men, brothers fighting to attain or defend the common good," Esolen tells his readers. Also, "He is made for a woman. It is the orientation of his body, in its sexual form. It is the orientation of his masculine being, developing in a natural and healthy way." "None of this should be controversial, no more than claiming that the noonday sky is blue … A boy grows up to be a man. A man marries a woman … [a] goal is stamped upon his body. Even savages without a doctorate in philosophy can figure it out," he states. "When husband and wife unite in the act of marriage … [t]hey do what their parents and grandparents did, and those ancestors are present in the heritage of the flesh," and while "[s]ophisticates may snort," Esolen says, consider "what kinds of men their sophisticated sons have made."

Writing in 2013 as a clergyman in a Jane Austen novel might speak, Esolen appeals to the fate of boyhood in the U.S. He concludes: "In this time, it is impossible to raise any real man without trying to raise a godly man. This is not icing. It is of the essence of manhood and womanhood." His last line describes the time as one during which a man must prepare his son "to build a home in a wasteland."[30] The warning is of a wasteland where no one has the good sense to understand a boy is by natural law made to be the sower of a field: "They are not the field, but the sowers." (Women are the field.) The essay links knowledge of Latin, old-fashioned common sense, a perspective on a father's "philosophical love," and eyes to see what human parts were, by natural law, created to do. This summons could have been modeled on the writings of Charles Kingsley at the birth of the term and contours of "Muscular Christianity."

The Witherspoon Institute is not AM talk radio, but a thinktank in Princeton, New Jersey, set up in 2003 through funding from conservative donors. The founders include Princeton University professor Robert P. George and Luis Tellez, who led a campus outreach for the conservative Catholic effort *Opus Dei*. A 2006 article for the *Nation*, "Princeton Tilts Right" reports on conservative efforts at Princeton connected to George. "Natural law informs much of George's 2001 book, *The Clash of Orthodoxies: Law, Religion and Morality in Crisis*." The essay quotes from the book: "The plain fact is that the genitals of men and women are reproductive organs all of the time–even during periods of sterility." And, "To curb sexual practices [George] views as immoral, including oral sex and masturbation (which he calls 'bad' sex),

George supports state laws banning sodomy, adultery and fornication."[31] Within five years of the founding of the Witherspoon Institute, the men had secured funding for headquarters in pricey Princeton, "bought for $1.5 million and renovated and furnished for an additional $1.3 million," as local reporter Deborah Yaffe wrote in 2008.[32] Princeton offers an obvious sheen for retrograde gender politics.

Most people in the U.S. have no idea who Kingsley was, though his classic children's fancy *The Water-Babies* is still as popular in England as the Winnie the Pooh stories are in the U.S. Before the YMCA "Keeping Fit" campaign of the Progressive Era in the U.S., Kingsley encouraged a newly urbanized, young, industrial male workforce to do daily calisthenics while imagining an adventure toward holy manhood in a foreordained Empire. Think "The Avengers" mixed with John Bunyan's *Pilgrim's Progress.*

Publishers took advantage of affordable book production to churn out inexpensive novels for boys and young men, with titles such as *The Heroes*, and *Hereward the Wake: Last of the English*. Kingsley was also able to combine the most politically serviceable elements of the new, evolutionary thought with other aspects of popular culture to offer a useful, overarching story of manifest greatness for men in England. Through the earnest, high adventures of his characters, Kingsley's stories made a struggle toward fitness appear providential, and, at the same time, crystallized English conceptions of progress for an expanding readership among the middle classes. His fairy tale realism narrated for a new generation the proper import of Darwinism in the English home. By Charles Darwin's own account, Kingsley is the "celebrated author and divine" of whom he wrote gratefully in the second and subsequent editions of *On the Origin of Species.*[33] The *Water-Babies*, Kingsley's enduring children's whimsy, was at the time part of a serious textual output for a generation of young men. These, joined with his homiletic call for a virile Anglicanism, helped create a version of Christian Darwinism that traveled to the U.S. decades later.

Kingsley's prose in *The Water-Babies* splinters with summary. But a few features are obvious. Darwin's science most comes alive when one has the eyes to see the intricate wonders of the natural world. The epigraph opening the 1864 edition reads all "unbelieving Sadducees" [sic] and the "less-believing

Pharisees" [sic] with their "dull conventionalities," should leave to her work "a country muse at ease; to play at leap-frog, if she please, with children and realities."[34] Children and realities are kept safe from brittle minds with the help of a rather stretchy version of God. As Kingsley puts it using William Wordsworth, "not in entire forgetfulness and not in utter nakedness" do we come into this world, but "trailing clouds of Glory," sent from the divine. For the child who knows this truth, "the great fairy Science" will do him only good and not harm.[35] Scientists who are asleep to the marvel of reality are silly: "folks' fancy that such and such things cannot be, simply because they have not seen them, is worth no more than the savage's fancy that there cannot be such a thing as a locomotive, because he has not seen one running wild in the forest."[36] To dress up a flying dragon in the name Pterodactyl does not erase the fact that it is flying dragon, the same beloved beast that supposedly "learned men" had been denying for years.[37] Finally, the natural world is best seen by someone washed clean, literally and figuratively, of all that soils their bodies and souls.

At the opening of the story, the main character Tom sees his reflection in a mirror and turns, angrily, to expunge this "little black ape" from the room of "the little white lady" who slept there.[38] Tom's realization that he is the "ape" sends him, by a circuitous route, on the under-watery journey to become a man, a "great man of science."[39] If he had remained soiled, and thus ape-like, Tom would have ended up like the efts, creatures who "will not learn their lessons and keep themselves clean" and thus devolve, growing not only "nasty, dirty, lazy," and "stupid," but also growing tails.[40] Larry Uffelman explains the purpose of the fairy tale: "Through the death, moral growth, and eventual rebirth of the central character, Kingsley links the principles of evolution in the physical world to the growth and maturity of the spiritual being," and so solves "the nineteenth-century conflict between science and religion."[41]

In a matching, whimsical tone, the *London Times* reviewed the first bound copy of The *Water-Babies* as displaying the truth that "the pleasantest things of life are as a rule unintelligible to us until we have lost them." Some of Kingsley's contemporaries suspected the new science would reshape English life. To use Kingsley's own words, "the great Fairy" known as science was "likely to be the queen of all the fairies for many a year to come."[42] It would behoove clergymen to note her allure and adapt accordingly. The "quiet sober people" who, as the *Times* describes them, "favoured Macmillan [magazine]," might have been "a little scandalized" by the "pure nonsense" of *The Water-Babies* when published serially in 1862, but, *the Times* reviewer declared, it was "by no means necessary to understand a book to know whether or not it is agreeable." The spritely work had a serious function. Kingsley saved Darwinism and Anglicanism with fancy. The English home could have its evolution and keep its idealized sense of boys, Mother Nature, and the children who were her gift. Kingsley was also able to layer on top of the evolution of the species the hierarchy within the species. Darwin's research had established monogenesis, that is, that the human species had one natural origin. So, what could the Church of the Victorian Era affirm that could connect evolution, monogenesis, and colonial rule? Kingsley provided both a "Natural Theology of the Future" and a fairy tale, covering all the bases.

I first came across an illustration by J. Noel Paton while digging through books in the St. Deiniol's library in Wales in 2008. Two of the young interns were shelving, and I asked them what they thought of the image. "Goodness," one said to the other, "doesn't he look like the face on the marmalade advertisement?" The young women's immediate response was that Tom looks like a caricature of an African child, a dehumanizing caricature similar to one known now in the United States as the dehumanizing cartoon "picanniny." In the United Kingdom, the dehumanizing image is known as a "golliwogg" cartoon. The caricature is named after the erstwhile marmalade advertising scheme that ran from 1910 to 2001, based on a series of children's books by Florence Kate Upton from the turn of the twentieth century.[43] Tom is not only dirty from soot, but soiled in a way that requires submersion and elevation. When the fairy queen who first attracts Tom to the water tells the other fairies about Tom, she explains, "He is but a savage now, and like the beasts that perish … "[44] The transformation of Tom the chimney-sweep is a transformation of evolution from sooty to clean, from savage to civilized, from working to middle class, and from more nearly black to obviously white.

There is a discussion on evolved human creatures between a fairy named Mrs. Bedonebyasyoudid, Tom, and Tom's beloved, Ellie. Mrs. Bedonebyasyoudid sums up the shape of savagery toward civilization in a way that draws on both an inherited and an acquired version of evolutionary theory. Groups fail to evolve when they pass on to future generations their stubborn incapacity to adapt. As Mrs. Bedonebyasyoudid puts it: " … there are two sides to every question, and a downhill as well as an uphill road; and, if I can turn beasts into men, I can, by the same laws of circumstance, and selection, and competition, turn men into beasts."[45] If Darwin had shown that beasts became men, so could Kingsley use this insight to turn men into beasts.[46]

The layering of racist caricatures is a distinctive combination of compressed and sprightly. Kingsley writes of "Jews' harps" and the loss of "Hardwork years" since "all the weakly little children had great stomachs, and then died." The beginning of the decline is the "land of Readymade." when "hardwork" had been lost. Kingsley's protagonist Tom is aghast "'Why,' said Tom, 'they are growing no better than savages.' 'And look how ugly they are all getting,' said Ellie. 'Yes; when people live on poor vegetables instead of roast beef and plum-pudding, their jaws grow large, and their lips grow coarse, like the poor Paddies who eat potatoes.'" The fairy

> turned over the next five hundred years. And there they were all living up in trees … "But what great, hulking, broad-shouldered chaps they are," said Tom; "they are a rough lot as ever I saw"… And she turned over the next five hundred years… they were fewer still, and stronger, and fiercer; but their feet had changed shape very oddly, for they laid hold of the branches with their great toes, as if they had been thumbs, just as a Hindoo tailor uses his toes to thread his needle.

The fairy of science shows them the eventual destruction of humankind: "But there is a hairy one among them," said Ellie. "Ah," said the fairy, "that will be a great man in his time, and chief of all the tribe." And, when she turned over the next five hundred years, it was true. For this hairy chief had had hairy children, and they hairier children still … Then the fairy turned over the next five hundred years … "Why," cried Tom, "I declare they are all apes."[47]

Tom learns that his fate would have been similar to the devolved creatures, the "efts," if he "had not made up [his] mind to go on this journey, and see the world, like an Englishman."[48] The sloth of one generation would come to bear on its extinction. Linking misery with "coarse" lips, and potatoes with imminent descent, those who "live on poor vegetables instead of roast beef and plum-pudding" become responsible for their demise.

The review of the book in the *Times of London* notes that it carries Kingsley's account of faith and moral aesthetics, what the review calls "the foundation of the theology of his school."[49] In his 1871 "The Natural Theology of the Future," Kingsley establishes the Anglican church's higher place among the religions, and explains how Christianity must evolve.[50] Through godly gardening, man is able to "root up the thorns and thistles" of "the race." If churchmen are going to keep apace, they must bring these natural and scriptural facts together to consider "questions of Embryology and questions of Race."[51] Churchmen will need to risk the disapprobation of some, some who think that the new finding "endangers the modern notions of democratic equality." There are those who fear the new findings, those who fear that "it may be proved that the negro is not a man and brother." Yet, Kingsley explains, according to "Mr. Darwin," "science has proved that he must be such." Common ancestry does not resolve the question of "democratic equality," rather, as Kingsley explains, "science is proving more and more the immense importance of Race; the importance of hereditary powers, hereditary organs, hereditary habits, in all organized beings, from the lowest plant to the highest animal." Science "is proving more and more the omnipresent action of the differences between races; how the more favored race (she cannot avoid using the epithet) exterminates the less favored, or forces [the less favored] under penalty of death, to adapt to new circumstances." The scientifically informed churchman must recognize that "competition between every race and every individual of that race, and reward according to deserts, is (as far as we can see) a universal law of living things." What is factual for "the races of plants and animals, so it has been unto this day among the races of men."[52]

When read through proper spectacles, the "painful facts" of science are evident at the heart of scripture itself, confirming both biblically and scientifically the superiority of Christianity. "The natural theology of the future must take count of these tremendous and even painful facts: and she may take count of them ... And what is the central historic fact, save one, of the New

Testament, but the conquest of Jerusalem." He describes "the dispersion, all but destruction of a race, not by miracle, but by invasion" as evidence that the Jewish people were "found wanting when weighed in the stern balances of natural and social law." He describes the passage "The kingdom of God shall be taken from you, and given to a nation bringing forth the fruits hereof'" as "the supreme instance, the most complex development, of a law which runs through all created things, down to the moss which struggles for existence on the rock."[53] A people incapable of winning the struggle of existence is replaced by a superior. The "central historic fact" of the "destruction of a race" is congruent with the "stern balances of natural and social law" now established by the new science of Darwinism. Kingsley shows the usefulness of Darwinian theology in an age marked for colonial expansion and Anglican dominance. If only "we clergy" will "summon up the courage" to tell this story, the "unknown x" left in the new science may be effectively replaced by "The Breath of God; The Spirit who is The Lord and Giver of Life."[54] The summons is clear. Churchmen must evolve, be courageous, and prescribe the proper mechanisms to cooperate with the divine arranger, the organizer of all that is, and Darwinism, as Kingsley interprets the science, will be the guide.

Churchmen later intent to preach a "gospel" of eugenics and laymen intent to provide a baptized guide for American progress through corporate monopoly had in Charles Kingsley's writing a resource. Science itself had given a way to read the bible as affirming that the fattest oligarchic cats were the fittest, that the race who won the West was providentially suited to rule, and that a "gospel" that would ameliorate the striving upwards of each individual and group not currently thriving was a dangerous, or at least unscientific way to proceed. Fellow-feeling is functional only inasmuch as it contributes to the overall "health" and "fitness" of a citizenry, and the engine for that fitness is competition.

"Chaos in the Family, Chaos in the State"

The clergymen who later praised and quoted Kingsley's "Natural Theology of the Future" were particularly obsessed with white people whose breeding allowed weeds to multiply, whether in cities or in Appalachia. Beginning in

Donald Trump's primary run announced in June 2015, questions about fitness and proper citizenship in the U.S. became obvious in bestselling books and within leading conservative periodicals. I had already been following the resurgence of language related to "white trash" on social media. In 2010, Jennifer Lawrence was heralded for her role as the heroine in *Winter's Bone*. The film reviewer for *The Guardian* was not an outlier in using the term "white trash" to describe the movie: "*Winter's Bone* … builds inexorably through successive stages of tension to an extraordinary finale of horror: a white-trash nightmare, featuring a chainsaw and a horrible visit to a moonlit lake."[55] What constitutes "trash" forms of whiteness? The *OED* gives the first use as 1821: "Originally and chiefly U.S. colloquial. derogatory." The phrase often includes the third word "poor." The editors include from 2006 in the *Florida Times-Union* (Nexis): "The other girl's mother told her.., 'Just stay away from her, they're nothing but white trash with money.'"[56]

By 2010, I had been teaching Lillian Smith's "Two Men and a Bargain" for a decade. This had prompted questions and confessions by men and women who recognized the description of the lessons they had been taught in their homes and churches about which white people they should care about and which ones they should "stay away from." Smith had written about the production and perpetuation of such distinctions in the 1940s. As Donald Trump gained the nomination for the Republican primary in 2015, pundits were drawing aesthetic and moral distinctions between "Trump voters" and the rest. By 2016, colleagues were recommending J.D. Vance's 2016 book *Hillbilly Elegy* as an expert account of what was ailing the country. A 2016 interchange featured in the conservative magazine *The National Review* outlines one of the obvious features of this time. The conversation is relevant going back to the Moody Bible poster of peaceable men in 1920 and forward into the myths of the West in Cowboy Church and into the Seattle launched "Fight Club Church" of Acts 29. How should a Christian man live "The Strenuous Life" if he does not share Teddy and Wister's Harvard degrees and family money?[57]

In his 2016 *National Review* article, Kevin D. Williamson announced one diagnosis with the title: "Chaos in the Family, Chaos in the State: The White Working Class's Dysfunction."[58] The accompanying illustration is a caricature of Donald Trump reading a bedtime story labeled "The Word of

Trump" to two white men sitting on Trump's knees, smiling stupidly. One wears a farmer's ball cap and a blue button-down work shirt. The other wears a yellow hard hat and suspenders. Williamson explained that his essay is part of an intra-conservative argument. He summarized Michael Brendan Dougherty's earlier essay, which ran under the headline: "How Conservative Elites Disdain Working-Class Republicans." Doughtery had suggested in his article that Republican strategists had no concern for people "rooted in their hometowns." According to such "elite" strategists, rooted men needed to join the "hyper-mobile world."[59] Williamson directly countered Doughtery. People rooted in their hometowns are not only stupid, but drug-addled and dishonorable. According to Williamson, Dougherty failed to recognize "the dysfunction and negligence—and the incomprehensible *malice*—of poor white America."

Noting that immigrants are not the major problem facing men represented by the caricatures in the illustration—Williamson also reported that working class white families are dealing with suicide rates and premature deaths by disease and toxins in a measurably drastic way. Williamson contrasted the two factors explicitly: "the effects of immigration overall are tiny compared with the effects of factors such as health-care expenses. In many lower-end occupations, overall compensation in fact has gone up over the years, but the additional compensation has come largely or entirely in the form of medical benefits." As widely reported around this time, Williamson summarized: "the life expectancies among non-college-educated white Americans have been plummeting in an almost unprecedented fashion." Citing the *Washington Post*, Williamson reported that: "the white people in Trump counties were likely to die younger. The causes of death were 'increased rates of disease and ill health, increased drug overdose and abuse, and suicide … '" His conclusion to this section of his essay reads as a lament: "This is horrifyingly consistent with other findings."

But then Williamson turned to his diagnosis of white working-class America. Why are white working-class people poor? They are breathing a miasma of amorality created by access to abortion and "liberal" divorce. "The divorce rate doubled over the span of a few decades," he intoned, "even as the marriage rate was declining." This, combined with "the violence of abortion, which fundamentally alters the relationship between men, women, and children, and what exactly 'family' means." He described "poor white America" as marred by "a social regime of illegitimacy, serial monogamy, abortion, and liberal divorce [that] has rendered traditional families optional, at best." Noting that "the great majority of divorces are initiated by wives, not by husbands," Williamson stated "welfare … supplanted [fathers] in their role as providers, assuming that they have the wherewithal to fill that role in the first place."

His conclusion was autobiographical and stark. "If you spend time in hardscrabble, white upstate New York, or eastern Kentucky, or my own native West Texas, and you take an honest look at the welfare dependency, the drug and alcohol addiction, the family anarchy …" a person will realize something crucial. His last paragraph reads: "The truth about these dysfunctional, downscale communities is that they deserve to die. Economically, they are negative assets. Morally, they are indefensible. Forget all your cheap theatrical Bruce Springsteen crap." He described "the white American underclass [as] in thrall to a vicious, selfish culture." "Donald Trump's speeches make them feel good," but "they need real change, which means that they need U-Haul."[60] The tone of his writing is part lament, part screed, with the confusing, to me, conclusion that people struggling with health care costs and high rates of unemployment in regions "like" West Texas, upstate New York, and eastern Kentucky need to pack up their families and go where the jobs are. Which is … where?

Jamelle Bouie asked a question in his 2016 article for *Slate*, entitled: "Poor Whites Trashed," with the headline: "Why conservatives are talking about struggling white people the way they usually talk about black people."[61] Bouie noted: "In the past, this is how conservatives have talked about struggling blacks. If inner cities and rural black communities were poor and dysfunctional, it was because of cultural deficiencies, not broad economic problems." Bouie continued: "With more effort, went the argument, they could overcome economic isolation and social stigma. And the evidence was success among low-income white Americans who'd overcome their station." Bouie began with a quote from Williamson's article, noting that "a dramatic decline in status, is happening." The "*National Review* did us the service of making [race and class anxiety] explicit." Bouie's conclusion rings still in 2026: "The big question—perhaps the single largest question of American history—is whether this will inspire empathy and fellow feeling with minorities or just become tinder for the ongoing racial reaction." My reframing of his question is this. Would white, working men recognize that the same blinkered logic of the Moynihan Report was being applied to them, and join with their black colleagues—men and women—to move beyond "empathy and fellow feeling" toward solidarity and organized action.

Which towns are disposable? It is instructive to read this as an argument among first generation, professional men about their fathers, brothers, uncles, and grandfathers. In Chapter 4, I draw on a distinction between "boomers" who exploit a region and "stickers" who remain committed to a region for good. This is a distinction from Kentuckian Wendell Berry, and he contrasts his own grandfather with James B. Duke.[62] As a placeholder until that chapter, note Berry's words: "The Duke trust exerted an oppression that was purely economic, involving a mechanical indifference, the indifference of a grinder to what it grinds … [and] any small farmer is only one, and one lost, among a great multitude of others, whose work can be quickly transformed into a great multitude of dollars."[63] Berry is describing a turn that Lawrence Goodwyn, in his description of populism in U.S. politics, links with "social control" and the "stigmas" associated being labeled "lazy." From Goodwyn: "It is clear that the varied methods of social control fashioned in industrial societies have, over time, become sufficiently pervasive and subtle that a gradual erosion of democratic aspirations among the whole population has taken place." Along with the erosion of the land and of entire regions comes also the "erosion" of meaning in the word "democracy," Goodwyn explains, the term became "increasingly obscure as industrialization has proceeded."[64]

Five years before this 2016 debate over which small towns should die, police officers, school teachers, and firefighters had joined together to fight the Republican governor's evisceration of labor unions in the state of Wisconsin. During the height of the Cold War, Wisconsin had been the first state to legalize collective bargaining for public employees. As ABC local KWOW reported February, 2011, "Police say nearly 70,000 people demonstrated at the Wisconsin State Capitol Saturday, most to protest the Governor's bill that would strip public workers of nearly all of their collective bargaining rights."

They were called chaotic and summarily fired by the hired goons who had taken over the state house. What counts as "chaos" in a man, or a group of men in post-industrial regions shorn of work with dignity?

A figure I turn to in Chapter 3 was initially set up as a model of Muscular Christianity in mainstream evangelicalism. Mark Driscoll's story of success in evangelism in the godless grunge-land of Seattle sold books and videos with the brand of Acts 29 until, at some point, he was too much. *Christianity Today* ran a podcast series focused on Mark Driscoll as an example of how *not* to be muscularly Christian. The text on the *Christianity Today* podcast website reads: "The Rise and Fall of Mars Hill" and describes Driscoll's brand as "founded in 1996, Seattle's Mars Hill Church was poised to be an influential, undeniable force in evangelicalism—that is until its spiraling collapse in 2014." "The church," *Christianity Today* says, "had a promising start." Alas, "Christian celebrity eroded and eventually shipwrecked both the preacher and his multimillion-dollar platform."[65] Historian Jodie Hatlem Boyer described the irony this way. *Christianity Today* running an exposé about Mark Driscoll's "Fight Club Church" is like the doctor in the Jurassic Park movie—the doctor who concocts the plan to bring dinosaurs to life—scolding the T-Rex for being too T-Rex-y. The multi-media corporation that is *Christianity Today* had promoted a worldview that made Mark Driscoll seem normal-edgy. Driscoll's brand became the focal point of the parabola of Muscular Christianity. Brand Billy Graham had created through showcased church "success" stories a built world in which "Mark Driscoll" was T-Rex, fitting in as the fittest of fit.

In 2014, Mark Oppenheimer reported in the *New York Times* about a related book-selling scheme. "*World* reported that $210,000 in Mars Hill church funds had gone to a marketing firm that promised to get *Real Marriage*, a book written by Mr. Driscoll and his wife, on best-seller lists."[66] In marketing terms, it was predictable. Pick an aesthetically normative spokesman. Make him successful in a region known best for a form of popular music associated with young male nihilism. Kurt Cobain had died in 1994, two years before Mark Driscoll founded a small church that then, with funding from outside donors with private jets, became a sensation. Unlike Cobain, Driscoll was built like a brick, talked brazenly and directly about his love of sex with his wife, and unapologetically encouraged men to stop whining about love or any other existential issue and be a man. When church work is set within marketing, and when Christianity becomes something that creates men better "fit" to run and jump and make money and pass on their good genes, why not go full-out and feature, as Driscoll's celebrated brand did, actual rings in which men could practice their mixed martial arts and declare a winner? Going back to the 1919 YMCA poster series, manly games are meant to be competitive, and fair. But why not go full nihilist and beat someone to a pulp?

 Goodwyn describes in *The Populist Moment* how people are divided in the U.S. as

> people discover they have far fewer opportunities than others of their countrymen (a not infrequent circumstance in capitalist systems of economic organization), they are told—as Populists were told in the 1890s and as blacks, Appalachian whites, and migrant laborers are told today in America—that they are "improvident," "lazy," inherently "deprived," or in some similar fashion culturally handicapped and at fault.

"These stigmas" have a history, in that "in earlier times [they] were also visited upon Irish, Jewish, Italian, and other immigrants to America," and they drive people "to undergo considerable indignity to earn sufficient status" to escape the stigma. "Accordingly," Goodwyn writes, people "try to do those things necessary to 'get ahead.' The result is visible in the obsequious day-to-day lives of white-collar corporate employees in America—and in the even more obsequious lives of the Communist Party … "

As a historian working from Texas to North Carolina, Goodwyn used his extensive research of the period of populism and agrarian revolt to describe the apparent lack of will that, as he notes, "traditionalists" find as a source of "glee." Goodwyn writes that such "traditionalists" use the word "apathy" to justify "maintaining things as they are." Why do people from Appalachian whites to migrant laborers to African American working-class people, people who are being horribly exploited at work, *not* join together and revolt? Goodwyn coined a phrase describing what I have seen in North Carolina—from pastors to parishioners, from churches with high steeples and churches renting space in a former supermarket. People do not join across divisions, together and refuse exploitation because we have been "instructed in deference."[67]

In *Guaranteed Pure,* Gloege documents a shift around 1860 in the conversations *about* working people by people with the economic means to shape the future of people working: "Concerns of urban atomization shifted to fears of social combustion; a concern for the masses had metastasized into a fear of the masses."[68] This is one of the ramifications of Social Darwinism, as industrialization came to the U.S. Goodwyn wrote in 1978 about the shift in the U.S. "over the last eight generations" "millions have been levered off the land and into cities to provide the human components of the age of machinery." He described and predicted that "industrial societies have not only become centralized, they have devised rules of conduct that are intimidating to their populations as a whole." Muscular Christianity describes Christianity used as a tool to prescribe fitness, shame the unfit, divide the striving, and intimidate populations as a whole. This form of religiosity is at times obvious and crass. But there are also toney, bow-tied versions. I will turn to respectable, revered monuments to Muscular Christianity in Chapter 4, on two Protestant cathedrals built during the Great Depression.

"Fit for Ministry?"

"Fit for Ministry?" was a 2001 cover article for *The Christian Century*: "A new profile of seminarians," the piece announced. The highlighted text on the first page runs "A recent survey of seminary students offers suggestions for dealing with the underlying causes of the problem of quality in the ministry." The article heads a series about the survey, with large charts. The first chart reads: "Mean age of entering students." The second is "Honors by age cohort," with a highlight for students entering as members of "the National Honor Society." The third compares "Honors: Rabbinical Students and Others" comparing "Rabbinical students" to "Others" by membership in the "National Honors Society," the "Dean's List," and those with "Honors Degree." Across many schools of theology, including Duke Divinity School and my *alma mater* Yale Divinity School, conversations focused on the quest to attract younger students, specifically recent college graduates.

The changing profile of seminary students has been much remarked upon. Whereas 50 years ago almost all seminarians in North America were white men who had recently graduated from college, today women are a major presence in seminary classrooms, as are (to varying degrees) ethnic and minority groups. Today's students are also substantially older by the time they get to seminary …

"Has this change been good or bad for theological education and for the churches' ministry? On this subject, there is much debate," readers were told.

The use of passive voice in the first sentence of the cover article is important. What had changed as of the turn-of-the-century survey was (and is) that there were (and are) fewer young, white men who had graduated from college. They were the demographic being "remarked upon." Remarked upon by whom? "Today" there are more women and non-white men, and older students who had graduated with their bachelor's degrees less recently than the "whereas 50 years ago" of comparison. Is this "good" or is this "bad," asks the survey, with no attention to who is asking the question. The source matters. The description of *Christian Century* online as of 2024 is "Thoughtful, Independent, Progressive." The *Century* is mainstream Protestant, positioned as centrist to *Christianity Today*'s mainstream evangelicalism. Elesha Coffman explains, "[In 1947] *Time* lauded the *Century* as 'Protestantism's most vigorous voice' and 'a beacon of level-headedness in a fog of misty thinking.'" "Nearly 3,000 libraries keep the *Century* on hand for research and leisure reading," she reports, "more than any other religious magazine can boast."[69] The report on this "good" or "bad" shift away from young, white men was funded by the Lilly Foundation.

Was the mainline attracting people "fit" for ministry if seminarians included as many women as men, and as many older students as younger students? The study made public conversations going on in admissions offices and within denominational bodies. These conversations were in violation of Equal Employment Opportunity Commission regulations against age discrimination at the time: "The Age Discrimination in Employment Act (ADEA) forbids age discrimination against people who are age 40 or older."

The ADEA had been in place since the heyday of young, white, college educated men—that is, since 1967.[70] With the posing of the basic question, and through the description of responses deemed "obvious" in the "what can be done" answers, the sense of "fitness" had to do with concerns about fitness and years of potential usefulness. Barbara G. Wheeler writes: "One obvious response is to recruit more recent college graduates. This survey shows that younger students are more likely to bring intellectual strength and strong educational backgrounds." She then summarizes an argument I had heard during many assessments: "They are also desirable simply because, if they enter and remain in church service, they will serve many more years than older students, thus 'repaying' more of the investment in their seminary training."[71] Clergymen and women are investments, the argument goes, appealing to potential donors concerned to fuel useful conduits for "the gospel." A top administrator for Lilly investments attended faculty meetings at Duke for years, sitting silently, watching who spoke up for whom in this period of assessment for excellence and stamina.

The back and forth between mainstream Protestants who call themselves "progressive" and mainstream evangelicals who "like Billy Graham" is one of the stories in the next two chapters. As church plants promised to attract "Tribal Men," both strands of mainstream Protestantism sought to shape their seminaries and congregations as fit for the future. To go back to Kingsley's call in his conclusion to "The Natural Theology of the Future," both strands of Protestantism have sought to "Evolve!" in such a way that they (we) are fit inheritors of the "American way!" of business.

2

Brotherhoods

History will prove that our current state government is the most corrupt ever and is "bought" by a few radical dominionist billionaires seeking to destroy public education, privatize our public schools and create a Theocracy that is both un-American and un-Texan.

"I'll Wear No Man's Collar" Texas State Representative (Republican) Glenn Rogers; Graford, Texas (2024)

In 2013, I had to choose between two events held the same weekend. Hundreds of (mostly) white, working class, Baptist men gathered in the foothills of Oklahoma for a conference called "Rewired," and a few hundred (mostly) white, white-collar men met in Washington D.C. for the New Canaan Society Washington Weekend. The promotional videos for the two events featured rock-like music and stills with similarly coifed and plaid-shirted men with guitars, and photos of men smiling, arms interlocked, kneeling and praying together. The icon for the Oklahoma conference featured a drawing of two eighteenth-century men (they are wearing knickers) in a boxing ring. The New Canaan Society symbol is a faux-classical outline of a muscled, shirtless man with bow and arrow. The Oklahoma video opened with two young men engaged in open-air karate, men bow hunting, skeet shooting, riding motorcycles, and riding horses. The New Canaan Society promotional videos featured men in a mahogany living room, sitting on a leather couch, rapt with attention while listening to an older, white man speak; more men in a bigger, lecture-style room with a speaker who is making them laugh; men sitting around eating a catered dinner, arms around one another; and, in a recurrent theme for the New

Canaan Society, one man lighting and another man sucking on a large cigar. At "Rewired," I saw more chewing tobacco than I had seen since high school, but no cigars. And, while there appears to be wine served at the D.C. conference, the "Rewired" video shows men sitting at long rows of school cafeteria-style tables drinking coffee from Styrofoam cups. The only woman in any of the promotional videos is in one slide from D.C. She is in the background, wearing a black uniform, pouring coffee.

I opted for Oklahoma. So, on April 26, 2013, I was driving north from Irving, Texas to the Oklahoma border to attend "Rewired," a conference for Southern Baptist men at a conference center in Davis, Oklahoma. Surfing the radio in my rental car, a man's voice announced that George Jones of Saratoga, Texas, had died. "He is best known for the greatest country song ever made, period," the disc jockey announced, then played "He Stopped Loving Her Today." The song is a heartbreaker about a man who continues to love the woman who left him long after she goes, ceasing only on the day of his death (which occasions the song). Any good Texan can tell you that Tammy Wynette was married to "The Possum," a nickname Jones earned for his propensity to pass out before a show, and that Wynette was most famous for her ballad "Stand By Your Man." I changed channels and heard Bryan Jonathan Fischer exclaim "This is *Muscular* Christianity!" (Emphasis in the original.) Fischer's show "Focal Point" is featured on American Family Radio, a self-described "Christian Conservative" talk radio station. That day Fischer was holding forth on the Hostess Brand story. Based in Irving, Texas, Hostess was still battling for survival against a greedy labor union, Fischer explained. The story of Hostess Twinkies versus Bakery, Confectionery, Tobacco Workers and Grain Millers' International Union had been running for months, an epic, quintessentially American battle that, for Fischer, was about men too stupid to save the company that employed them. This was one of many moments when the intersection of men, work, and evangelical messaging was clear. George and Tammy, singing about the ties that bind a man and a woman, in misery tangled up with devotion. Idahoan Bryan Fischer reclaiming with gusto a phrase first coined for a Victorian churchman. A struggle between labor and management over fair wages, at a company whose signature product (the "Twinkie") has become a synonym for "weak."

I had picked up a *Ladies' Home Journal* at the Dallas/Fort Worth airport, and the regular "Can this Marriage be Saved" spot featured a husband who had lost his job and a wife who resented his ensuing depression.

This chapter is on ministries to men using a "Western" theme. There are not many actual men in the U.S. working with a horse to move cows. But there are ministries to men built around the myths of a supposedly simpler time. This has been the most appealing part of my research for many people curious about "Muscular Christianity." The term "Cowboy Church" has punch.

If a man enters a church that looks more like a barn than a church, he does not have to take off his hat. That is a simple explanation for "Cowboy Church," but it is symbolic. Paul Gauntt is a long-time correspondent for the magazine *Baptist Progress* and for the *Waxahachie Daily Light*, both out of Waxahachie, Texas. He wrote a 2009 piece on the "History of Cowboy Church Movement" that helps introduce the effort.[1] This also has the benefit of being from the locale credited with the beginnings of the effort. Gauntt's wording is evocative, "the movement is spreading faster than a dry Texas prairie fire—and it had its origin right here in Waxahachie." His history links to what is now considered the largest "Cowboy Church" in the world. "Beginning in March 2004 in what became known as the Cowboy Church of Ellis County," Guantt explains, "the simple agenda of the movement is to reach people who have a bent toward the outdoors with riding and roping … [and] has had astonishing success in reaching a sector of the population that may not have otherwise set foot inside a church house." Gauntt relates that Ron Nolan, who founded the Ellis County church in 2000, attributes the idea to his son, Matt, who told his father that his own friends in the team roping community had no interest in anything like "church": "He told me that those guys there would never set foot in a church." He also quotes a man named Frank Sanchez, "who for 42 years, never walked inside a church" and serves in leadership for the movement: "Unchurched people view a traditional church as an organization that just wants their money and they also feel that the institutional church is too 'righteous' for them," he said. "What we want to do in the cowboy church is to lower those barriers built up between the church and the unchurched, and make people feel comfortable—that they can come as they are." As of 2024, the Texas Baptists have a website dedicated to Western Heritage Ministries, with training for and recruitment efforts to grow the movement with new church plants.[2]

Rewiring "the West"

The period on which "the West" is based is short. As Victoria Lamont writes in her *Westerns: A Women's History*, "open-range cattle ranching proved to be an unsustainable practice that eventually led to conflicts among large and small ranchers, homesteaders, and so-called rustlers."[3] These conflicts are the backdrop for *The Virginian*, written on the side of large ranchers. Foregrounding these tensions is one way to rewire myths of Muscular Christianity in "the West." What makes a "Western" a "Western" is a question about which scholars of history, literature, and film make careers. And the question matters.

Consider as a story of otherwise the short story and film "Brokeback Mountain." Diana Ossana, Larry McMurtry's long-time writing partner, insisted McMurtry read Annie Proulx's "Brokeback Mountain" after it first appeared in *The New Yorker* in 1997. Together they wrote the screenplay, bringing the story to the big screen, vivifying Proulx's wind-scoured, skeletal prose with details like a J.C. Penney's wedding dress and a Mr. Coffee machine.[4] In an early scene, the screenplay reads "WE SEE: ENNIS, horseback, being an exemplary sheepman, a sickly lamb across his saddle, trailed by the blue heelers."[5] Proulx, Ossana, and McMurtry draw on the West as a place where tending well, hunting humanely, and slaughtering discriminately are part of the code of a good man. The treatment of animals is fundamental. The note draws on a shorthand "WE SEE" regarding how Ennis is "exemplary." The reader and viewer can judge a man by how he treats "his animals" and, in this case, the animals he is paid to keep alive. Ennis's father had forced Ennis at age nine to look at the body of a man dismembered alive, and he made sure Ennis knew why. Ennis and Jack each marry women not only out of economic necessity, but out of survival, and their fathers, each one, raised their boys by a code that included being respectful of animals and that, on threat of brutal death, precluded homosexuality. Proulx's story ends with a reality that McMurtry and Ossana thread through the screenplay: "There was some open space between what he knew and what he tried to believe, but nothing could be done about it, and if you can't fix it you've got to stand it."[6] Jack tries, finally, to live both tending cattle and loving a man, and, off screen, his wife's father makes sure he dies alone, disfigured, drowning in his own blood.

When Jack and Ennis leave their summer jobs after falling profoundly in love, Ennis cannot walk "half a block." Both Proulx's story and McMurtry's screenplay read "he feels like someone's pulling his guts out, hand over hand, a yard at a time." The notes for this scene in the film read:

> A COWBOY passes the alley. Pauses, looks at ENNIS.
> ENNIS glares at him.
> ENNIS
> (growls)
> What the fuck you lookin' at?
> The COWBOY moves on.[7]

I had read McMurtry's 1961 debut novel *Horseman, Pass By* when I was a teenager. His cinematic note struck me. McMurtry could have passed on this effort. He became part of a team effort (over years) to bring a story to screen in which "the Cowboy" does not move on. McMurtry typed these words about the story in the notes on the screenplay: "I was the more stunned when I read 'Brokeback Mountain' because I realized that it was a story that had been sitting there all my life, fifty-five years of which have been lived in the American West. There the story was, all those years, waiting in patient distance for someone to write it."[8] The story had been there waiting for someone to make a "Western" about two men in love. The movie is a love story, a tragedy, and a Western, argues John White in his Routledge Film Guidebook on *Westerns*.[9] White notes that the film "brought a challenging short story by Annie Proulx to a mainstream audience and took the Western into new territory with regard to issues of gender and sexuality … " And he goes on to explain why the film is within the genre: "*Brokeback Mountain* is intimately concerned with the myth of the West, with romanticized notions of the cowboy and pioneering life … The dramatic battles to defend high ideals found in classic Westerns are contrasted here with the struggle to stay alive in the face of stultifying prejudices." He also writes about the masculinity of the film: "What is on sale here is male potency … The intensity of the bipolar opposites contained in the cultural oxymoron 'gay cowboy' are ever present beneath Ennis's surface presentation of self." He gives as a key detail in the film the reaction of Ennis's wife when she sees the two men kissing: "there is a shot of her face as she attempts to come to terms with what she has seen. To her left is Ennis's cowboy hat hanging on a peg on the wall: her struggle is to square this kiss with all that the hat stands for in cultural terms."[10]

In *Brokeback Mountain*, the two protagonists are not fighting "dramatic battles" but involved in daily, small efforts to pass for the form of man that is symbolized by that cowboy hat. They are each and together involved in "the struggle to stay alive." There is another form of "male potency" in the short story and the film. The screenplay ends: " … on the back of the closet door, WE SEE THE SHIRTS, on a wire hangar suspended from a nail, and next to them, a postcard of Brokeback Mountain, tacked onto the door. [Ennis] has taken his shirt from inside of Jack's, and has carefully tucked Jack's shirt down inside his own. He snaps the top button of one of the shirts. Looks at the ensemble through a few stinging tears. ENNIS: Jack, I swear …"[11] The "male potency" of the story is not the survival of the fittest, not the social Darwinian testing ground within which the myth is supposed to be set. It is the survival of Ennis's love for Jack.

Here is a second way to reset the myth of "the West." Why not "Shepherd Church"? Why did church marketing strategists recommend a niche brand of "Cowboy" rather than a niche brand of "Shepherd?" One obvious answer is that the Marlboro Man became a mass marketed icon of masculinity, selling tobacco from the 1960s forward. National Public Radio ran a series "Present at the Creation" that featured archival work into the creation of pieces of Americana. In 2002, the series ran a piece on the Marlboro Man, by Kathleen Schalch.[12] She reports on the advertising conundrum facing executives when they needed to sell their filtered cigarettes, originally aimed at women, to men. They knew it was a matter of minutes before studies linking tobacco to cancer emerged, and they needed to hook customers on a "safer" cigarette. The original "Marlboro Man" featured diverse working men, but, by the 1960s, they homed in on a man on a horse in a cowboy hat: " … as American politics became more complicated in the 1960s, Jack Landry, the Marlboro brand manager at Philip

Morris, saw an opening into which the cowboy fit like a glove." Schalch quotes Landry: "In a world that was becoming increasingly complex and frustrating for the ordinary man … the cowboy represented an antithesis—a man whose environment was simplistic and relatively pressure free."[13]

The image continues to evoke a "simpler" time today, and in the case of many "Cowboy Church" products and preaching, a "simpler" form of "the gospel." Many of the sermons from Southern Baptist congregations following this brand present a form of "the gospel" that can appeal to a sense of Christianity that is "simplistic." This jangles discordantly, as the words fall in the midst of lives and regions that are pressure laden. "The Marlboro Man" bookmarks "the 1960s" as a decade of demise, later in the 1980s for writers like Anthony Esolen in his lament about sexual confusion, to Kevin Williamson in his diagnosis that small towns are dying (and deserve to) because they have lost their way through the liberalization of divorce laws and the accessibility of reproductive choice, to evangelical sociologist James Davison Hunter's binary between cultures in a societal war of lefty secularists versus traditional religionists. The 1960s, a time that brand manager Jack Landry names as "increasingly complex and frustrating for the ordinary man," works as a jump in the timeline between what is simple, old common sense and the befuddling nonsense of anti-war protests, desegregation, gay pride, and women's liberation. As Landry words it here, "the cowboy fit like a glove."

The Marlboro Man is by 1965 decidedly a cowboy.[14] This is in spite of the fact that, in the language most spoken immediately before Texas became Texas, "pastor" means shepherd. The answer to why not a "Swineherd Church" may be obvious. But sheep are as Texan as cows. The Texas State Historical Society is a non-profit in existence since 1897. Their entry for "Wool and Mohair Industry" explains a shift in the region now known as Texas from shepherding as ancillary to cattle work toward shepherding as an industry in itself. They include details about the growth of sheep work and concomitant wool work. From 1850 to 1885, the numbers had increased from 100,530 sheep to 6,620,000 sheep. The "industry" of wool and mohair includes sheep and goats, together, the author explains, and my hometown of San Angelo became the center of production, and "the headquarters of the Mohair Council of America, an organization designed to promote the virtues of mohair."[15]

Growing up, I passed billboards along the regional highway across West Texas repeatedly that read "The Mohair Capital of the World!"

Elmer Kelton wrote from his home in San Angelo as a journalist and novelist of books in the genre of "Western." His journalism focused on the varieties and varied tending and trading of sheep and goats, and he wrote for *The San Angelo Standard Times*. The *Wall Street Journal* ran Kelton's obituary in 2009, explaining his appeal and noting the writers who define the genre considered him the best of the best. They quoted him as saying, "I can't write about heroes seven feet tall and invincible. I write about people five feet eight and nervous." They also note that "in 1995, based largely on the accomplishment of 'The Time It Never Rained,' the Western Writers of America voted him the greatest western writer of all time."[16]

Kelton wrote about the critical reception of his 1971 novel *The Day the Cowboys Quit*. The novel is historically informed. In the 1986 edition's introduction, Kelton characterizes the criticism "that it was out of character for cowboys to strike and that therefore the novel was a transparent attempt to place modern-day labor-management problems in the context of a Western." Kelton explains that the book's setting is an actual strike in what is known as "the Texas Panhandle in 1883."

The Texas panhandle is the northwestern part that looks like a squared-off handle on a frying pan. The striking cowboys are "the hub around which the story revolves," but, as Kelton explains, the story describes a time when "free men" had been "downgraded and fettered in a manner they refused to accept." Kelton's voice as a journalist comes through in the introduction, as he teaches about the period. Smaller ranch settlers had won their claim "through hard work, boldness and—in some cases—outright theft." Kelton puts the change in the decade around 1880: "Handsome profits attracted the attention of Eastern and European investors. The 'Beef Bonanza' lured millions of dollars to Texas and Western ranges. However welcome the money might have been at the time, it came with strings attached." His introduction to the volume notes "newcomers … saw him as no different from employees in a shoe factory or a cotton mill. To protect their own interests they began imposing rules of employment which took away freedoms and privileges the cowboy had regarded almost as a birthright." That birthright included "the right to have cattle of his own" and the liberty to ride.

> Often the cowboy was denied even the opportunity to keep his own horse in the company remuda. Thus he was robbed of his mobility. If he quit or was fired, he was stranded and afoot, an awesome prospect for a man who had spent his life ahorseback. That old freedom to saddle up and ride away was compromised. [The 23 rules posted in 1888 at the XIT ranch] became a red flag, an implication that the cowboy was chattel …

Kelton states that "viewed only for immediate effect, the [1883] strike was a failure." The strike meant that "unemployed cowboys were riding the plains looking for work" and "owners quickly fired the strikers and replaced them with men eager for a job." Eventually, "the strikers scattered, blacklisted and unable to find jobs on ranches in the upper Panhandle. It was clear that the cowboys had lost." What also "gradually became clear" was that "the ranch owners had not won an unqualified victory. They were unable to force all the former strikers to leave the country. These men by and large had the sympathy of a growing number of small ranch operators and homesteaders who saw the big ranches as a common enemy." The moment in history reverberated as "strikers became farmers and small ranchers" such that "there were many more cowboys, farmers, and small town businessmen than ranch owners." "In county after county," Kelton relates, "big owners found themselves facing a hostile local political climate. In terms of taxation, of inability to win court judgments or obtain convictions of those who transgressed against them, they found that in the long run they too had lost the strike."[17]

Memorials Matter

There is no monument or memorial in Texas for the day the cowboys quit. The strike of 1883 merits a brief entry online in the Texas State Historical Association website with a tonally beige conclusion: "Whatever the causes of their failure to organize effectively, the strikers were finally unable to overcome the obstacles they found in the cattle industry. While some historians claim that the strike reflected the international labor movement, others consider it an interesting but isolated incident that had no lasting repercussions for either cowboys or the cattle industry."[18] "Failure to organize effectively" intimates that there was an active organizing effort and some possibility or measure of "effectiveness" at this time in the disputed territory. The "while some …. others" balance ignores which economic perspective a historian might hail from. And "isolated incident" appears as the closing word to reassure anyone looking for evidence of labor unrest in Texas.

For comparison, within seven years of the 1886 labor-related Haymarket Affair citizens had erected a Martyrs' Monument in Illinois. The battle for an eight-hour workday in the postbellum Midwest now has as one of their markers a National Historic Landmark. The application to the United States Department of the Interior, National Park Service in 1997 describes the site: "The predominant figure is a woman who is standing over the other figure, a bearded male worker. Below the bronze figure on the upper step is inscribed the date 1887 with bronze palms below it." The inscription below both reads: "The day will come when our silence will be more powerful than the voices you are throttling today," words attributed to upholsterer and labor organizer August Spies before his execution there.[19] The site of the strike in Tascosa, Texas, is obviously not Chicago. Yet this is context to understand which stories people told and still tell about their region and who struggled against whom.

This also relates to the fact that "the West" was a place where some postbellum dignitaries would erect monuments to the Confederacy. The fact that there was from 1916 to 2017 a monument to the Confederacy in Helena, Montana, is also context for how "the West" functioned in the half-century after the Civil War. Larry McMurtry did not pick his two cowboy heroes in his Pulitzer Prize winning *Lonesome Dove* out of a hat. They are both former Texas Rangers with service in the Confederate army. The *Texas Standard* noted in 2023 that "*Lonesome Dove* is one of the most popular Texas novels of all time with many millions of copies sold since it was first published in 1985. The miniseries that followed in 1989 was the second most popular miniseries of all time, behind *Roots*."[20] McMurtry named the "Old West" as "still the phantom leg of the American psyche" and was abashed that critics and readers considered it "the *Gone with the Wind* of the West."[21] But that is an apt description. Two Texas Rangers? Check. Two Confederate soldiers? Check and check. The story carries nostalgia for a time-that-never-was immediately postbellum when men were men alongside one another in a fight against the elements—when they were not also fighting Mexicans and American Indians.

Here is another way to shift perspectives on the myths of the "West." Why is there a Confederate monument in Montana? The Intermountain Histories Project features a heartening collaboration of journalism, archivism, and national landmark work.[22] A section by Makoto Hunter links five locations under the heading "Confederate Markers in the Intermountain West." The introduction names my initial confusion. "One might not expect to find commemorations of the Confederacy north of the Mason–Dixon Line, let alone west of the Rocky Mountains … Where did these Confederate markers come from, and why were they in the American West?"[23] Hunter explains "Helena's local chapter of the United Daughters of the Confederacy … had fundraised for the fountain since 1903 and donated it to the city." "In a dedicatory speech," Hunter explains the spokeswoman "said the fountain was the Daughters' gift to their new home, and she praised the city's American spirit of unity in which there were no bad feelings between the American North and South." Her words christen the West as claimed for a particular kind of "home." "On behalf of the Daughters of the Confederacy," she concluded, "I present this fountain to the city of Helena as a token of our esteem toward our new home."

In his 2003 book *Race and Reunion: the Civil War in American Memory*, David W. Blight works decade by decade through primary documents—speeches, newspaper reports, and memorial wordings themselves—to explain the pressure exerted by business and federal interests to repeat the words "reconciliation," "regeneration," and "reunion" postbellum. Blight explains the effort in part by way of Grant's nomination for President. He describes Grant's conclusion to his speech as employing "the splendidly ambiguous slogan of his campaign: 'Let us have Peace.'" By 1868, the "Republican Party retrenched onto a platform of order and stability; they would now be protectors of a status quo rather than innovators."[24] Blight notes "the prevailing theme was the equality of soldiers' sacrifice on both sides." This was particularly intense in Gettysburg: "As regimental monuments began to mark the landscape at the

Gettysburg battlefield, soldiers' dedication speeches and tourist guidebooks portrayed the site as the 'Mecca of American Reconciliation.'" The Mecca of *White* Reconciliation, and in ways that were, as Blight clearly notes in his title, about race. These pageants of reconciliation between veterans were intentionally about "peace," order, and stemming the tide of interracial organizing. Blight recounts: "At many dedications of the common soldier monuments in Northern towns, such as one in Sharon, Connecticut, in 1885, orators celebrated how after twenty years the 'unutterable bitterness and destruction' could now be 'obliterated … forgotten,' how the results of the war had been rendered permanent, 'the error of slavery ended; every foot of our soil free to labor.'"

Larry McMurtry would have a character say "what total horseshit." African American writers were composing words against this false unity in every form they could give—in song, newspaper, essay, book. Blight quotes an editor from June 1888, "No God-knows-who-was-right bosh must be tolerated at Gettysburg. The men who won the victory there were eternally right, and the men who were defeated were eternally wrong."[25] The bosh won, but not fairly.

These connections from "past" to present require concerted effort. The Illinois Labor History Society was formed in 1969. Their mission statement includes "preservation," "study," and "history," but also the intent "to arouse public interest in the profound significance of the past to the present." As with the Intermountain Histories Project, they invite collaboration with colleges and universities. One early collaboration is listed from 1974—"In collaboration with the Film Department of Columbia college, produced 'The Memorial Day Massacre of 1937,' a 17-minute documentary film containing the unedited version the Paramount newsreel of the event." In 1977, they collaborated with the University of Chicago for an event studying the 1877 Railroad Strike or "Great Upheaval."[26]

For his part, Timothy Tyson has helped to trouble the mythmaking of the Confederacy in North Carolina. While researching this section on the memorials of Confederate soldiers in "the West," I continued hearing his words about why the land of Billy Graham has so many Confederate monuments, erected decades after the Civil War. The memorials were erected to eclipse facts. He explains: "If you added up the African Americans, the Unionists, the anti-Confederate rebels, the anti-war crowd and those who simply hated what the Confederacy did to their home state, they might have outnumbered the hardcore Confederates." In his 2017 article for the *Raleigh News and Observer*, "Commemorating North Carolina's anti-Confederate heritage, too," Tyson recounts "during the actual Civil War, the Confederacy bitterly divided North Carolina, the last Southern state to secede and the one with the highest number of battlefield deaths and the highest desertion rate. At times the conflict in North Carolina literally became 'a war within a war.'" He continues: "The Confederate Conscription Act, which exempted prosperous slaveholders from military service, turned many more Tar Heels against the war. That autumn of 1862, North Carolina's own internal civil war began to rage." This history is barely told and is crucial for understanding the "legacy" of the state: "From the coastal swamps to the wilderness of the Blue Ridge, anti-Confederate guerillas, Unionists and runaway slaves battled the Confederacy; parts of North Carolina became virtually ungovernable." He links the time before the "memory" of the erected memorials to the time of the memorials through into the present: "The notion that the Confederacy represents white North Carolina's heritage is not historical but instead political."[27] The placement of a Confederate memorial in Montana in the early twentieth-century is pertinent for the myth of the individual cowboy and the myth of "the West" marketed by Southern Baptist churches from Georgia to Nevada in the early twenty-first century.

"The Farmer and the Cowman"

I taught my daughters to sing "OAK … lahoma … where the wind comes sweepin' down the plain" when we crossed the Oklahoma border. The song was a scrap of a myth of a myth that I had heard sung by friends. The Tony Awards website for 2019 celebrates Daniel Fish's production of the Rodgers and Hammerstein 1943 musical *Oklahoma*. Fish's production won "Best Revival of a Musical." Fish created a straight-up reckoning of the libretto. "There's still 'a bright golden haze on the meadow' … but here there are also fully stocked gun racks up on the walls, just to remind us how the West was really won" reports *Variety*. The musical is set in the "sweeping prairies of the Oklahoma Territory, poised on the verge of statehood in 1907," and Fish's "production style is decidedly naturalistic, with a strong undercurrent of violence." The review states plainly: "In this context, the killing that ends the show is no facile *deus ex machina*, but a real statement about the making of America and the settling of the Wild West."[28]

An *Oklahoma!* song stuck as I sorted the niche marketing of "Cowboy Church." The local judge in the musical begins "The Farmer and the Cowman" with an earnest entreaty set to a continuous square dance cadence: "territory folks should stick together; territory folks should all be pals; cowboys, dance with farmers' daughters; farmers, dance with the ranchers' gals." A local rancher sums up the stakes. Once a mere territory becomes part of the United States, a farmer, a store owner, and someone who works with cattle—everyone must "act like brothers." If being a good, white, male citizen in the U.S. means being "brothers" across a region, why have a church called "Cowboy"? Why not Farmer Church? Why not a square dance that includes farmers, cowmen, and merchants?

Oscar Hammerstein II and Richard Rodgers won viewers and critical acclaim for their mythmaking by describing mainstream American culture within a fantastical setting. As Rob Weinert-Kendt words this in a 2018 essay for *America Magazine*, "they captured the nation's broad-shouldered postwar confidence as well as its perennial mix of idealism and nostalgia." Their mythmaking continues to connect with mainstream viewers. Weinert-Kendt explains: "The question of whether their work has transcended the square, segregated era of its making—a purportedly halcyon age that some people in this country have in mind when they talk about making America great 'again'—has partly been answered by their musicals' continuing popularity … "[29]

Why market a brand of evangelicalism that focuses only on a cowman? The simple answer is that "the Cowboy" still works as a unifying myth. As Gary West insists in the title of his 2012 article for the *Fort Worth Star-Telegram* "Are the Cowboys still America's Team?: The answer is yes. Other teams may try to claim the title, but there is only one America's Team."[30] He explains that Bob Ryan "coined the Cowboys' famous nickname while editing the team's highlight film for the 1978 season, which concluded in Miami with a Super Bowl loss to the Steelers." "They appear on television so often their faces are as familiar to the public as presidents and movie stars," West quotes from the film, "They are the Dallas Cowboys, 'America's Team.'" Ryan asserted that the Cowboys "appeared more frequently than any other team on national television, had the most visible players and sold the most merchandise. Their popularity crossed regional borders, it veritably soared, and their fan base became national."

The Dallas Cowboys, many of whom are not from Texas and most of whom do not show up in cowboy hats, work as manly avatars. They represent a form of patriotism for men and women across the U.S. in a way that is not even available to the "Patriots." Teddy Roosevelt was from New England, but it was "the West" that made him a symbol of muscular Americana. Gary West connects these ideas succinctly: "this team with the pristine logo, a blue star suggestive of independence and individuality, had become a symbol not just for winning but for progress … It probably helped, too, that the cowboy was an iconic figure in American history."

When I checked in for the 2013 Davis, Oklahoma, Baptist men's retreat I was handed an actual item that reads "Man Card." It is a laminated card with red lettering in a font that matches the Marlboro Man advertising campaign.[31] The logo for "Rewired" itself in 2013 is also red but in a stylized form of linked letters together so that R-E-W connect as circuitry and R-E-D connect as circuitry, with the I standing alone in the middle. The background of the "Man Card" is the same as the cover of the book we each received for the conference. The title of the book reads in all capital letters "THE FIGHT FOR BIBLICAL MANHOOD" with "Biblical" in the Marlboro font. The drawing on both is of two shirtless men in a boxing ring wearing knickers. The style of the flooring they are standing on is wooden and the overall impression is old-timey. One of the men could be "Pa" on the television series. When I asked friends older than I am to describe the image, they said "fisticuffs," "breeches," and the "Marquess of Queensberry Rules."

The theme of the "Fight" was pornography. The schedule for the retreat and the description of the speakers and worship leaders are bound together with a book by Tim Challies, produced by Cruciform Press called *Sexual Detox: A Guide for Guys Who Are Sick of Porn*. The author has as a core assertion in his narration of the poison to which he is offering the detoxification that James

Dobson, the founder of conservative conglomerate Focus on the Family, is wrong about masturbation. Masturbation, Challies contends, is *not* "normal." When I read this book my first night, I thought that the book probably would connect to most participants as a remedy for "sin" if any man who masturbates is included under that diagnosis. Does the Marlboro Man have time to masturbate?

At the Rewired event, I met Southern Baptist pastor and strategist Keith Burkhart and explained that I was writing about forms of ministry specifically aimed to reach men. Burkhart is part of the Baptist General Convention of Oklahoma and worked in a role called "Family and Men's Ministry Specialist" for a decade. He has also led the Oklahoma Faith Riders, a motorcycle ministry and has been a chief strategist for the yearly Rewired Men's Conference.[32] The event is held at the Baptist Falls Creek Conference Center in Davis, Oklahoma. The Center was established in 1917, around the time when boys wore knickers. Burkhart explained that the Southern Baptist Church had been reaching men where they are. He calls this, in his document about the efforts, "Reaching Tribal Men." This is "mission work" that Burkhart situates as akin to learning about a group of people "outside the United States," explaining that success in "partnerships" with churches elsewhere involved attention to the context. In preparation for a mission trip, he had "diligently studied about the people, their language and their customs." He gives the following as a summary of the plight facing men in the U.S.

> For every 10 men in the church… 9 will have kids who leave the church; 8 will not find their jobs satisfying; 6 will pay only the monthly minimum on credit cards; 5 have a major problem with pornography; 4 will get divorced, affecting 1,000,000 children each year; Only 1 will have a Biblical worldview; All 10 will struggle to balance family & work.

Burkhart understands men as subscribing to different realities, depending on their particular "tribe." If "Rule #1 in Missions" is to "Know Your Location," a person (man) seeking to reach a group of men needs to specialize in ministry to a particular group, or "tribe."[33] He states "in every community there are tribes of hunters, fishermen, golfers, bikers, sportsmen, cowboys, and a variety of outdoor adventurers." The second aspect of Rule #1 is to know where tribes gather: "On any given night or weekend you can find villages of men at bike nights, golf courses, hunting/fishing events, rodeos, NASCAR races, etc."

The retreat was structured around this assumption of segmentation, with "Pre-Event Activities" from Trout Fishing, Cowboy Camp, Shotgunning, Video Gaming, and Skateboarding. The former student who suggested I attend did so because I was noting how around 2008–2012 United Methodist leaders were pressuring churches to employ marketing strategists to target a particular demographic. One way to read the Moody Bible Institute poster from 1920 is that the men are described according to their particular "tribe" and who they are, by their tribe, able to reach. My objection to this pattern within United Methodism was, at that time, that it was wrongheaded and tacky. Paying people from schools of business to help a congregation "pitch" itself to a particular segment of the population troubled me aesthetically as well as theologically. Here was Pastor Burkhart from the Southern Baptist leadership making it all sound so commonsensical. You cannot expect a man who likes trout fishing to minister to men who like skateboarding … But you might craft a net to catch most if you call masturbation a sin.

The formal presentations included "Manhood from a Coach," "Velocity and Me: How to Win as Men," and "Fight For Your Family!" as well as practically named sessions on "Reaching Men Through Small Groups" and "Sharing your Story in a Way that Will Win Others to Christ." I could not attend every session, so I had to choose. Two sessions among the many stand out.

At a conference against pornography, one of the central presentations in the large auditorium was a video mash-up of animal snuff films.[34] During a baffling video presentation, the speaker insisted that hunting was the most masculine of sports. In "Predator: Be the Hunter, Not the Hunted," he gave an introduction explaining that his work is dedicated to "evangelizing hunters." He told the auditorium full of men ahead of time that his presentation was for men, not "girls." He laughed about a time when a group of teenage girls had cried when he showed footage of "a sow taking a shot to the head." His presentation consisted of twelve straight minutes of animal after animal shot with a gun or a crossbow. He repeated twice that this was "a man thing"—that, if his young son and daughter were watching, his daughter would be "scarred for life." The focal point of his presentation was repetitive, disjointed images of the moment of animal death, with his exclamations of "Yeah!" and "Did you see that one!?"

Davis, Oklahoma, the town nearest the campsite, is eight miles from the Chickasaw Cultural Center.[35] The opening image of statues and sculptures at the Cultural Center is of two Chickasaw men hunting with bows and arrows. The description reads: "They're Hunting—Owwatta. Throughout the Mississippian Period, 900–1400 A.D., hunting was necessary for food and clothing. The bronze statue by James Blackburn features two hunters carrying bows with stone-tipped river cane arrows and river cane-woven quivers."[36] In personal correspondence with a friend who hunts for food, he explained that the celebratory mash-up we viewed was a category error—a depiction not of hunting but of something else, perhaps the ritual before staking a severed head on the wall. This was a point, again, when the conceit of "Muscular Christianity" rang false. If someone is practicing Christianity in a muscular way, according to a concept of "best man wins"—whether in the boxing ring or on the range—then the form of "the gospel" appearing on the screen and around the presenter's words about "being the predator not the prey" seemed more like someone who might "like Billy Graham" but who knows nothing about the practical work of hunting animals for food. This series of animal snuff films seemed not only to me but to some of the men in the room to be at least as problematic as bare breasts and butts. I sat at the back of the auditorium so I could think about how the farmers, cowmen, and trout fishermen were receiving this message. At least one in five of the men there were not looking at the screen but instead to the side, or down; some of them were looking at the ceiling. Two men in the auditorium walked out.

The other presentation that stood out was by Lew Sterrett, who uses his craft of horsemanship to explain ministry and leadership.[37] This presentation also involved mammals, but this time featured them alive. Equestrian Lew Sterrett offered a "Bonus Session" at a section of the conference grounds designated "Cowboy Camp" a presentation on "How to Make a Lasting Positive Impression." Sterrett is originally from Pennsylvania, now headquartered in Anadarko, Oklahoma. His 2013 business card features a photo of him riding a horse in traditional cowboy gear of hat, leather jacket, and chaps, with a logo of a horse racing around a cross. It reads "Sermon on the 'Mount' with

Dr. Lew Sterrett." He demonstrated Christian leadership models using well-trained horses and an untamed gelding. One of his opening lines is "Eat your heart out. *This* is the original Harley!" The day I caught him in action, he used a persistent, beautiful mare to lead the gelding, positioning the gelding to follow right at the back of the mare's lead, basically following her rump. He had a microphone connected to his head so that he could explain what was happening as he related horse training to ministry. I heard "she is leading," "he is following," and then again, "she is guiding," "he is learning to … " A friend who knows both horse training and farming said in personal correspondence about this display: "on a farm, functionality favors survivability." Sterrett, he said, was being functional. His lead horse that day was a mare, so he used the mare. Lew Sterrett explained later also that a mare will well train a stallion, adding "nothing will tear apart a mustang like a band of mares."

This again reveals a contradiction within some forms of Muscular Christianity. If "Muscular Christianity" draws from the "natural law" revealed to Teddy Roosevelt by "the West," or as it was revealed earlier to Charles Kingsley, then, by the basic "fitter and better" world built by the language system functionality should be key. Recall that when the head of Motor Racing Outreach asked me around this same time to recommend a book on single fathers from a Christian perspective, I could not think of one, and the question was clarifying. Within the binary of gender there is male and female, with males as breadwinners and women as homemakers. Never mind that this is not the reality of many men and women even in gender traditional churches. The two words together "she" and "leading" jangled in my head. I knew the networks I was studying reinforced the manhood in Roosevelt's "the Strenuous Life." A man who is the primary caregiver for children, a woman who is leading a younger man in a training exercise—in the world of meaning created by mainstream evangelicalism, these scenarios seem unnatural.

By 2013, I had read and heard many sermons and tracts that made clear males are built to lead, females built to follow. I had heard sermons where preachers had gone out of their way to make clear that God's love cannot possibly be likened to a woman's love for her husband or a mother's love for her children. God is sovereign and male. Men, built in his image, are built to lead. Lew Sterrett's no-nonsense decision to use a mare to make a point about

God's work of discipline stood out in a way that brought into contrast this messaging. I hoped to find that his form of ministry was characteristic of the "Cowboy Church" part of the effort to "reach" men as if they are in "tribes." It is not. Visiting "Cowboy Church" across the U.S., I was not, thank God, subjected to another video of an impaled animal, but neither did I encounter another showcased speaker like Lew Sterrett and his leading mare.

I have two mementos from Rewired that stand out—a horseshoe and a sweatshirt. Two men were at "Cowboy Camp" with a horseshoe ministry. We talked about the difficulty of men to be open with their real struggles. One named this as the expectation that men will be "Stoic." Their item is a bona fide horseshoe, with a standard engraving of "John 3:16" on each of the ends. They then engrave a name at the top of the "U." The card attached gives a translation of John 3:16: "For God so loved the world that He gave His only begotten Son, that whosoever believeth in Him should not perish but have everlasting life." On the other side of the card is a list that could serve as a lesson in basic evangelical theology. The script reads: "<u>The ABC's to Becoming a Christian</u>: **A**dmit to God you are a sinner. Repent ... **B**elieve that Jesus is God's son and that God sent Jesus to save people from their sins ... **C**ommit your life to Jesus ... **S**urrender your life to Christ." I asked why a horseshoe rather than a cross? They suggested a horseshoe is more immediately incarnate, or earthly. The cross appears to many men, they explained, as the opposite of incarnate, as disconnected to real work and real hands. The cross seems spiritual or too emotional, disconnected from real men. Their personalized horseshoes open more "real" conversations, they explained.

This connected to a distinction made by my host at "Rewired." She and I talked about divorce, children, and how much both of us enjoy being around groups of men doing athletic things. Several of the men recommended I return for the "Women's Retreat." "They don't have these activities at the women's conference," she explained, "and I am pretty much a tomboy." There are other Southern Baptist women in Oklahoma who love their horse or motorcycle, and their gun, and who would also find pleasure doing more than sitting around, knitting, talking about their prayer lives. We agreed with one another about this point. This "sentimental" programming, my host explained, is why she does not enjoy the women's conference. But there is an imposed male/

female contrast going on. The underlying story runs this way. Women are more spiritual/emotional and men are more carnal/rational. Christianity is about things spiritual, and women are better at spiritual things than men, so men's ministries must appeal in a targeted way to men's carnality. In many cases, that appeal has to do primarily with telling them, as has been the case in Western Christianity in other times and places, how and when to think about women and how and when to have sex. This pattern is not unique to Southern Baptist strategists in Oklahoma, of course. And, it remains part of the story.

It was colder at the camping site than I had anticipated, so I bought a sweatshirt. It is hanging by my editing table as I type, reminding me that this book matters. In Acts 29 churches, I have heard sermons specifically address the importance of proper obedience in the workplace. I heard scant of this at Rewired and little mention of work in "Cowboy Church" sermons. Yet "work" is everywhere, with tools hanging on walls and bathrooms made to look like horse stalls. Where, when, and how men work is part of the design. My Rewired 2013 sweatshirt is raw. The large image across the front is a length of large, strong looped chain in the form of a circle with the word "REWIRED" as part of the chain. Inside the circle is a large cross made up of two parts: a hammer and a double open-end wrench marked ¾ and ⅝. Across the wrench are the words "REWIRED—AMERICAN MADE." The tag inside reads "Made in Pakistan."

Poaching

In a 2020 student project in journalism for "The Carolina Connection" radio, Annabeth Poe visited with me about Western-themed ministry and interviewed the minister of a nearby Cowboy Church. The accompanying photo reads: "Willie Pickard preaches a Christmas message at Stockyard Cowboy Church in Siler City, NC." Annabeth Poe begins: "One of the fastest growing trends in religion mixes Christ with cattle. They're called Cowboy Churches and according to one fellowship group, more than 200 are now operating around the United States." Her report is edited for concision at 2.58 minutes, but she spent hours on the effort. Poe summarizes well the setting: "baptizing people in livestock watering troughs, taking offering in milk pails instead of gold plates, and adorning the service with country gospel music instead of a choir." Tammy Taylor, who sings with the group names the allure: "you can wear a ball hat, you can wear a cowboy hat. It doesn't matter what you look like because God doesn't look at what you have on. He looks at your heart … " She explains: "I love the cowboy culture because it brings in people that may never even darken the doors of a church." In Poe's clip from our visit, she highlights my main concern, a concern that connects with a faith she and I share, about the simplification of Christianity in the messaging. She then answers my concern with the pastor's plain words. "But Pickard, the preacher at Stockyard, says the gospel itself is simple. That it's just about asking Jesus to be your savior." Pickard notes: "A lot of churches have made it hard. They teach that you need to do this or that first, and then accept Him. But no, you just need to accept him. He will do the changing." Poe's conclusion is perfect: "Even though he preaches in cowboy boots, and the floor is dotted with manure, it still is holy ground."[38] Not incidentally, Annabeth Poe won second place in the Hearst monthly competition and an award from Radio Television Digital News Association of the Carolinas for Best Feature Story.[39]

In her adept contrasting of my desire for a more complicated, biblically attentive version of "church" and Pickard's answer, she has noted we are answering different questions. Is "the gospel" simple? Yes. In this belief, strange as it may sound, Pastor Pickard and I agree. Tammy Taylor and I are also in agreement that people must be welcomed to church as they are, hat or no hat. But I do not think people are simple. A presumption of much in this network is that the "sorts" of people drawn into these ministries are themselves "simple." I do not believe that anyone's life, once they have come to "accept Him," as Pickard words it, becomes magically simpler, or simply changed.

An elder Southern Baptist pastor at a storefront Cowboy Church in Reno, Nevada, helped me understand another aspect of the effort. In February 2014, I flew to Reno to visit an Acts 29 church plant and a "Cowboy Church." "Cowboy Fellowship Church" met in a strip mall with a 7-11 convenience store. The group shared the small, functional meeting space with a Spanish speaking congregation and a Russian-speaking congregation. Eddie Miller, the fellowship's pastor, explained that the Russian and Cowboy congregations share ministries, including to women who have found themselves in the U.S. as "Russian brides," women who have married American men. My notes on the church bulletin from that Sunday are sparse because I was drawn in as a participant in the gathering. We sang from a physical hymnal, with no drums or microphones. Miller preached sitting down. More accurately, he "taught" sitting down. He "preached" in a way that I have only seen Jewish rabbis preach. (The word "rabbi" is a transliteration from the Hebrew, and the Hebrew word means "teacher.") People opened bibles, and he read through the passage from the New Testament book of Romans 11:33–12:2, giving commentary from the original Greek. The theme of his sermon series for that part of the year was "Living Sacrifice," and people responded with comments and questions during the sermon time. One of his emphases in the lesson was that, if our lives are a "living sacrifice" then this means "living, and living is not predictable." He taught that a life of faith is not "easy," or "perfect." I wrote on the bulletin: "opposite of bossy life coach." Miller treated the people at the gathering as people who had come to learn, and who had things to ask related to the actual text for the day.

In conversation after the service, I asked about the idea of "reaching" men through niche marketed churches. Miller said many of the church schemes were not so much "reaching" men as converts as they were "poaching" them from other churches. He wrote in email correspondence, "Most of the folks attending Cowboy Church today were attending church somewhere else and were drawn to the Cowboy Church because of schedule, dress code, and lifestyle issues … " For background, Miller served for thirty years as the "area missionary" for the Sierra Baptist Association, retiring in 2022. The Sierra Baptist Association covers Western Nevada and Eastern California, spanning 30,000 square miles.[40]

I asked Miller about dividing of men by "tribes," sharing that I was skeptical about the wisdom of that method. He wrote about the history of this idea. "Your statement regarding dividing people up seeming wrong goes all the way back to the '70s when the foundation was laid for this movement. In my first semester of Seminary at Southwestern in 1975 I had such a violent reaction to this concept that was just then being taught in the missions classes that I dropped the class." He continued, explaining that, when he was in training, "the concept of people group outreach and population segmentation was just beginning to be taught as the foundation for reaching the world for Christ, and while I see the great value in knowing a culture and reaching people in their heart language and culture, this concept has really come of age in the Purpose Driven type churches." "While the cities are more effectively reached theoretically by some of these strategies," he conceded, "the proliferation of these kinds of efforts into rural, and suburban locations has served to further divide people in what I believe to be unhealthy ways." Miller also named a specific threat to the health of congregations: "We are on the brink of stopping all cross pollination among believers of different cultures and population segments. The great weakness is that targeting a single group makes it okay to turn your back on the other groups in the area not served by any church's ministry." He summed up the problem in scriptural terms: "I think the Bible was serious when it said that in Christ there is neither male nor female, bond nor free, Jew or Greek. This concept is not displayed much in the evangelical/ free church of the 21st century in America."

My second concern was about the simplicity of the messaging. Miller responded:

> We do not use much of the Cowboy Church material available today because it is very thin theologically, and it tends to support an anemic view of following Christ day to day. Many of the people in the Cowboy culture are like other cultures in that they are experientially oriented and are drawn to emotional and charismatically (popular usage) driven worship experiences.

He explained this in clear terms: "Lot of emotion, not much Gospel. They also have a strong work ethic so earning their salvation is very important to them even though it is impossible."

Miller wrote that many people "are looking for something for themselves rather than an opportunity to make a difference in the Kingdom" contrasting two related commitments within many Baptist circles. Does a human being most need a commitment to a confession of faith in Jesus Christ as savior, and does this commitment resolve their predicament as a person on this earth for all time moving forward? Does a human being also need a commitment to help people and be helped by people around them as they move forward? Is that commitment of mutual aid, of upbuilding together in a congregation, part of the story of becoming "Christian," or at least of being "Christian"?

When the pastor in Siler City characterized his message as "simple," he stated a belief in the conversion of a person as requiring a simple affirmation and acceptance of Jesus as savior. There are fully queer affirming evangelical churches that retain this affirmation of simplicity when it comes to the connection between God and an individual. It makes logical sense within this world of thinking that a person would seek a setting "for themselves." Miller explained that for some forms of these ministries people come to be served. There can be a passivity about the settings, where people come to hear and feel something for their own sake. Why else go? Because, Miller noted, there is also a call within the Baptist tradition to "make a difference in the Kingdom." In the case of the congregation that gathers on Sunday mornings in that storefront church, they reach out. A common term is "outreach." Miller noted the importance of a group of people gathering in the name of Jesus to reach out, and not only to secure more butts in a pew. Their outreach includes, as he explained, meeting people where they work, in casinos, to name one example, and to offer help, as he explained in person, to "Russian brides."

The bulletin and the website for the church have the words "Cowboy" and "Church," and the church is listed as a "Cowboy Church" at a search tool for people looking specifically for a ministry related to "the West" at: http://www.cowboychurch.net/nevada.html. Yet he noted that the congregation is also made up of people who came related to "outreach" and who may or may not have any interest in "the West." He explained that their location is a basic matter of availability, of functionality. As he related, they are "off target" for the usual "target group" of people who are working with livestock, "but we have practiced incarnational evangelism as opportunities have arisen and have a mixed group as you saw." I will explain in the next chapter the "target group" for Acts 29 churches. Some of the other churches I have visited have been "a mixed group," drawing from people of different races and backgrounds. What sets apart Cowboy Fellowship in Reno is that this mixed group was not there for a show. Worship was not a performance. The circled chairs, the shared prayer concerns, the questions and answers, this was unique—more like a bible study (with actual bibles) mixed with a Quaker meeting. Their "incarnational evangelism," as he called it, means that they brought that sense of trust outward by teaching English as a Second Language classes and thinking together about how to reach people at casinos. It is not a grand strategy. I am not sure someone determined to "count" success would see this ministry as "successful."

He also wrote: "While we are aiming at a particular kind of person that is lost we are seeing all kinds of people that are lost respond. Shocking isn't it? The area where we serve is about 95% lost." What does Miller mean by "lost?" Are people literally wandering around Reno without a map? When he says "shocking, isn't it?" he is being ironic. He is saying that it is not at all "shocking" that when people are treated with basic human dignity they feel, rightly, that they have been "found." This language of "lost" is connected to "lost and found" parables in the New Testament. The most well-known in Methodist circles is about a shepherd who has lost one of the sheep in his flock. The shepherd takes time to find the lost sheep, rather than writing them off as "lost." Miller stated that the focus on a particular "tribe" has been a form of missiology since he was a student at a Baptist seminary in Fort Worth, Texas.[41] He related this strategy to "population segmentation." That is probably a self-evident term. But he also explained that this decreases "cross-pollination," that a focus on one set of cultural tropes risks segmenting people such that church is no longer a setting for people to learn from one another across boundaries within mainstream evangelicalism. Another striking aspect is his concern that these schemes may divide mainstream evangelicals from ethnic groups moving to Reno to work in casinos. "The great weakness is that targeting a single group," he explained, "makes it okay to turn your back on the other groups in the area not served by any church's ministry."

One word for Miller's perspective on missions, service, immigration, labor, and "cross-pollination" is "catholic" in the small "c" form of that word. The *OED* has as the first definition the most common use: "Since the Reformation, the term 'Catholic' has chiefly been used to denote the part of the medieval Western or Latin Church which continued to be led by the Pope."[42] The non-ecclesiastical use means "Of, relating to, or involving the whole world; worldwide, universal."[43] Without romanticizing the Roman Catholic Church, consider this connection between the two uses, ecclesiastical and non-ecclesiastical. When driving to and from Dallas/Ft. Worth to visit cousins we would regularly pass by St. Joseph Parish in Rowena, Texas, off Highway 67. The architecture would be beautiful anywhere, but due to the terrain we could see the church for miles before arriving. In "Indian Creek, Rowena and Ballinger: Discovering history gems in small West Texas towns" Michael Barnes of the *Austin American-Statesman* evokes the setting:

> Motoring alongside the flat cotton fields on U.S. 67 from San Angelo to Brownwood on a recent West Texas road trip, we spotted in the distance a tall, dark church spire. It looked out of place. More like something you'd see in parts of Europe, maybe, not West Texas… The spire belonged to St. Joseph Catholic Church in Rowena, a town of fewer than 500 souls.[44]

St. Joseph is a cowboy church. Men and women may arrive on a Sunday morning for mass after having tended cattle, sheep, or goats. Due to the parish system, people worship together—bankers, cattle people, shepherds, mechanics, restauranteurs, people who wash dishes at the Lowake Steak House all attend together. The bulletins feature businesses supported by the parish. For April 7, 2024, some include Frey Cattle Company, Top Tier Grain and Feed, Jones Plumbing, Olfen Sausage, Kit's Body Shop, Byler Dozer Service, and the Joe A. Vancil Ranch. The ranch includes the icon of a cowboy kneeling before a cross and his horse behind him.[45] Michael Barnes tells his readers that, "during the terrible drought of the 1950s, St. Joseph became an anchor for the whole surrounding area." Barnes explains the current demographic of the parish: "Now a little over 200 families—mostly of German, Czech or Mexican origins—attend the church." St. Joseph is both upper-case C Catholic and lower-case case c catholic in a way that helps to describe the "cross-pollination" Miller, a Southern Baptist from further West, describes.

I attended what has repeatedly been called "the largest cowboy church in the world" while visiting Texas to attend my uncle's funeral. Ellis County Cowboy Church is in Waxahachie, a small city or large town that is halfway between my destination of Irving, Texas in the Dallas/Fort Worth Metroplex and Cedar Park, Texas, where my parents now live. I honestly picked out the church because I had only ever driven past Waxahachie, never properly visiting. I did not choose the church intending to contrast a small cowboy church in Nevada with "the largest cowboy church in the world." My father had told me that the Ellis County Courthouse is beautiful. By 2022 I had visited multiple cowboy churches including in my hometown of San Angelo, Texas; in rural Georgia; Ponder, Texas, outside of Denton, which is outside of the Metroplex; Tyler, Texas, in East Texas; and, of course, Reno, Nevada. The Ellis County church welcomed everyone into the large, no-nonsense structure with coffee and donuts. It was the first cowboy church to hand me a bumper sticker and the second to give me a copy of a 1992 version of a 1927 book by Oswald Chambers called *My Utmost for His Highest*. The only recognizable similarity between Eddie Miller's Southern Baptist church in Reno and the largest cowboy church in the world was the word "cowboy." Ellis County Cowboy Church is the largest version of the brand I had seen elsewhere, with seats all pointed toward a large stage on which one man in a hat preached a long sermon with visual prompts on a screen. People filed in, sat and listened, and filed back out. It was more like a show than an interactive bible study. In this way, it was also more like worship at Duke Chapel than it was like the storefront gathering in Nevada.

Vouching

I open this chapter with the words of three-term Texas State Representative for District 60, Glenn Rogers, who Christopher Hooks describes as "a Texas A&M–trained rural veterinarian and sixth-generation rancher … conservative … pro–border wall, antiabortion, anti–gun control [who] in the family of man … comes from the Hank Hill branch."[46] Rogers had the chutzpah to oppose Texas Governor Abbott, particularly the governor's plan to siphon off more public funding away from public schools into a voucher program. Hooks explains: " … when Abbott pushed hard for his voucher program … dragging the House into two miserable special sessions in which he promised retribution unless representatives such as Rogers went along, Rogers refused to bend." Glenn Rogers "became one of twenty-one rural and small-town Republicans who said the proposal would permanently weaken the Texas public school system on which their communities depend." In the 2024 primary race, funding poured in to bring to heel the twenty-one rural and small-town Republicans who had opposed the privatization of public schools. Sixteen of the twenty-one ran in the primaries for reelection in 2024.[47] The funding came from outside of the state and within. *Texas Monthly* reported "Jeff Yass, a Pennsylvania billionaire who runs a Wall Street trading firm and was an early investor in TikTok, a Chinese-owned social media company" sent money, and money flowed across Texas from "two billionaire oilmen, Tim Dunn and Farris Wilks."[48] Glenn Rogers called these men "radical dominionist billionaires seeking to destroy public education."[49]

This story is not the blockbuster version of oil country that "There Will Be Blood" offered in 2007. It is a true story from small town oil country. Perhaps consider it a *High Noon* story in real life. Glenn Rogers had to stand out, and alone, in trying to protect the goods held in common that are the public-school systems in his district. My father is from Palo Pinto County, Texas, eighty-nine miles west of Ellis County. He was ten when the 1952 movie *High Noon* came out, and he remembers sitting transfixed in the Grand Theater in Mineral Wells, Texas.[50] He calls it "the best in the Western genre" and mused to me recently that Larry McMurtry probably loved the movie. The population of Palo Pinto County was counted at 28,409 in 2020. District 60 of the Texas House is 185,732 and includes Palo Pinto, Parker, and Stephens Counties. The Palo Pinto Independent School District announced in 2023, "Palo Pinto Elementary–U.S. News Best Elementary School 2022. According to U.S. News and World Report, Palo Pinto Elementary ranks among the top 30% of Texas elementary schools."[51] The journalist who visited his Graford ranch in the days after he was targeted during the primary explains that "Rogers felt betrayed by constituents, including his neighbors in Palo Pinto County, who ought to know him but many of whom believed the attacks."[52] And quotes Rogers, "If you tell a lie often enough, it becomes the truth," he said. "It's not the truth, but it becomes their version of the truth."

Gary Cooper plays Marshal Will Kane in the 1952 classic. As critics and film studies scholars have noted repeatedly, Cooper appears genuinely frightened, vulnerable, on screen. Cooper is not a stoic version of a town marshal; he is in a low-to-high-grade panic as he tries to rally help to keep the town safe from a killer returning for revenge. The film is played in real time, as the clock at the train station ticks periodically onscreen toward noon, when the train carrying the killer will arrive. At the halfway point, Kane stands at the front of the town church with his neighbors in the pews. The town parson is standing in the pulpit, and the town mayor is standing in the front with Kane. Kane's new Quaker wife, played by Grace Kelly, resists jumping into the verbal fray of all the men standing and arguing, but she stands up, visibly livid, "Don't you remember when this wasn't a fit place to bring up a child?"[53] Thomas Mitchell plays Mayor Jonas Henderson, and it is his closing speech that leaves Kane abandoned. The viewer, like Kane, does not know exactly where the mayor is going to land with his words: "It is our problem because this is our town. We made it with our own hands out of nothing. And if we want to keep it decent, keep it growing, we've got to think mighty clear here … " He continues, "Now, people up North are … thinking about sending money down here, to put up stores and build factories … but if they're going to read about shooting and killing in the streets … They're going to think this is just another wide-open town. And everything we worked for will be wiped out." He then tells Will to leave town in order to keep the peace.

Cooper has looked miserable in front of the fray, as neighbors hurl absurd accusations of greed and incompetence at him. But there is a glimmer of hope in his eyes until the exact point when the mayor says the words "Now, people up North … " It is then that Kane knows exactly where the mayor is going to land. Cooper looks subtly sideways at the mayor, then he looks down at the floor. He will have to go this alone. The story in the film is as much about the mid-twentieth century in the U.S. as it is about anything related to "the West."[54] When Glenn Frankel's book *High Noon: The Hollywood Blacklist and the Making of an American Classic* came out in 2017, journalists sought to crystalize the story for busy readers.[55] In a piece for the *New York Post*, "How 'Commie' writer turned 'High Noon' into subversive Hollywood hit," Larry

Getlen writes "The cowardice of the townspeople and their betrayal of Kane wasn't just a figment of screenwriter Carl Foreman's imagination. It was a very real and frightening depiction of his personal experience getting caught up in the film industry's communist witch hunt of the late '40s and early '50s … " Foreman found himself hauled in to testify before the House Un-American Activities Committee during the creation of the film.

An impetus for this chapter is my belief that people attracted to themes of "Cowboy" deserve preaching and teaching worthy of the best "Westerns," whether a novel written by Elmer Kelton or a film written by Carl Foreman. They deserve the complicated word of God worth their time in their complicated, often beleaguered settings. They also deserve settings in which they can talk together and openly about what they most *need* for themselves and their towns. In the words of Quaker Amy Kane, "Don't you remember when this wasn't a fit place to bring up a child?" In this, Texas is a "bellwether," as Texan journalist Lawrence Wright put it. Consider how much money it has taken to convince voters that support for basically well-funded public schools in their cities and towns is a sign of "socialism." Every small town with a high school in Texas has revolved for decades around the football program. "Friday Night Lights"—the book, the film, and the television series about the Odessa Permian High School football team of 1988 is set in the backyards of the two Texans Glenn Rogers names as "radical dominionist billionaires seeking to destroy public education."

Tim Dunn teaches Sunday School in Midland, Texas, and Farris Wilks is, as reported by *Texas Monthly* "the pastor of his own church, the Assembly of Yahweh Seventh Day Church, near Cisco, Texas."[56] *Forbes* also reports that Farris and his brother Dan "have acquired more than 672,000 acres of land in six different states across the West, becoming America's 12th-largest landowners." Through their petrochemical fortunes, they have managed to convince many voters that support for the actual public schools surrounding the local football teams is itself a sign of weakness—that support for this common good is collaboration with those forces poised to storm their homes and take away their independence and their guns. It would be laughable if it were not so utterly grim.

This also connects back to the time historians often term the "Second Red Scare," the House Un-American Activities Committee, and the musical *Oklahoma*. I am editing this section of the book during the time when most of the movie-going public in the U.S. learned for the first time about the studious murders of members of the Osage Tribe in Oklahoma. Most people in the U.S. became aware of this history through the 2023 Martin Scorsese film *Killers of the Flower Moon*. In a 1994 review of a book on the murders, Margo Jefferson wrote for the *New York Times*: "The terror began in 1921, when an Osage woman was found at the bottom of a canyon with a bullet in her head. By the time the FBI began an investigation four years later, 60 rich Osages had been murdered and their land had gone to local white lawyers and businessmen."[57] Jefferson names the setting as "the lethal, wild West."

Hear, then, the 1953 lyrics from the theme song for *Oklahoma*. The musical is set only a decade before this history: "We know we belong to the land, and the land we belong to is grand!" "Plen'y of air and plen'y of room … "[58] The man who co-wrote this jingoistic lyric was required to attest to his patriotism. Rob Weinert-Kendt recounts that "in 1953 Hammerstein drafted a 30-page statement to the [U.S.] State Department not only disavowing any former association with Communist-affiliated organizations but expressing support for the current 'police action' in Korea and stating, in a plaintive self-assertion that is humbling to read, 'I have helped write many of the songs of this nation.'"[59] "Oklahoma" is one of the "songs of this nation." The committee to which Carl Foreman the screenwriter and Oscar Hammerstein the lyricist were summoned was about what is and is not "American." As Jim Harrison writes in his essay on "Geopiety" for *West of 98: Living and Writing in the New American West*, "there is no more otiose line in the history of American poetry than [Robert] Frost's 'The land was ours before we were the land's.'" Rewiring "the West" for the sake of any truthful, small "d" democratic sense of "brotherhood" must involve reckoning with each of these intertwined stories. Who owns the land, and the petrochemicals underneath, in "God's Country?" Will mayors and parsons in towns like Palo Pinto, Texas, and Davis, Oklahoma, encourage parishioners to stand up to, as Glenn Rogers calls them "radical dominionist billionaires seeking to destroy public education," men who pay other men, like Governor Abbott, to cast public school advocates as unpatriotic?

Oil Rich

In the 1956 movie *Giant*, James Dean's oil wildcatting character taunts rancher Rock Hudson: "I'm rich, Bick. I'm a rich 'un!" Who wins in the American version of business? Cowboys? Farmers? Wildcatters? *There Will Be Blood* from 2007 is included among the best films on critical lists in part because it rang jangling chords about manliness at that precise time in U.S. history. Does the myth of "the West" result in a true laboratory of success for fitness? The film won awards in the middle of two ongoing, intractable wars in Iraq and Afghanistan. This, during the oil baron, Texas Rangers, Bush dynasty. If "the West" is a Social Darwinian laboratory, oil wins. If, to use Teddy Roosevelt's jingoism from 1899, the nation needs to reproduce settings where men can prove their fitness through a "Strenuous Life," then an oilman has usually won.

In *Anointed With Oil: How Christianity and Crude Made Modern America*, Darren Dochuk writes that "late twentieth-century oil's prime movers remained tethered to a language that accentuated the oil-rich nation's special moment in the sun." He continues: "Forty years after Spindletop, in February 1941, magazine publisher Henry Luce would give that moment an enduring name: the 'American Century.' Luce, the son of foreign missionaries sponsored by the Rockefeller family, used the pages of his *Life* magazine to compel his fellow citizens to 'create the first great American Century.'" Dochuk tells readers "Luce heralded oilmen as the vanguard of pure American values, praising their 'dynamic spirit of freedom and enterprise' and 'sense of illimitable roundness of the world.'" Luce, by Dochuk's narration, had described for the magazine reading public in 1941 that if "harnessed by God-fearing patriots … oil had the capacity to transform the world into something godlier and better …. [oil was] the source of its prophetic mission."[60]

I graduated from high school in oil country the year of "The Crash of 1986." In his book *Texas Oil, American Dreams*, historian Lawrence Goodwyn describes that time, "It is not an easy task to describe the psychological as well as economic consequences of this shock, other than to suggest that fallout from the crude price crash of 1986 has influenced in large or small ways every subsequent development affecting independent producers down to the present." The reverberations shaped everything from local franchises to hospital nursing staff. "Bankruptcies coursed through every sector of the drilling industry," Goodwyn writes, "including, of course, wildcatters."

Houston had an NFL team from 1960 to 1996 named the "Houston Oilers." Their icon was an oil derrick. Beginning in 1968, they played in the Astrodome. In a 1965 essay entitled "Love, Death, and the Astrodome," Larry McMurtry describes the structure as a "huge white dome" that "poked soothingly above the summer heat haze like the working end of a gigantic roll-on deodorant." He continued "it seemed a bit conscienceless for a city with leprous slums, an inadequate charity hospital, wretched public transportation … to sink more than thirty-one million dollars in public funding into a ball-park." McMurtry called this "not, however surprising" given that Houston "is the kind of boom town that will endorse any amount of municipal vulgarity so long as it has the chance of making money." He calls the dome "*echt*-Texas."[61]

With this much money behind a team named the "Oilers," and with this much petrochemical "boom town" money running through the region, why not "Roughneck Church" or "Oilers Church?" "Cowboy Church" works as a myth and as a distraction. "America's Team," the Dallas Cowboys win (and the Houston Oilers do not exist anymore) in the struggle for fitness in brands because they provide a distraction from the reality of the lives of fans. "Cowboy Church" works from a form of nostalgia. "Cowboy" wins in the game of fisticuffs because it is a distraction from the reality of Texas politics and geopolitics in the U.S.

Muscular Christianity has never been about facts. McMurtry's Pulitzer Prize winning *Lonesome Dove* is a comic book version of what Teddy Roosevelt sought when he went out to the Dakota territories after the death of his wife and mother. The besotted Pulitzer committee found a mythology of a region, not the complex reality. If asked to imagine a different reading world beyond manly heroism set in the West, I would recommend McMurtry's Thalia novel *Duane's Depressed* (1999). This is not a utopia set on a different planet but set in the reality of Texas in the twentieth century. I agree with McMurtry's answer to the question of his "best book," a question he was asked frequently in the last decades of his life. Duane is an oil man McMurtry had written while seventeen-year-old Duane was in his senior year in high school, a man who eventually ends up striking oil and, in the book after *Duane's Depressed*, manages the new arrival of a herd of African Rhinos in *Rhino Ranch*. The book includes a Texas Ranger who cannot ride a horse. The shifts in Duane's life from a fatherless teenager working on oil rigs to a rancher with his own oil rigs to a rancher with oil rigs and rhinos are each plausible. The Rhinory in Fredericksburg exists: "Our family settled in the Hill Country over 150 years ago. We are proud to continue the ranching and farming tradition, albeit by raising rhinos instead of cattle and wine grapes instead of hay."[62]

Judith Wynn wrote a synopsis of the novel for the *Boston Herald*: "Sixty-two-year-old Duane Moore is depressed. His wife, Karla, thinks that he wants a divorce. His four grown children think he's insane. His five grandchildren think he's weird. All these noisy dependents live under Duane's roof and drive him crazy. So he decides to stop driving. From now on, he'll walk … " Foregoing motorized vehicles in the land of the truck is bizarre, but Duane Moore accepts Karla's insistence, eventually, to go see a therapist. This is bizarre on bizarre, and it is Pulitzer material. Duane only trusts the therapist, we are shown, not told, through her connection to a convenience store he has visited almost daily since he was himself a roughneck. McMurtry writes trenchantly about the internal life of Duane throughout:

> His main worry, when he thought of going to a psychiatrist, was that he'd just sit there and not be able to think of anything to say. After all, he had been brought up *not* to talk about his troubles, which were nobody's business but his. And he never *had* talked about them much. He might get into the doctor's office and find that he was unable to shrug off a lifetime of reticence.[63]

Recall that the men who gave me the horseshoe hanging next to my door, from Rewired, told me the same thing. By the metrics of the Commonwealth Fund, Texas has one of the lowest-rated healthcare systems in the U.S, right there with Oklahoma.[64] Go to intensive, thoughtful, long-term, in-person therapy in Waxahachie, Texas, or Davis, Oklahoma? On whose dime?

3

Sovereignty and Submission

He kicks you in the head then, while you are down on the ground, he picks you back up! You don't want to miss him!

Conference organizer for Advance 13, regarding Matt Chandler, then President of the Acts 29 network (2013)

Submit

I have a sweatshirt and a horseshoe from my time at Rewired in Oklahoma. The fee I paid was small, and they offered me coffee, barbecue, egg burritos, and camaraderie. I found their focus on pornography and masturbation as the sins most warranting attention unfortunately predictable. The underlying notion of the retreat, that men must be divided by "tribes," is problematic in that it segments people within a region. Still, I did not leave the retreat worried about the state of Baptist men in Oklahoma. I did not depart thinking there was something wrong at the core.

Acts 29 is different. Most of the churches in the Acts 29 network are also Southern Baptist. They are also a niche-marketed brand, or a form of "reaching" men by "tribe." But camaraderie is thin on the ground. The leadership and strategists in this network are people who not only "like Billy Graham" but who are expected by their strategists to out Billy Graham Billy Graham. A competitive fight for fitness in Acts 29 is part of the whole setup.

I first realized this when different Acts 29 churches were vying for access to Sunday morning auditorium worship space in downtown Durham, North Carolina. J. D. Greear won. His multi-campus Summit Church secured the historic downtown Carolina Theatre in Durham for one of the Summit Church campuses around the same time Greear won the presidency of the Southern Baptist Convention.

There is no 29th chapter of Acts. Acts tells a story in 28 chapters about the earliest followers of Jesus. "Acts 29" is the name of a network of city and suburban churches branded as the rightful heirs to the early church. Self-sacrificial submission to authority is so a part of the DNA of Acts 29 that it is written into the Trinity itself. In 2017, on the website for "The Resurgence," a program for training and continued education for pastors and laity in the network, their second distinctive reads, under the heading "JESUS-MODELED LEADERSHIP": "God exists in a perfect community; we call this the Trinity. The three persons of the Godhead are all equal in power, glory, and righteousness, yet each is distinct with different roles. The Son submits to the Father, and the Spirit does the work made possible by the sacrifice of the Son." This understanding of submission within the "three persons" dictates hierarchy and submission as within God's plan from the get-go. Therefore, "God calls for this kind of community in church government and Christian households."[1]

Obedience is key, from submission to God's sovereignty, to submission to the authority of the lead pastor, to recognition of the headship of bosses at work, and to recognition of the leadership of a husband in a family. Acts 29 has been marketed to attract young, aspiring lower-middle-class men who have newly arrived in a city. J. D. Greear explained at the Acts 29 "Advance 13" conference in 2013, "By changing the man, you change the family, and thus you change and save a city."

The Advance 13 event filled the main auditorium of the Duke Energy Center for the Performing Arts in Raleigh, North Carolina. There were hundreds of abridged, advance copies of J. D. Greear's then-forthcoming book *Gospel*. A brochure sits next to my other materials from the event, a reminder that Acts 29 is part of a larger setting of manly culture. There were stacks of fliers around the auditorium for the "BROADWAY SERIES SOUTH." The flier featured "The

Tenors" looking chiseled in leather bomber jackets on their "Lead With Your Heart Tour." Mr. "WHITESNAKE" is below the tenors, arms raised, bathed in red lighting, with "YEAR OF THE SNAKE" announced. *Men are from Mars, Women are from Venus*, "The Hit Show based on the Best-Selling Book by John Gray" appeared with "Two Shows!" "By Overwhelming Demand!"

The one woman featured is Jillian Michaels, "A unique live experience sharing her keys to HEALTH, SUCCESS & HAPPINESS." Jillian Michaels's claim to fame is that she is "The Star of NBC's Hit Show *The Biggest Loser.*" In other words, she is famous for having lost a significant amount of her own body weight. Technically, she is not the only female image on the flier. There is half a cartoon face of a feminized image on the "MARS/VENUS" announcement. And *50 Shades! The Musical!* runs at top and center with an accompanying image of a necktie. On the necktie is a stylized outline of a woman presenting her ass to a stylized image of a suited man with a bullwhip.

Acts 29 speakers and preachers often used the phrase "man-up." At the National Prayer Breakfast in Washington, D.C. in 2013, I was introduced to Doug Burleigh, one of the leaders of the National Prayer Breakfast network and past head of Young Life. When I told him I was researching ministries to men, he looked down at my 5'2" self and declared that the two problems facing men today are "passivity and pornography." The message that the plight facing working-class and struggling middle-class men in the U.S. is of their own making is part of these networks in a way that is more barefaced than in any ministry I encountered related to myths of "the West." As that conference organizer referenced in her recommendation of Matt Chandler, the messaging is like a kick to the head.

Matt Chandler took over as the leading face of Acts 29 in 2012.[2] As of January 11, 2025, the church at which he is the "Lead Pastor" in Flower Mound, Texas has ninety-eight people on staff. In 2013, I visited the main campus of "The Village Church" for Sunday morning worship. My 21-year-old daughter went with me to visit an Acts 29 church in an Atlanta suburb in 2023. She had never been to a church with this recipe. As we walked down the stairs into the dark auditorium worship space, she shook her head. "What? This isn't a church?" Then the praise band started. She was having the time of her life, dancing, clapping, arms waving, and she shouted into my ear (the music at these churches is really, really loud) "This is great! wait, is this going to be all music? I might have to come back here!" Her expression was jubilation mixed with surprise. Then we all sat down in our chairs. Two minutes into the sermon she looked at me with a grimace and mouthed the word "Ewwwwww."

It was at Matt Chandler's Village Church in Texas that one of the lay ministers answered a question I had been sorting through for months. At Advance 13, J. D. Greear had given a long, impassioned, thoughtful address to the giant auditorium about the importance of lay ministry. Meaning, he had stressed the importance of people who are not ordained pastors. Afterward, I asked one of the members of Greear's staff, standing with a table full of "content samplers" for Greear's book *Gospel*, about a puzzle in Greear's address. Why, if the non-pastors in a church are an important part of what makes a church a church, does the multi-campus church plan that is Greear's "Summit Church" pipe in Greear on a screen at each of their non-base locations instead of entrusting an associate pastor with the sermon? Why does it always have to be Greear, even when Greear is not actually present in the building?

The guy laughed at my question. "You don't think Greear makes these decisions, do you? He does what the marketing team tells him to do." When I asked a lay minister at Village Church about Matt Chandler's leadership style, he said that it is not Matt Chandler who really heads up the Acts 29 network. He then indicated with his chin toward the double glass doors. "That guy is in charge of things … Tyler Powell. Mark Driscoll hired him in Seattle and then, when Chandler became President [of Acts 29] they moved him here. His office is next door."[3]

This structure of control puzzled me. How are these churches "Baptist?" That I was baffled requires a history lesson about Baptists. Most of the churches in the Acts 29 network have been affiliated with the Southern Baptist Convention. J. D. Greear himself was head of the Southern Baptist Convention from 2018 to 2021.[4] In many of the descriptions of Acts 29, writers describe the tradition as "Calvinist." Some leaders themselves use this term. Meaning, the network follows a form of theology based on the writings of French Protestant Reformer John Calvin (1509–1564). But in the very term "Baptist" there is a history that relates to independence from governmental or even established churchly authorities.

The *OED* explains that the word "Baptist" as a noun is a more neutral term originating from the pejorative use of the term "Anabaptist" to describe groups that variously dissented from the established churches across England and Western Europe. The definition includes two Baptist distinctives. A "Baptist" is "a person who believes that baptism should be administered only to people old enough to fully understand the sacrament" and "a person who rejects Anglican doctrines."[5] Another term that historians use for Baptists is "Free Church," meaning free from state control or "Nonconformist."[6]

In his *Routledge Encyclopedia of Protestantism* entry on "Baptists, United States," American church historian Curtis Freeman gives the count of Baptist associations, or "bodies" as "more than fifty," and adds that, despite many divisions, there are distinctives held in common across groups of people meeting as "Baptist."[7] "Although Baptists are known to be contentious and fissiparous, they nevertheless share an amazing consensus around a set of convictions and practices" Freeman writes, and includes among these shared items "congregational polity," "soul liberty," and "separation of church and state." While a local Baptist church is often associated with one of the bodies connecting Baptist churches, Baptists generally agree that a local church decides the things that matter. By "soul liberty," Freeman means that an individual human being must have the liberty of their soul—an ability to practice their conscience. Freeman then gives this detail to explain the connection between belief in "soul liberty" and belief in "the separation of church and state": "It has been suggested that if historians were to ask who was responsible for religious liberty in America, their answer would be 'James Madison,' but if the question could be put to Madison he might very likely reply 'John Leland and the Baptists.'"

Given this history of Baptists, going back to before the founding of the United States, a structural system that gives marching orders to members across a Baptist association is strange. That role of holy band conductor, in a congregational polity system, is for an individual church's leadership. The individual pastor and a team of official advisors or "deacons" are the "deciders." Many Baptists will aver that their political structure requires all the baptized members to be responsible for decisions in the church. There is no need to romanticize "congregational polity" as "the best" for Protestantism. But it is distinctive. The notion that someone other than the lead minister would be telling a lead minister what to do, or that the person heading up the Acts 29 network could be someone who is not listed as such, struck me as both odd and troubling. When the man at Advance 13 laughed about my question regarding what I presumed to be J. D. Greear's choice to have himself displayed onscreen rather than trust his associates with preaching, he was likely laughing at my naivete. An Acts 29 pastor in Oklahoma had told me in 2012 that the model is akin to a franchise, with a particular formula held across every locale. But I sentimentally assumed that any church plant schemer who told a Baptist preacher how to run his church would be told to take a hike.

Another way to explain the oddity of a franchise model for brand control among Baptist churches is to point out that Canadian novelist Margaret Atwood recognized "Baptists" as part of the resistance in her 1986 dominionist dystopia *The Handmaid's Tale*. While watching the state-enforced television, the book's protagonist, known as handmaid Offred (of Fred, who owns her) hears that the army "the Angels of the Apocalypse" are "smoking out a pocket of Baptist guerillas" in the "Appalachian Highlands." Atwood also includes "Five members of the heretical sect of Quakers have been arrested" as part of the newsreel in the built world of "Gilead."[8] Anecdotally, when teaching that novel, I have also found that people who grew up Baptist, whether African American or white, are the most likely to recognize where the authorities in "Gilead" have transmogrified words from the bible into slogans for political control. In other words, Baptist preachers are not commonly known for their submission to hierarchies, including hierarchies within their own congregational associations.

For this research, I visited Acts 29 church plants in different parts of North Carolina, Atlanta, Seattle, Oklahoma City, Reno, and in various cities in Texas. Some of them were renting space in schools as a temporary beginning spot. Others were in their own, often adapted structures. Each of the preachers kept to a particular line when preaching about manhood. The churches consistently keep to a description of the challenges facing their target demographic: young adult men.

The speaker designated specifically to speak about masculinity at Advance 13 was John Bryson, who *Christianity Today* described in 2013 as "founder and pastor of Fellowship Memphis, a multicultural church in Tennessee, and … an executive board member of the Acts 29 church planting network."[9]

Speakers used the language of "deployment" often during the two-day conference. Hundreds of people, mostly men, sat in the stadium seats and were told how to attract and train the best men to be deployed. John Bryson went into detail about the challenges facing newly professional class young men who had been brought up by working class men in the U.S. "Young men are confused." There is "lack of clarity" about their roles. They will "use boyhood behaviors to try to make themselves men." He then named the apparent camaraderie that men could share when telling of their sexual encounter, their first time having imbibed to become actually drunk, the first time they killed an animal. Bryson moved expertly to how men have grown "lonely" because their own fathers were failures. In this loneliness, men were using "technology instead of intimacy." He said this is all going on while "no one knows what is going on under the hood."

Then he shifted to a different tone, about men growing "soft." In my notes, I wrote "what? soft?" "Confused men," as Bryson named a generation, "commit 99% of crimes" and "88% of robberies," and "90% of DUIs." Men are "lonely" and "drifting" and "create major problems." His preacherly lecture then shifted to the altar call to which he would return, accelerating: "What in the world is wrong with us?" "There is no knee bended to God."

And at this point, John Bryson shifted from a Bruce Banner professorial persona to a Hulk for Jesus baritone, moving into an extended contrast between Jesus, who "Took the initiative!" and Adam (the first human/man) who was "Passive!" After the industrial revolution, he explained, boys no longer saw their fathers at work and women had to "fill in the gaps." Then came "feminism," which left men "unsure about how to act." But "God models masculinity." God "looks into chaos and he acts! He does something!" Bryson called Adam a "metrosexual" who "stands there with his manhood pants down." Like Adam, men are "cowards" and "childish consumers." Jesus, by contrast, has a "showdown with Satan" and teaches how to "lead a home," how to "lead a wife." (There are many exclamation marks in my notes, because Bryson shouted much of this.) "God formed you to work!" he told the audience. "Men solve problems! Men do not complain, they fix! Men do not pout, they endure! Men do not blame, they own! Men do not wish, they do! Men do not just start, they finish!"

He had given an impressively nuanced summary of the Greatest Generation's failure of parenting due to their emotional unavailability. Bryson had tracked almost point for point concerns that U.S.-based mainstream egalitarian feminists had written, but then turned around and gave an antidote to the mess that he had described. The antidote is "Work!" All of his descriptions of Jesus and of good men who follow Jesus were about activity, initiative, and work. Not once did he describe Jesus's emotional availability. Having depicted Adam's main vice as having a penchant for talking things out rather than stomping on them (or on it—the talking snake in Eden), Bryson could not end with an appeal to correct the Greatest Generation's error by listening attentively to one's wife or children. It would have sounded sissy.

This was a point in my research when I heard my soul break and then slowly reassemble itself. I steeled myself and asked one of the lead organizers about the gig economy and the lack of sustainable jobs for men. North Carolina had the highest unemployment rate in the South at that time. Bryson had narrated the story of the fall as in no small part Adam's failure to recognize that he should have been working before the snake showed up. Bryson transformed Reformist John Calvin's stock story of justification by grace and works born of gratitude around backwards and made work to sustain a family the original gift of God to man.

This is a theologically and even biblically questionable take on labor, I explained to the man standing in front of me. But from a prosaic, practical standpoint, what if work is not to be had? Or what if it becomes dehumanizing and unsafe, as it did at the North Carolina Smithfield meat-processing plant before the workers unionized? Or what if your work as an executive marketer at Pfizer requires you to lie? His answer to this set of questions was that the young men he knows who cannot find work adequate to provide for their families are insufficiently enterprising and unable to recognize the importance of "value added" effort. They need to be willing to move anywhere or do anything that remotely fits their gifts, he explained.

Bryson had emphasized during his talk that young men need to marry early and procreate often. So, I asked this lead organizer, should men who cannot find work that will sustain a family strike out on their own and move wherever there is labor to be had, as they did during the Great Depression? If so, what would that mean for their task of being the relational leader of their household? How are they supposed to lead their wives from across several states? His answer? "Yeah, I know, times are hard, but that may be what they have to do." Men are unemployed or underemployed because they have "too many conditions and not enough initiative." They do not want to move where the jobs are or want only to work particular hours. Apropos of I am not sure what, he ended our conversation by telling me he has an M.B.A.

Supermarkets

Matt Chandler's church in Flower Mound, Texas, meets in a building that was previously an Albertson's supermarket, located between a Sonic Drive-In and the Massage Institute of Texas. With giant buildings left shuttered across the Metroplex, this is a regionally helpful reuse of concrete. If pressed to name something good about these kinds of church plants, this would be it. For sprawling suburbs "gone to seed," as one friend from the D/FW Metroplex said about Irving, planting churches amid seeds may be helpful. In the case of Irving, the "seeds" in "gone to seed" are mostly immigrant families who have moved there in the last two decades, leaving mainline churches built in the 1950s as commuter congregations who must decide whether to reach out to the neighbors around the church building or basically ignore them. The existence of empty supermarket buildings links up with the financial difficulties facing working people in the cities and suburbs where the churches are planted. The shift of such work from a career with a team to isolated and isolating distribution centers has shaped the realities with which men must navigate their sense of themselves as men. This background matters for understanding the marketing of the Acts 29 brand.

In my own backyard, the home region of J. D. Greear's Summit Church, friends and people next to me in the grocery store lines were discussing longstanding rumors that the people controlling the conglomerate that owns both Kroger and Harris Teeter supermarket chains were planning to close all the Kroger stores in the Triangle. I overheard many people musing about whether the generic Harris Teeter brands were better than the generic Kroger brands. Were the supermarket gurus reacting to the growth of Amazon by going with the small stair-step upscale Harris Teeter over the more prosaic Kroger?

Then someone explained a factor that no one in mainstream media in the Triangle was covering. As the "Is it Union?" website notes, two-thirds of Kroger employees have a labor union, the United Food and Commercial Workers International Union (UFCW).[10] Harris Teeter employees do not. In conversation with people working at Kroger during the last months before closure, people explained that they would have to find another job or move away from their friends and family to keep a labor union position with Kroger.

Susan Faludi is a journalist best known for her 1991 tome on reactionary responses to feminist gains, *Backlash: The Undeclared War Against American Women*. She was the 1991 Pulitzer Prize Winner in Explanatory Journalism. This was for a 1990 *Wall Street Journal* article "on the leveraged buy-out of Safeway Stores, Inc., that revealed the human costs of high finance" (as described by the Pulitzer committee).[11] The full title reads: "The Reckoning: Safeway LBO Yields Vast Profits but Exacts A Heavy Human Toll—The '80s-Style Buy-Out Left Some Employees Jobless, Stress-Ridden, Distraught—Owner KKR Hails Efficiency." Reporting from the bellwether state of Texas, Faludi contrasts a new form of robber baronry with an on-the-ground detail from the "80s-Style Buy-Out": "63,000 managers and workers were cut loose from Safeway, through store sales or layoffs … A survey of former Safeway employees in Dallas found that nearly 60 percent still hadn't found full-time employment more than a year after the layoff." She tells the story of "James White, a Safeway trucker for nearly 30 years in Dallas …. [who] marked the one-year anniversary of his last shift at Safeway" by committing suicide. "Safeway was James's whole life," said his widow, Helen. "He'd near stand up and salute whenever one of those trucks went by." When Safeway dismissed him, she said, "it was like he turned into a piece of stone."[12] Mikhail Vaynberg was also among those fired, a refrigeration engineer who, Faludi reports, had "invented a new cooling system for the stores that cut energy costs 35%, saved $1.6 million a year, and was copied by many suppliers." She describes his life in the period after: "Now Mr. Vaynberg, still unemployed, spends his days in a painfully clean living room, prowls the halls at night and avoids old friends and neighbors. 'I am ashamed,' he says, staring at his big empty hands. 'I am like an old thrown-out mop.'"

Faludi's reporting connects to her 1999 tome *Stiffed: The Betrayal of the American Man*. This is the book I have taught for decades to students studying at Duke Divinity School, a school set in a region stricken by waves of factory closures and other economic shifts that have hollowed out small towns and driven working-class people out of gentrifying cities. In her (critical) review of *Stiffed* for the *New York Times*, Judith Shulevitz called it "a lament for the lost and distinctly unfeminist characters who stumble through its pages": "downsized aerospace engineers; suburban teen-age sexual predators; football fans whose teams have skipped town; male porn stars whose livelihood depends on their waning sexual powers … gang members; Promise Keepers." Shulevitz notes that, by Faludi's telling, "these men and boys have in common … [being] pushed by forces they don't understand into roles in which their masculinity has nothing to do but roil and fester."[13]

Faludi's next book is the third in a trilogy that began with her 1991 *Backlash: The Undeclared War Against American Women*. *The Terror Dream* details the reactionary gender politics in mainstream media following the national emasculation that was 9/11. She traces the use of mythology of "the West" across everything from branding Bush and Cheney as valiant cowboys to the vaulting of first responders into mythic heroes. In 2024, on a website called "9/11 Families for a Safe and Strong America," the curators include as part of their effort a 2008 excerpt from *The Terror Dream*: "The firefighters entered the World Trade Centre armed with 15-year-old radios that were well known to malfunction in high-rise buildings. When the South Tower fell, the firefighters in the North Tower had no idea what had happened." This history is one of the facts hidden by the mythology. "When the fire chief radioed a Mayday order to evacuate the North Tower, almost none of the firefighters heard it … Firefighters made the same point in their oral history accounts; they said they were 'clueless' and knew 'absolutely nothing' of what was going on outside."[14]

The labor unions representing firefighters had been pushing for updated equipment prior to 9/11. The isolation of "a firefighter" as a hero was a myth wrapped up in a lie about how safety works in the profession.[15] What the brotherhood of first responders may offer for men at work some men seek through church, especially in the anti-union South and Southwest. There is a sense of purposelessness, of alienation and atomization that Faludi described in both her reporting on Safeway Stores and across many different sectors and decades in *Stiffed*. In 2024, there were reports in every outlet to which I am privy on the dearth of friendships between men. *Time Magazine* ran an essay on February 16, 2024, under the straightforward heading: "Why Men Struggle With Friendship." The author Rhaina Cohen links to studies under the titles *Deep Secrets: Boys' Friendships and the Crisis of Connection* by Niobe Way; *Buddy System: Understanding Male Friendships* by Geoffrey Greif; and APA GUIDELINES for Psychological Practice with Boys and Men, a long literature review from the American Psychological Association.[16] A reader does not have to ascribe to the idea that men and women are inherently, fundamentally different (I don't) to appreciate how definitions of "what makes a man a man" in the U.S. matter.

When I parked at the Duke Energy Center for the Performing Arts for the Advance 13 event, what I noticed first was the number of church vans. Groups of men had driven in from across the southeast in small vans with the names of their churches on the side, smaller town churches from across different denominations. I passed Baptist, Church of Christ, Assemblies of God, Nazarene, and at least one United Methodist church van. When I walked into the swanky Duke Energy Center, what I noticed first was that the lobby was a giant market of mainstream evangelical technology—booklets on everything from church lighting to missions to seminaries to counseling centers to church marketing—most with banners with their social media tags, and curriculum in every form, digitized collections, and the old-fashioned paper kinds. There were rubber bracelets and buttons and plastic tote bags. And, although the price of the conference was in the hundreds of dollars, there was not even free coffee. The talks were interspersed with videos and still images selling things to participants. That, and really loud music.

This is linked to what John Piper, a spokesman for these circles, called the importance of human "insignificance." A former student had explained to me that the really loud music is part of a formula that also includes shining a light onto the preacher so that the preacher often cannot even see the congregants. Ryan Quanstrom had served as an intern on staff at a 2,000-member church with a well-known praise worship musician. This musician explained to him that they keep the music level at 111 decibels so that people cannot hear their own voices or the voices of the people around them. For context, the U.S. National Institute for Occupational Safety and Health states, "Workplace noise is hazardous with repeated exposures of 85 dBA or higher."[17]

One of the many advertisements was for a digital library for sermon preparation from a company called LOGOS. The spokesman told participants that the premium package included the best of "Piper and Keller." John Piper and Tim Keller are household names for this network. At this point, a group of men behind me, dressed in t-shirts and blue jeans, started talking. There was a lull in the music and visual pyrotechnics. One of them said, "This is all cool, but depressing; we can't afford this stuff." The connections between the basic, no frills church vans from towns, smaller cities, and exurbs across North Carolina and this young man's words rang in my ears during the next segment, on global missions and markets.

Andre Mann spoke to the people assembled in the Duke Energy auditorium about the "impact" of their donations to evangelical-adjacent work in other countries. Mann is described in 2024 on the "Faith Driven Investor" website as a "Managing Partner" at Melior Capital.[18] Melior Capital's website describes the institution as "a Swiss domiciled company investor and advisory firm focused exclusively on the global life-science sector."[19] There are advantages to being a "Swiss domiciled company." The Swiss government does not require that a company be invested in the actual region as a place to live and breathe and be accountable to one's neighbors, their tax system allowing for an elastic use of the word "domicile."

Mann first delivered a brief lecture on the history of "missions" and informed them with a sense of exasperation that "on average Baptists give $42.00 a year for sending the gospel." Citing the New Testament verse from the book of Acts 8:4—a line about early followers of Jesus becoming dispersed, or "scattered" as the New International Version words it—Mann told listeners that "the gospel occurs in the marketplace, not in the church." His interpretation of Acts 8:4 was that "the early church grew because businessmen went out" to share "the gospel." Mann linked together this line of the bible with examples from other business-related mission endeavors, including the Basel Trading Company out of Basel Switzerland, founded in 1815.[20] The wind-up was on the importance of intertwined efforts of global markets and "the gospel." Mann's lecture was the most TED-talky of the conference as he flashed the performance hall screens with numbers, global maps, and a description of global capitalism (a term he did not use) as a worldwide opportunity for "mission." Business leaders appreciate connections to "gospel" missions because, he explained, people who are connected to these networks in "unreached markets" receive "character training" that makes them more reliable workers. He might as well have used the word "peaceable."

The term "mission" as used in mainstream evangelicalism may itself be unfamiliar to some readers. For readers in the U.S. the association may first be with NASA, the U.S. space program. Within mainstream Protestant teaching and preaching from the mid-twentieth century through to today, the "mission" endeavor can mean anything from sending a group of church teenagers to the Mexican border to hand out water to migrants, to sending them to report those kinds of missionaries to the federal authorities for punishment. In common parlance, it usually means something along the lines of helping people who are the kinds of people who do not attend the congregation itself. As with NASA, a "mission" involves someone traveling.

Mann's pitch to the attendees at Advance 13 included a screen-wide map indicating the populations of regions on the continents of Africa and Asia. He announced that "God has orchestrated a strategy!" That strategy, Mann explained, is the movement of business overseas. Through business expansion across countries with large populations, God is providing "deep spiritual integration," "character training," bringing about "winning in the marketplace and winning in ministry." He repeated after showing graphs and arrows indicating the movement of industries across the ocean. "God orchestrates history!" and named in particular "new markets in China." At this, Mann reiterated to the audience "Yes, I said China!" His call was for "free enterprise to advance the kingdom." Under my breath, I countered "It wasn't God who orchestrated NAFTA."

While the average age of the Advance 13 participants was around 35, there were some men in that auditorium who lived through the regional ramifications of the North American Free Trade Agreement of 1992. During the 1992 Presidential debate between Democrat Bill Clinton, Republican President George H.W. Bush, and Independent candidate Ross Perot, Perot had linked the phrase "giant sucking sound" to NAFTA. It was the first question in the debate, and Perot went into detail, or, as he called them, "the brass tacks." Perot said in 1992,

> if you're paying $12, $13, $14 an hour for factory workers and you can move your factory south of the border, pay a dollar an hour for labor, higher young—let's assume you've been in business for a long time and you've got a mature workforce—pay a dollar an hour for your labor, have no healthcare—that's the most expensive single element in making a car— have no environmental controls, no pollution controls and no retirement, and you don't care about anything but making money there will be a giant sucking sound going south.[21]

I was at Yale Divinity School in 1992 and endured much razzing as a fellow Texan. But many people in Texas were not laughing. Both Mexican American and Anglo friends and parishioners were dead serious about the implications facing the Southwest with the arrival of NAFTA. Someone convinced Fleetwood Mac to come together to play their 1977 hit "Don't Stop Thinking About Tomorrow" at the inaugural ball for Bill Clinton in 1993.[22] The song had been played often during Clinton's run for president. As young volunteers (I was one) teared up with the music, some elders winced. They *were* thinking about tomorrow, and they knew Perot was right.

Andre Mann had opened his lecture to the gathering with a bible quote about the difference between "tent fakers" and "tent makers." Mann was referencing a use that the *OED* gives from the 1884 book *A Christian Home*: "Paul was a tentmaker, and he was not ashamed of it."[23] The phrase is from a line in the New Testament book of Acts (18:3) about the early apostle Paul staying with a household in Corinth who made tents. Because Paul also made tents, it makes sense that he spent time with people in Corinth who made tents. That is a simple, no-nonsense reading of the text. The use of the term "tent maker" has become a symbolic catchphrase within mainstream evangelicalism for mission work that also involves some kind of work with things. In his lecture, Mann used "the gospel" to make global capitalism into "tent-making." He did this while speaking to people domiciled in a region shredded by global capitalism.

Recall that one of the on-stage running advertisements at Advance 13 was for an online library of sermons and texts, with the selling point that the premium version included John Piper and Tim Keller. John Piper has been for decades one of the most celebrated mainstream evangelical scholars in the U.S., also promoted abroad. He is the son of an evangelist and a graduate of Wheaton College in Illinois. Piper is also a spokesman for "The New Calvinism," often shortened to "neo-Calvinism." Speakers and writers in this network related to Acts 29 may not indicate up front that they are connected to the Southern Baptist Convention, or even explicitly note that they are an Acts 29 church plant, but they frequently will describe their theology as "Calvinist." This network is obviously related to marketing, to markets, and to supersizing churches with large screens and more people in the stadium seats. That is one way to think about the strangeness of leaders of Baptist-related churches taking orders from outside their usual polity structure. It is about markets. And, adjacent to this, and the selling of sermons and books by John Piper is the marketing shift toward "The New Calvinism." What connects being "kicked in the head" during preaching, being told that young men are losers in the current economy due to lack of initiative, and older men hearing that God has orchestrated a global economy that has decimated their region is an emphasis within neo-Calvinism on divine sovereignty and human submission. The message that human beings are fundamentally disobedient and that what God most demands is submission has been given a megaphone.

Most of the focus of criticism of neo-Calvinism and of Acts 29 in particular has been on hyper-masculinity and misogyny. The 2022 *Christianity Today* podcast series on the original face of Acts 29, Seattle pastor Mark Driscoll, focused primarily on the blatant sexism and obvious misogyny of Driscoll, and on the apparent lack of accountability within the network for bullying and verbal abuse in the original churches for whom he was the spokesman. They retread what Alison Sargent had reported a decade before in *Bitch Magazine*. Sargent had written about what was amiss in this network from the beginning of the marketing that made "Acts 29" a network in the first place. Her 2012 article is entitled "Oral Sex, Yoga, and God's Eternal Wrath: Inside the New Hipster Megachurch That Tells Modern Women to Submit." Sargent noted there the significance of the Acts 29 origin story: "After Driscoll and his wife, Grace, founded the church in 1996 in their Seattle home, it grew at a rate of about 60 percent a year," significant given "Seattle is one of the most left-leaning cities in a state that, according to a 2004 Gallup poll, ranked as the third least religious in the nation." She reported in 2012 that "Mars Hill now has more than 5,000 members, with campuses in Portland, Orange County, and Albuquerque." She rightly describes Acts 29, as a "'church planting' network that trains men who wish to open churches," which "led to the creation of the Resurgence, an online training resource with links to sermons, blog posts, music, and forums— essentially, a Mars Hill starter kit." She also notes that the network had gone global. Sargent described the aesthetic of the brand in the 2000s–2010s as "strict Calvinist doctrine allows congregants to occupy a unique, rebellious niche between middle-aged conservative Christians and their secular liberal contemporaries." She continued "Mars Hill members talk about sex, drink alcohol, get tattoos, and swear. They also believe homosexuality is a sin, men are meant to lead, and wives must submit to their husbands as the church submits to God."[24] Acts 29 was a notch more overt and a shift more aggressive than movements such as Promise Keepers, who in the 1990s had similar gender politics but more emphasis on manly "humility" in marriage, a word trending in evangelical circles in the 1990s.

The megaphone message of SUBMIT was created by preaching in former supermarkets and through super marketing. Alison Sargent wrote that the Acts 29 network was built upon "strict Calvinist doctrine." John Piper encapsulated this aspect of mass-marketed neo-Calvinism in the U.S. in a lecture to the Religious Newswriters Association in 2009. John Piper gave a lecture on

"The New Calvinists" at the meeting on September 11, 2009. The session was called "The Young and the Reformed" and the announcement included this description: "They're called the New Calvinists; this subset of young evangelicals … Why is Reformed thinking making inroads among the Southern Baptists? And why are women invisible in this movement?" The moderator was Julia Duin of *The Washington Times*. Carolyn Custis James of the Synergy Women's Network, Inc. and WhitbyForum, John Piper of Bethlehem Baptist Church, and Collin Hansen of *Christianity Today* were the panelists.[25] Piper told the group that neo-Calvinism is offering a word about God's power that is "profoundly steadying in a world like ours," and he specifically referred in the lecture to September 11.[26] During a time such as ours, during "a world like ours," as survivors of 9/11, which message is most "profoundly steadying?" he asked. Piper then used two scraps of popular culture. Holding up an "Arlo and Janis" syndicated comic strip, with a couple walking through an evening snow, John Piper read the text bubble: "Ever notice that the best moments make you feel insignificant?" He paused to look out at the tables of people, both lecturing to them and appealing to them to hear the supposed salience of this insight. Then, turning to a Nature Valley Granola advertisement, Piper pointed out the "tiny little figures" on the "vast terrain" of a rocky climbing site, noting "they look unbelievably fragile; they could topple off at any moment." Then he read the caption: "You've never felt so alive. You've never felt more insignificant."

This spokesman for "The New Calvinism" expertly summed up the messaging for the journalists. The message of insignificance is significant. The combined message of individual insignificance and submission to authority is layered as a transparency over the different pages of the Acts 29 playbook. Members submit to pastoral leadership. Wives and children submit to husbands and fathers. And pastors themselves submit to the assessment and plans of men like strategists Tyler Powell. Human beings are fundamentally "insignificant," and what makes a human being feel "alive" is this experience of being small. This link between "the gospel" and being "tiny" has been an effective supermarket of submission. The Acts 29 "gospel" has delivered an anti-prosperity message of success. What the world needs most to hear is not a word of encouragement toward success—a message about God's unique plan for your individual life—but a word of obedience—a message about God's overarching plan to bring your family into a hierarchical structure of authority. It is a striking contrast of form with content that a movement showcasing a revolving spectacle of one male leader (alone on a stage, with screens of his large, projected face and body) has had a continued emphasis on human "insignificance."

A feature of the National Prayer Breakfast Fellowship Family is the use of men as tools. Men at every level are instrumental, meaning useful inasmuch as they function according to their capacity to market "the gospel." This emphasis extends to upper-class, highly economically advantaged men. Even in the highest circles of the Fellowship Family, as they have been recorded on camera or in interviews, there is the avowal that each man is most properly a tool, to be employed depending on the serviceable things at his disposal. This description of useful things ranges from his smile and height, to money or family wealth, to an artistic gift with a musical instrument, or a tomb in the wealthy part of a burial ground. The resting default in this form of Americana meets "the new Calvinism" is the insignificance of an individual man. A man gains significance as a human being if he submits to be used to redeem his city, his town, his region, his nation, up to the World Economic Forum's various plans to determine "who owns the moon."

In my notes from Advance 13, I have arrows from Andre Mann's lecture on why working-class white men should give more money to support the exporting of their jobs overseas—"Yes! I said China!"—to Larry Osborne's lecture scolding them for judging any man richer than they are. Larry Osborne said, in effect, stupid white working-class men assembled to learn how to grow your churches, shut up and be grateful. You never know when a very rich man may be useful for the purposes of the Sovereign. The Sovereign's "orchestration" encompasses global maps of exports and imports and the conversion of rich men who may prove useful with their donation of tombs.

The Christian Post's article on Osborne's closing talk at Advance 13 gives in the article's title the theme, "Pastor Larry Osborne Urges Christian Leaders: 'Don't Become Accidental Pharisees [sic].'" Katherine Weber describes Osborne: "Pastor Osborne began preaching at his Vista, Calif., megachurch in 1980, and he now speaks to a congregation of over 6,500 per weekend."[27] Within the Acts

29 world, these numbers serve to credential a speaker, as the words "best-selling author" or a Harvard B.S. would for others. The biblical personality Osborne focused on for his talk was Joseph of Arimathea. According to one reading of the Hebrew Bible's prophetic book of Isaiah, the Savior had to be buried in the tomb of a rich man. If not for Joseph of Arimathea, Jesus would have been tossed into a pit of dead people. Joseph was a member of a select few, Osborne explained, and was seeking Christianity in secret, for fear of losing his power as one of the elites in the Roman Empire. In Osborne's account, Joseph served as a placeholder for Christians with more power and money than the average, overtly pious Baptist Christians sitting in the Raleigh auditorium for the conference. He explained that Joseph's fear of coming out to accept the consequences of his alliance with Jesus was part of God's overall plan.

The bible story that still rings in my ears today is from Mark 10, about a young man with "many possessions" who came to Jesus asking about eternal life. "Jesus, looking at him, loved him and said, 'You lack one thing.'" Jesus *looked at him*. We do not know the end to this rich man's story, but Jesus apparently did not look on him as a placeholder within a providential grand strategy to reinforce God's sovereignty. Jesus, looking at him, loved him, and told him what the man perhaps most dreaded, but most needed to hear. Jesus told the young man to sell all he had and give the money to the poor.

Measuring "Real"

In Billy Joel's 1982 hit song "Allentown," he narrates the effects of the slowdown of the steel industry in the Lehigh Valley of Pennsylvania. Joel sings about "the promises our teachers gave" that if boys "worked hard" and they "behaved" they would be able to make a living wage in their home region. What the teachers did not teach, as Billy Joel wrote, was "what was real." Joel names "real" as "iron and coke, and chromium steel."[28] Along with the text in the New Testament book of Mark, "Allentown" rang through my brain during Osborne's talk. This mega-church "success" preacher from Los Angeles was schooling ministers and their ministerial teams who had driven miles in their church vans to learn about how to measure up in their own post-industrial hometowns.

NPR's *All Things Considered* ran a retrospective on Billy Joel's "Allentown" in 2023: "The boom and bust of the area's steelwork that made much of the country's biggest landmarks until its sudden collapse in the '80s and the lives that were never the same when their stable jobs were taken away." Julian Abraham continues: "The song is mainly about Bethlehem Steel, a nearby steel factory that used to be one of the biggest in the world. At its peak, it employed over 30,000 people." After interviewing people in Allentown, including the mayor (who hates the song), Abraham ends the piece with Joel's perspective on the song's significance. Joel said soon after the song became a hit that it represents not only that specific valley in Pennsylvania but other post-industrial areas. Joel's words counter the poverty shaming in *The National Review* and by people intent to find truth in J. D. Vance's exploitative description of Appalachia in *Hillbilly Elegy*. Abraham ends with this line: "We're not moving out or giving up, [Joel] said. We're going to try."[29]

A volume of essays announced in response to J. D. Vance's book that *Hillbillies Need No Elegy*.[30] The volume's introduction explains the basics of their dissent: "Every now and then, America remembers Appalachia exists. Reporters seek statistics on the opioid epidemic. Politicians talk about unemployment at a breakfast restaurant in the mountains … TV producers scout for a reality show."[31] Meredith McCarroll's introduction to the volume reads: "One of those moments came after the 2016 Presidential election, as America looked around—a bit stunned—wondering why the rural working class had helped put in office a wealthy businessman from New York." She continues, "*Hillbilly Elegy*, was newly on shelves, there to explain the region for us: a story of a kid born into instability and drug abuse who joined the Marines, went to law school, and eventually made it out of Ohio. It was a runaway bestseller."[32] Vance's book was marketed as "real."

In my role teaching people training for some form of Christian ministry, I have sought to address what is "real" in the systems of power they are often already navigating in their internships with congregations. Even what we call "second career" students who have already been in the "real world" are often shocked by the crassness of people in charge of determining which churches "count" and how to "count" who counts in a congregation. Measurement systems of networks like Acts 29 make their way, sideways, into mainstream white Protestantism. Outlets like "Outreach" report on "the country's Fastest-Growing, Largest and Reproducing churches—a salute to church health and kingdom growth," and many leaders in mainstream Protestant circles develop pulpit envy.[33] The counting of butts in stadium seats and eyeballs on big screens makes its way over to Methodist bishops and Presbyterian elders counting butts in a pew and eyeballs on hymnals.

Here is one story. A group of parishioners at Trinity United Methodist Church in historic downtown Durham, my home parish for two decades, had an ongoing conversation about the "success" that many of them would pass on their drive downtown on Sunday mornings. The church is the mother ship of white Methodism in the county. I was a morning Sunday School teacher for the older couple's class until they had all passed or left for assisted living. They were at the time in their seventies and eighties, and they had watched their congregation shrink in size from the heyday in the 1950s. What they most noticed when driving by buildings in which the Acts 29 Summit Church people were gathering were the young adults visiting on the lawn or crossing the street to one of the downtown venues. "They must be doing something right" was a phrase these older Methodists said in one version or another repeatedly. How could their congregation also be successful in bringing in young people? At one point, some of the members who would not step foot into a megachurch were seriously contemplating adding large screens to the front of the historic sanctuary to try to match what they thought might be a recipe for "success."

It was in part due to this sense of loss and irrelevance that some key members of the lay leadership at Trinity later fell for a stunningly ill-conceived plan to begin a church plant in a particularly queer, hipster center near downtown, to be sponsored by the historic downtown church.[34] The aging mainline congregation was assigned the task of hosting a clergy couple only recently declared United Methodist who had, prior to their seminary training, succeeded as inspirational speakers to mainstream evangelical parachurch groups across the country. Trinity United Methodist was told to coordinate with a gender-conservative, evangelical organization called the Association of Related Churches, whose stated purpose is to "strategically resource church planters and pastors to help them reach people with the message of Jesus" in cities like Durham. The organization's website in 2023 featured articles like "Future Faith—Three things Gen Z wants from your church" and "Pioneers to Prophets: Building a spiritual foundation for numeric growth."[35]

The church plant was called "Pioneers," and set up shop in a historic building that had once been a car dealership, with beautiful floor to ceiling windows across the façade.[36] As Sarah Edwards described the situation in her article about the closing of Pioneers in February 2024, "Pioneers, with its shared business designation, neighboring proximity to a swath of avowedly queer businesses, and rose-gold messaging tailored to affluent transplants, proved a perfect storm."[37] A flier affixed in 2022 to the door of Pioneers and posted around the adjacent neighborhood had as the title line: "Why we oppose Pioneers church in this location." The document reads: "Pioneers is a church plant, funded by the greater United Methodist Church along with ARC, the Association of Related Churches, a business model used to plant churches." The authors named that the new church planners "are positioning themselves to capitalize off of the growth and money that is now flowing into the neighborhood," adding that the "model of 'redemptive entrepreneurship' is a façade for the purpose of raising money to fund a discriminatory church that does not welcome all residents equally."[38] Over thirty clergy members from the area signed an urgent letter to the United Methodist leadership for this area that noted the following about the plan: "LGBTQ+ people decry the presence of this non-affirming and non-inclusive church centered in the middle of Durham's most prominent LGBTQ+—inclusive neighborhood. People of Color call out the church's intention of 'city renewal' in a city still recovering from the systemic destruction of Black communities and the broken promises of urban renewal."[39]

It was a clustermuck of bad church plant planning and United Methodist politics during the pandemic. Many clergy in the Durham area were worried the leadership would simply tell them to close their doors and sell their buildings as membership and attendance dropped. Trinity UMC had the benefit, at least, of having their sanctuary be officially historic. That was of little comfort as historic buildings had been torn down to make way for exorbitant condominium complexes across downtown.

Local news coverage of the plan led to such a righteous uproar that the new bishop of the conference, who did not himself approve the baffling plan, ended up issuing a formal apology to the people of Durham. The letter acknowledged UMC leadership had been "slow to entirely comprehend the unique nature, values, and makeup of this neighborhood." They noted that they were "not initially attentive" to the actual location in which they had planned a "plant." "We are sorry that we were not initially attentive to the harm that might be done when a new congregation was started," the letter read, "which was not fully affirming of the LGBTQIA+ community and inclusive of marriage equality, in a neighborhood which is known to be safe and affirming for LGBTQIA+ community members."[40]

The evangelical-hipster couple who had been assigned to the church ended up leaving the United Methodist Church for a denomination that better fits their gender conservatism.[41] Members who had nothing in common except that they had each asked questions about the feasibility and suitability of the plan asked me whether they had done something wrong. The couple had been citing one bible verse at them, from the book of Matthew in the New Testament, chapter 18, to instruct them to speak first to the clergy before speaking in a committee meeting. This is counter to Methodist polity. Methodists are named for method, and we are methodical about committees. When I called leadership about my concerns, a person on the bishop's cabinet gave me a lecture on marketing.

There is a 2006 episode of Mike Judge and Greg Daniels's animated television series *King of the Hill* that epitomizes the interplay between megachurch evangelicalism and mainstream Protestantism in the U.S. The setting of the series is "Arlen, Texas" and as Mike Judge told the *New York Times* in 2009, Arlen is based on Richardson, Texas, a suburb of Dallas, along with Judge's childhood in Albuquerque, New Mexico.[42] The 2006 episode is entitled "Church Hopping." The IMDB listing provides this summary: "After having a falling out with Reverend Stroup, Hank leaves Arlen First Methodist and joins a Mega-Church ... only to be overwhelmed by its nonstop demands on his free time."[43] Some background is helpful. Reverend Stroup is the first clergywoman assigned to Arlen First Methodist Church. That storyline is itself hilariously on-point, as members reckon with what it means to have a "lady preacher." First Methodist in Arlen does not have bells or whistles, but simply pews and hymnals and church casserole covered dish suppers. Peggy Hill, usually practical, has had enough with Reverend Stroup's apparent refusal to take her advice "for adding some pizzazz to that church" and suggests they move their church attendance to a 5,000-member megachurch. Peggy warms to her suggestion: "They have their very own coffee shop, florist, mini-mart, bank, and a dry cleaner that accepts all competitors' coupons." Hank responds: "If I wanted to go that route, I could just walk around the mall and think about Jesus." This being a predictable series, reliable Hank and Peggy end up back at First Methodist.[44]

There was a widely shared, cited, and weirdly revered report in 2010 that linked Methodist "vitality" with viewing screens during worship: "High vital churches are more likely to use multi-media in their contemporary services," adding that churches with both "traditional" and "contemporary" worship services were statistically more likely to be "vital."[45] As one United Methodist News piece summarized the consulting report: "The study also found that contemporary services work best when the music echoes what people hear on pop radio. Such services can use traditional hymns, but they had better have a backbeat."[46]

The writers for *King of the Hill* had created a scenario where a fictional mainstream, Methodist clergywoman resisted the push to emulate evangelical marketing strategists, and yet some key leaders of the denomination took up this steeple/big screen envy with verve. The "leadership" "vitality" "success" combination during this time was part of both a trend and fad, regardless of the frequent protestations by people promoting the words and growth schemes from 2008 to 2018. It was a denominational amalgam of MTV meets Business School meets a denomination worried they had lost their status as "America's Team." It was also a high-data version of the Moody Bible Institute poster from 1920— clergy positioned as instruments to increase numbers for a version of "gospel."

In 2012 the United Methodist News Service ran a report on the denomination's efforts to "reverse declining U.S. membership and revitalize its congregations."[47] The opening image is of a consultant in a bright green suit: "Laura Nichol, a member of the Call to Action Interim Operations Team, facilitates a conversation about the cultural changes The United Methodist Church needs to reverse decades of declining U.S. membership." Next to her is a large yellow pad of paper with the handwritten words for the gathering: "Denominational Goal: 1) Stop Decline 2) Encourage Growth." And below these "Strength of Will—[indecipherable] is in growing the church." The article names under the heading "Facing a Culture of Fear" the most significant part of the plan. This was a push to encourage and/or require that local clergy report weekly church attendance and other numbers on a "dashboard" that would be viewable by their bosses and colleagues. This was sold at the time as a method to provide deeper "insight, support, and accountability." In the bright, upbeat video shared to promote dashboarding, the narrator, a woman who sounds white and middle-age, says this last word in the phrase, "accountability," with a tone of schoolmarm seriousness.[48]

It was this sense that clergy were insufficiently "accountable" that many bishops and other cabinet members repeated during this time. The 2010 study set off an alarm: "The consulting firm Towers Watson measured vitality in terms of attendance, growth over five years, professions of faith per member and annual giving per attendee. Of the congregations it analyzed, Towers Watson classified 4,961, or 15 percent, as 'high-vital' congregations."[49] There is a section in the report that reads under the heading "The Importance of Metrics." The Methodist Church was once a force for higher education across the U.S., from Vanderbilt, American University, Emory, Duke, and University of Southern California. The report's attestation of biblical warrant suggests no such scholarly heritage:

> Jesus lived and taught by the numbers. He withered a fig tree because it was not bearing measurable fruit. It had leaves, but not signs of vitality—fruit. Jesus taught about talents and that multiplying talents was a sign of faithfulness. The scriptures often included numbers—5,000 fed, 10 healed, 12 disciples made. Jesus said, "You will know them (disciples) by their fruit." (Matthew 7:16).[50]

As one former student noted ironically, if we muster the "will" to do so, the UMC can push ourselves back to the year 1960.

The United Methodist Church News Service shared the news that churches who wished to get with the "Vitality" program needed to emulate "pop music." Vital congregations will include "contemporary" services that emulate "what people hear on pop radio." And "traditional hymns" must include "a backbeat."[51] During a point where I almost gave up on my home denomination, the United Methodist Church began celebrating U2charist. The title is a play on the evangelical pop led band U2 and one of the fancier names for "the Mass," "Eucharist." The liturgy is "Mama Mia" but instead of using Swedish pop band Abba they created a Bono themed liturgy.[52] Only "Mama Mia" does not purport to be about the physical presence of God.

Steve Albini wrote an essay on the music industry published in 1993 for *The Baffler*. It is entitled "The Problem with Music."[53] When he died in May of 2024, the *Irish Times* ran an obituary with the title "Steve Albini taught thousands of musicians that ethics and politics are embedded in business and art" and the follow-up tagline: "Producer provided a counterpoint to those stars who preach while avoiding tax or the consequences of their own work practices." The description under his photograph for the piece reads "Steve Albini came from a politically conscious Chicago punk scene that shunned the mainstream as vapid and shallow and the music industry as essentially exploitative."[54] Albini described himself as an "engineer" who should be paid "like a plumber." Rock journalist Jim DeRogatis wrote in an interview from 1992 that Albini refused to take royalties on albums. "He says that his fee depends on the band's ability to pay and whether or not a major label is involved."[55]

"Some of your friends are probably already this fucked." This is the last line of Steve Albini's 1993 *Baffler* essay describing the setting of major record companies as "a trench, about four feet wide and five feet deep, maybe sixty yards long, filled with runny, decaying shit" through which the artists must swim, in competition with one another, toward "a faceless industry lackey" holding a contract. One of the details of his work as an acoustic engineer connects with the marketing of "the gospel" and the measuring of "success." He described the music industry from the late 1980s to the year of publication of this article in 1993: "Then vintage microphones were all the rage … Compression by the ton, especially if it comes from a tube limiter." He continued, "It doesn't matter how awful the recording is, as long as it goes through a tube limiter, somebody will claim it sounds 'warm,' or maybe even 'punchy.' They might even compare it to the Beatles … I hate it. It makes everything sound like a beer commercial."[56]

Albini noted how a form of artistry—music—can be funneled so that it becomes something other than art. It becomes uniform, predictable, "commercial." This connects to the "trendy thing" that went on in some mainstream Protestant circles from the early 2000s into the present, as people assigned the task of planning to save mainstream Protestantism sought methods to make their ministries marketable. Some of my friends and former students trying to follow the fads, or to refuse them, have indeed been "fucked." What happens when clergy submit to marketing plans that turn "the gospel" into something so pop-generic it sounds like a beer commercial?

Hank and Peggy Hill depict white, middle America. Judge has them attending First Methodist because Methodism is generic local church. Their foray into a mega-church is brief. They return to Methodist potluck dinners and hymnals. The show first aired in 1997, eleven years after the United Methodist Council of Bishops produced a controversial not-vanilla political document. Their words made the front page of the *Washington Post*. "Methodist Bishops Blast SDI A-Arms."[57] The article by Marjorie Hyre ran April 30, 1986. "The Council of Bishops of the United Methodist Church, spiritual leaders of the nation's second largest Protestant denomination," Hyre reported, "denounced yesterday any use of nuclear weapons and the Reagan administration's Strategic Defense Initiative, popularly known as 'Star Wars.'" She noted the scope of the letter, written to "9.2 million members of the church in the United States and 15 other countries" and that "the bishops rejected the doctrine of nuclear deterrence, the linchpin of the United States' modern military policy, as a 'position which cannot receive the churches blessing.'" The letter noted the loss of spending on social goods: "U.S. arms are now being purchased with food stamps, welfare checks, rent subsidies, Medicaid payments, school lunches and nutrition supplements for poor mothers and their children." The letter was "the strongest statement any church group has made on nuclear war and has received widespread attention." The full eighty-seven-page accompanying text is available in many small Methodist church libraries to this day. It is also available as *In Defense of Creation: The Nuclear Crisis and a Just Peace* through the internet archive.[58] This was a moment in the largest mainline Protestant denomination in the U.S. when elected representatives risked sounding less like a beer commercial and more like punk rock.

In a 2004 article for the *New York Times*, Laurie Goodstein and David Kirkpatrick reported on a reactionary thinktank set up in the 1980s to counter such courage.[59] Carl F. H. Henry, evangelical and founding editor of *Christianity Today*, was among the group who began the Institute on Religion and Democracy in 1981.[60] In "Conservative Group Amplifies Voice of Protestant Orthodoxy," the *Times* named donors and the purpose of the organization, which effectively split the Episcopal Church in the U.S., the mainline Presbyterian denomination in the U.S., and the mainline Methodist denomination—the United Methodist Church: "the flashpoint is homosexuality, but there is another common denominator as well." Goodstein and Kirkpatrick reported, "a small organization based in Washington … helped incubate traditionalist insurrections against the liberal politics of the denomination's leaders." They continued: "With financing from a handful of conservative donors, including the Scaife family foundations, the Bradley and Olin Foundations and Howard and Roberta Ahmanson's Fieldstead & Company [the IRD has had] a pivotal role in the biggest battle over the future of American Protestantism since churches split over slavery at the time of the Civil War." "Methodist, Presbyterian and Episcopal churches have 12.5 million members," the report read, adding "for decades they and other mainline denominations have provided theological backbone and foot soldiers for liberal causes like abortion rights, racial and economic equality, the nuclear freeze, environmentalism and anti-war movements." They quote church researcher Alfred F. Ross on the goal: "The mainline denominations are a strategic piece on the chess board that the right wing is trying to dominate." The Institute was created to control "the Sunday pulpit," "millions of dollars of capacity … with control of church newsletters and pension funds," and "foreign missions."

They complete this last point with the note that the missionaries carry with them "their brand of Christianity" throughout the globe. Goodstein and Kirkpatrick interviewed two of the matriarchs of the effort, listed as Mrs. Ahmanson (Roberta, wife of Howard, a banker from California) and Mrs. (Diane) Knippers. Each defines the group's role as defending Protestantism from the supposedly fringe left. The argument for the organization ties together the loss of numbers in the mainstream churches with "churches' liberalism," a force that the donors say "has contributed to their steep decline over the last 30 years even as more conservative evangelical churches have grown." Mrs. Knippers explicitly names that theological education was within the crosshairs of their efforts by 2004. "In the seminaries, what replaced the liberation theology of the 80s was a radical feminist theology," she said, linking writings for justice for poor people and writings for justice for female people together as signs of decadence. Mrs. Ahmanson also blames the "elite." "Christians should stick to the fifth century St. Vincent of Lerins's orthodox standard of "what has been held everywhere in every time by everyone.'"[61] The *Guardian* reported in 2003, "between 1997 and 2002, the IRD, set up during the Cold War to fight the spread of communism, spent at least $2.5 million to monitor and resist the liberalisation of America's churches" and specifically names the Ahmanson family as bankrolling the effort.[62]

The Crotch Shot

Texas Monthly ran a series of text and podcast essays in 2022 on the Dallas Cowboy Cheerleaders. I listened as a distraction then realized a connection. There are large screens at the front of the Cowboy Church in Ellis County, Texas (celebrated as the largest). Most of the cowboy-themed ministries I visited had a simple screen to display the lyrics of songs the people there to attend were to sing, and an image or two—a bronc rider or a calf-roper, sometimes a highlighted bible verse. The high-tech, large screen worship spaces I visited were in Acts 29 churches.

In the *Texas Monthly* series "America's Girls, Episode 7: All-American Sexy Girls" the grabline reads: "From honey shots to swimsuit calendars, sex has long been part of the cheerleaders' brand."[63] Sara Hepola interviewed, Sharon Grigsby, "the metro columnist for the *Dallas Morning News*." They discussed "the Jumbotron at AT&T Stadium," which, when the stadium debuted in 2009, "was the biggest high-definition video board in the world." "We are talking about something that goes almost from end zone to end zone," she adds. Grigsby tells Hepola, "Most anyone I've ever talked to who goes to the game, ends up watching the game on the Jumbotron."

The giant screens at Acts 29 gatherings not only reproduce the image of a man on a screen. They magnify his masculinity. Given that the men in the network do not wear clerical robes, this means the jumbo screens display his body very much enlarged. He serves like the icon on the Brawny brand of paper towels, Mr. Clean, or the Jolly Green Giant. What Blumenthal and her husband termed "the breast board" at Cowboy games reinforces a particular version of femaleness. Something that confused me—the pattern of pulling back to show a pastor's entire body on the big screen—made new sense. The church version of the jumbotron does not only show their "breasts." It shows their crotch. In conversation with another clergywoman who has had to deal with the steeple envy in her own denomination, we both agreed. If you do not have the proper equipment to produce the shot, you cannot be on trend.

One way to explain a muscular Christian shift in culture at Duke about 2007–2010 is through the unspoken code of dress for young men. By 2010, the brand of the school had, through marketing and intentional recruitment, shifted younger, and significantly more male. The 2010 entering class was 63 percent male. As the Fund for Theological Education study on "fitness" had noted, the "traditional" young male student of the 1950s and 1960s had been replaced by a truly diverse group of people.[64] The young dean of Duke Divinity School sought to recruit a "fitter," younger class of students through marketing. The missional wording changed from "A Community of the Love of Learning and Desire for God" in the late 1990s to a set of words that were tonally different. "Excellence," "coaching," and "leadership" became foundational words for recruitment. *Divinity Magazine*, started in 2002 as a vehicle for alumni, donors, and potential donors, carried an increasing emphasis on leadership and features to attract young adults. L. Gregory Jones secured funding for the Center for Reconciliation, "launched" in 2005, and the Center for Faith and Leadership, founded in 2007. They became barnacles bigger than the ship of the school itself, with websites swankier than the basic Divinity website. It took a student savvy about website design to point out to faculty that the websites for the two centers did not offer a "back to Divinity" option. Once you clicked on either of the two new websites, you were at the main event. These efforts coincided with the opening of a significant new building on Duke Divinity campus.[65]

The cover of the Spring 2006 issue of *Divinity Magazine* announced, "Resurrecting Excellence: A New Effort to Cultivate Ministry's Best." Perhaps in an editorial attempt to reassure readers, the opening page of the issue, "From the Archives" features photos of women studying, with the note "Women divinity students, whose numbers increased fivefold between 1971 and 1973, study in the student lounge." The cover article begins on page 3 and features primarily a book co-written by Dean Jones entitled *Resurrecting Excellence*. The staff writer explains "Nationwide, numerous programs focused on excellence in ministry are already underway. Typically funded by Lilly Endowment Inc. or other foundations." Jones notes the decline in mainline Protestant churchgoers and names as a primary problem "complacent and ineffective ministry." The director of the religion arm of the Lilly Foundation, himself a Duke Divinity graduate, is quoted as calling the issue "mediocrity masquerading as ministry." The article continues "Make no mistake, excellent ministry happens all across the country, Jones and Armstrong contend in *Resurrecting Excellence,* and they cite numerous examples. When you see excellent ministry, the two authors say, you know it. It has its own aesthetic."[66]

The aesthetics of excellence took a confusing turn as the school's brand changed. The Winter 2011 issue of *Divinity Magazine* noted "The sessions from the 2010 Convocation & Pastors' School are among the most widely downloaded audio recordings from across all of Duke University. As one alumnus reflected in a post-event evaluation: "The speakers really addressed a very wide spectrum of listeners. I am non-denominational/semi-evangelical and felt totally welcomed."[67]

The evangelical rock star on the list was Rob Bell, a graduate of Wheaton College (Illinois), the motto for which is "For Christ and His Kingdom." In 2011, *Time Magazine* named Bell one of the 100 "Most Influential People in the World." "Is hell real? It's a question that has vexed the Christian church for two millennia," *Time* reported. They continued, "Interesting stuff, to be sure, but hardly notable in the world of theology—except that Bell, the man raising these issues, is an Evangelical pastor with a huge and growing young following." How was Bell so influential? "Bell, 40, is the founder of Mars Hill Bible Church in Grand Rapids, Mich.; a master of social media; and the author of a current best-selling book, *Love Wins*." They describe the aesthetic: "Wielding music, videos and a Starbucks sensibility, Bell is at the forefront of a rethinking of Christianity in America."[68]

By 2011, Duke Divinity was heavily recruiting from schools like Wheaton College and Calvin College, both in the Midwest and each drawing from students who had grown up in non-denominational churches with links to neo-Calvinism. Bell was a superstar to many of our students, male and female, and had a clear "aesthetic" of excellence. When I asked a colleague familiar with non-denominational churches in the Midwest to explain the view, she explained much of it had to do with "the crotch shot." It was a crude way of noting something that I had vaguely noticed in the attire of many of our youngest male, white Divinity students. They were wearing tight blue jeans, even while preaching. It was a significant shift in preaching attire.

The aesthetics of excellence for mainline churches included numbers. Duke Divinity Faculty received a report each year from the Director of Admissions, often with a director of the Lilly Foundation also in attendance, and we were told, with great pride, that we had the youngest entering class of students from across our peer institutions. The report from the 2001 Auburn Study called on seminaries to address the dearth of young adults entering the ministry. It was around this time, between 2005 and 2011, that we were shifting the demographic toward men. "Coaching." "Excellence." "Leadership."

Daniel Vaca begins his book *Evangelicals Incorporated: Books and the Business of Religion in America* with a story about the mainstreaming of a form of evangelicalism through a combination of forms of marketing related to superstar figure Rick Warren, whose 2002 book *Purpose Driven Life* was

Figure 3.1 *Rob Bell in the February 2014 issue of O, The Oprah Magazine. Credit: Bryce Duffy. Used with permission.*[69]

catapulted to success in part through the marketing of Oprah Winfrey Incorporated.[70] Oprah, whose face and apparent openness about her own struggles with spirituality and doubt, combined with oodles of money, can make an author an evangelical household name. Her brand makes an author part of what Daniel Vaca calls "ambient evangelicalism." When I used a private search engine to find an image of Rob Bell, preacher, this is one of the first to come up.

The photograph is from the February 2014 issue of *O, The Oprah Magazine*. The article begins with a description of Rob Bell.

> Bell moved to California a little over two years ago from frigid Michigan; he tries to get in the water every day. It usually happens sometime after he makes "a proper breakfast, a proper smoothie, or French toast or eggs" for his three children, ages 15, 13, and 4, and drives them down a mountain to their respective schools in his 2001 Toyota Sequoia—a car for which he traded in his Land Rover, since the Sequoia's rear window allows access for paddles and surfboards. At 43, Bell looks more like a moneyed California surfer dad than one of America's most popular spiritual leaders, an author-sermonizer who built a megachurch in a former shopping mall before he was 30, has sold 1.2 million copies of his six books, is developing a spiritual TV show for OWN, and has preached the good word at the Viper Room (which, for anyone who was not a teenage girl in the early '90s, is the L.A. nightclub where River Phoenix died of a drug overdose). Bell has the uncanny magnetism of a cult leader or a U.S. president, tempered by the earnest humility of a seeker. He often seems to be plugged in to some bottomless spiritual-energetic power source.

This is one way to describe the resurrection of excellence. The term "frigid Michigan" contrasts effectively with the warmth of the accompanying photograph. Readers are reassured that he cooks his children breakfast, that he drives a reliable, sturdy, Sequoia, and that his previous vehicle had been a Land Rover. Sensible, and the author notes a man who seems more "California surfer" than an "author-sermonizer." Bell also "built" something; he "built" not just a church but a "megachurch." The location of that thing that he built is also sturdy, reliable, a "former shopping mall." The author adds this flourish to the facts. For any "teenage girl in the early '90s," he may be known by his proximity to another god-like figure, a tragic one. Rob Bell can cook up the bacon, fry it up in a pan, build a megachurch in an abandoned shopping mall, and never let you forget he's a man. "Uncanny magnetism." "Cult leader or a U.S. president." But with the "earnest humility" of someone who is searching. And he is also the Energizer Bunny of Spirituality.

The accompanying image is worth a thousand words. In the online version of the article, Pastor Bell is shot from below, with a bluebird sky behind him, accenting his blue-on-blue board shorts, riding low on his midriff, showing a line of sunny hair up to his large, brown cross sturdily resting on a brown rope, between his abdominal muscles and his ample chest. The look on his face is determined, even his watch is set off in a way that highlights his hands, holding a long, dark paddle. In the magazine print version, Bell is haloed by large white words, in capital letters "HEAVEN IS A PLACE ON EARTH." The pastor who came to be known as the man willing to take on evangelicals who insist on the existence of hell is posed as a muscular angel here on earth.

When I explained this photo to a Buddhist friend who grew up Episcopal, he asked, "did these people learn nothing from the story about the golden calf?" How, he asked me, is this any different than crafting a calf of gold and showcasing it as the location of God's presence? What strikes me most about his question, as a Christian Ethicist, is what does it mean that this one human being is supposed to take on that kind of presence? How is this not making a human being into an impossible icon?

In my book on the marketing of mainstream domesticity in the U.S., I asked about the use of better mothers and gardens as icons of homey holiness. Another friend at that time suggested that a helpful concept for what I was describing there is the anti-icon. He explained that an icon is supposed to take the viewer deeper into God, deeper into the unfathomable presence of God. What an anti-icon does is reverberate back onto the viewer, presenting a boomerang of self-scrutiny.[71] Rob Bell's "Love Wins" message was to be one of reassurance. Yet with the emphasis on his success, and with this emphasis on his physique, he becomes a kind of anti-icon. If that seems too theoretically dense, perhaps simply ask whether Pastor Bell has been posed as a golden calf.

It is not an easy combination to mix a call to submission, the insistence on honoring the sovereign, and something approaching real humor. The marketing of holy masculinity in mainstream evangelicalism requires a sense of solemnity in order not to veer into the range of spoofery. Mainstream Protestants in the U.S. are not generally known for our humor. But there is an edge to the Acts 29 forms of spectacle that necessitate the recognition of authority without whimsy, without a strand of the absurdity of life. There is a dead-earnest chirpiness to much of the praise music. The accompanying musicians in bands at these churches clap, smile, and "yeah!" but their words insist repeatedly (meaning with many repetitious refrains) on "kneeling before the throne," "obey Him," "know the King." In order for a man on a stage, appearing alongside a giant video of himself, or appearing streamed in from somewhere else, not to seem like a caricature of a superhero preacher man, there is a fine line he must walk to be reasonably winsome and authoritative. From the songs to the very loud music to the professional visuals, the messaging is steeled.

Going back to Western-themed ministries, the conceit of a rodeo is written into the architecture and the branding images. The "West" remains today tied to calf-roping, bull riding, and pig chasing. And, in those settings, any man, woman, boy, or child will be able to accurately name, if asked, who the true heroes are in any rodeo. The clowns. It is the work of the clown to attract the attention of a dangerous mammal and to direct attention by the audience away from a human scrambling, limping, or crawling to safety. Without the clown, a rodeo would be more like a cage fight between competing mammals. Humor, a sense of the lunacy of the entire endeavor, runs alongside the athleticism and skill of the competitions at a rodeo.

Entertain Us!

Attention to items put together as insider-comedy may describe for an outsider the formula of mainstream, evangelical auditorium worship. A creator on YouTube named "Church Soundguy" has a video posted in 2012 that provides the basic elements of worship services at churches in the Acts 29 network.[72] Another from 2020 is the "Worship Song Song," also on YouTube, attributed to "Random Action Verb Worship" (a play on trendy church names) created by comedian Shama Mrema, directed by Robert Therrell, with music by Andrew Simmons.[73] The basic elements condensed in each of these videos have also been incorporated in mainstream, older churches attempting to achieve this particular "aesthetic of excellence" in order to keep up and be judged as "vital." From the specificity of the two videos, it is clear that people with a background in these worship productions created them. The videos came to my attention because former students who had worked in these church networks as sound engineers, musicians, sermon ghostwriters, and recruitment specialists sent them to me.

In "Contemporvant" from 2012, the off-screen narrator is a man speaking like one of the male disc jockeys on a classic rock station, the kind of DJ on a two-man team who makes crude jokes in between songs by Rush and Pearl Jam. He announces "You can't stop it. It's coming to a town near you. It used to be called 'contemporary.' Some call it 'Relevant.' We're so cool, we call it 'Contemporvant.'" The on-screen words are in Papyrus font. The font matters, as the style is linked in evangelical circles to man things—gravity and biblicism.[74] The visuals show manly hands setting up sound equipment, a balding man in his thirties looking into a compact mirror while brushing his forehead with a make-up brush. He has a pierced lower lip. Four white men are playing classic rock style music, three with rock t-shirts; the lead, pierced guy is wearing flannel. The opening song concludes, and a hip Asian American man comes on stage with a red t-shirt and blue jeans. He is wearing black, rectangular glasses. The white male preacher with a full head of brown hair comes next onto the stage. He is shown sitting next to a glass table, no pulpit, then standing, then hitting his fist on the top of the glass table. Then there is a video within the video, playing during the time when congregants may put their money in offering plates. The visuals for the video being played inside this YouTube video are black and white, scenes from inside a car window driving down a city highway, driving over a city bridge, and then the video goes back to the main preacher.

The words in the video describe the components in the script for the video. Cool young hip guy says the words "cool young hip guy welcoming all with gravity, and cool glasses; I welcome everybody with arms wide open, revealing my tattoo so you know I have a past." The lead singer sings "Opening Song! Opening Song! Lights and Big Drums! You know it's cool because you've heard it on the radio!" Next, "This is the song that everyone knows, the song that everyone knows," and then, "This is my new song that nobody knows, I want you to learn this song and buy my record in the bookstore … after the service." The senior minister says, "One man has all the answers. I have all the answers. I am showing a picture of a puppy and a baby from an impoverished Third World nation. I am speaking softly to draw you in, and then EMPHATICALLY driving all my points … whispering, whispering, pausing … pained expression … long prayer." The closing credits announce that the church has won the "Winner" for "Papyrus Font Award," along with awards for "Informally Dressed Pastor" and "Edgy T-Shirts."

The creators of this YouTube video have hit all the points of the recipe, the formula for success presented at every Acts 29 congregation I attended, except for one modification going on over the last fifteen years of my research. That modification includes aesthetically normative women on stage, sometimes singing, sometimes playing a bass guitar, sometimes using a tambourine.

The second video that provides a script for the mainstream evangelical contemporary worship recipe was posted in 2020 on YouTube as "Worship Song Song." The online video provides a transcript link and full attribution for the creators of the video, which runs for 3.5 minutes.[75] The video has been viewed 680,000 times as of January 11, 2025, with 1,274 comments. The comments on this post are from the point of view of church attendees and people involved in worship musical teams. @TheGeekRex concurs with the formulaic quality of the brand:

> The key change part really stood out to me, as someone who makes music in my free time. The number of times I've watched the woman standing in the front of the church stand up and raise her hands in time with the big key change/crash symbol combo has pretty much convinced me that modern worship music is nothing but self-centered musical hypnosis. I can play a specific three-note chord or change the bassline midway through a song and it'll give me the same chills. You might as well just time the air

conditioning to the big musical moment, just to really fill people with the holy goosebumps.

The video features eight young adults playing soft rock style instruments—keyboard, three guitars, drums, and a pop-up from a tambourine guy. As with "Contemporvant" the words are what they are doing: "This is the first verse of the worship song song. The words are simple so sing along long." The first substantial lyric might sound odd to an outsider, but it is recognizable for the commenters on the YouTube site: "I am terrible, but he is able." Another repeated line is "Life's got me down I'm at the end of my rope. Here's an out of context Bible verse about Hope!" along with "it's repetitive it's repetitive it's repetitive [pause] all my problems are gone." Then vocalist Abby Gilbert, with perfect church hipster young woman long blonde hair, sings "I'm a rich blonde female, singing about how I fail, things are bad again, I am struggling, I'm a total mess, my life's a train wreck, I'm pure garbage [pause] I need him again!" At this point, one of her bandmates pauses briefly to look like "Huh?" But the line is perfect, as this is the basic role for many women serving on these musical teams. They are not there as symbolic of holy power, but of submission to the sovereign.

An Acts 29 pastor had explained when I visited their church in 2011 that the network involves conformity akin to that of a fast food franchise. There is a recent episode of Rian Johnson and Natasha Lyonne's 2023 series *Poker Face* in which a central character at a Subway franchise, located in rural New Mexico, finds joyful creativity in improving the standard recipes required by corporate.[76] Customers remark that he has improved on the usual fare. The setting is not magical realism. While a sandwich composer at a Subway franchise at a regional airport could not get away with this, the truck drivers who drive through rural New Mexico are hardly going to report inconsistency to the national headquarters. The network of sovereignty and submission plants churches in regional hubs and cities. Tiny town truck drivers are not their aim. And, the requirement of predictability in messaging, music, even the form of mission hand-outs and images on the screen during prayers—this requirement of overseen sameness means that pastors in the network have less freedom than a Subway chef in rural New Mexico.

The uniformity of these muscular Christianity church marketing formulas is emasculating. They are forms of submission. Susan Faludi writes that an astronaut serving as the "celebrated post-war flyboy" for NASA was "supposed to be the representative man … experiencing space for all his brethren."[77] "Heroic," they did not even have control over the machinery. They were expendable, but also necessary for their properly handsome faces and able bodies. NASA needed their version of a praise rock band. These versions of manly, holy heroism do not even serve well the men who can measure up to the crotch shot aesthetic.

News Matters

The recipe for "community" in many multi-campus churches in suburbs and cities is to create a "community" within a region using one highlighted senior male minister around whom a team gathers small groups to connect people across a multi-campus church. The growth of this church model has accelerated at the same time local news outlets have been bought by national chains or have shuttered their services altogether. The elevation of preachers and pulpits has coincided with the evisceration of local journalism.

Social media moguls know this. Election profiteers know this. The Cambridge Analytica scheme to micro-target political advertisements using a combination of social media data and evangelical church data depends on this reality. In a 2020 documentary directed by Charles Kriel and Katharina Gellein Viken entitled *People You May Know*, Matt Engel, the Director of Gloo Labs, speaks to Katharina Gellein Viken about the use of data collected through data mining conglomerates: "We are sitting on mounds of information." The "we" Engel means here are people like himself and Gloo founder Scott Beck, people with the skills to set up, as Beck has described Gloo, a "global faith ecosystem."[78] In the interview, Engel defines "wisdom" as "just having more information than another person." He directly addresses the reason why a marketing plan like Cambridge Analytica would draw on data collected from faith-based organizations: "Churches have the one thing that most companies are absolutely desperate for, which is relationship. We own the relationship space, like, we own it. That's the church."[79] As of 2024, Gloo is one of the keystones of the "He Gets Us" advertising and data mining effort, covered most extensively by muckraking journalists at the Baptist News Service.[80]

Without a town square, shorn of even a local shopping mall, and without a local news outlet, churches fill a vacuum. The loss of local news shapes the influence of local church leaders and the people they "own," to use Engel's description. The Local News Initiative out of Northwestern University allows viewers to pinpoint states, counties, and parishes to note the presence or absence of local news coverage. As of their 2023 report, "Texas has 29 counties without a news source, and 131 counties with only one." In a small city like San Angelo, Texas, there remains one daily newspaper, the *San Angelo Standard-Times*, established in 1884 and now owned by Gannett Company, Inc. out of Tyson, Virginia.[81] Gannett also owns the *Austin American-Statesman*. Gannett Company and The McClatchy Company, the two largest owners of newspapers in the U.S., announced in 2024 that they would no longer carry content from the Associated Press beyond that of limited election reporting.[82] In North Carolina, McClatchy owns the *Durham Herald-Sun*, the *Charlotte Observer*, and the Raleigh-based *News and Observer*. McClatchy thus owns the daily newspapers of three out of four of the state's largest cities. Greensboro, North Carolina is the fourth, and their daily newspaper, the *News and Record*, was purchased by billionaire Warren Buffett, then sold to an Iowa-based company. As Andrew Carter of the *News and Observer* wrote in 2023, "ACC tournament the biggest story in Greensboro. There's barely a hometown paper left to cover it."[83] The loss of local and regional journalism also shapes coverage of large, evangelical churches and faith-based organizations.

The Summit Church website in May 2024 welcomes online visitors with the words: "One Church. Many locations." The opening image is a video of a praise band, the lead singer wearing a baseball hat backward, jumping around in a circle, holding his microphone—all in the style of Adam Nathaniel Yauch, aka MCA, of the 1980s hit band The Beastie Boys.[84] The jumping baseball hatted man has an aesthetically normative white woman on stage looking at him and smiling. The next image is of an older white woman standing with her back to the camera, praying with two hipster looking young white men. The next image shows young people in a row of seating, standing and singing together, followed by a young white man being submerged in a baptismal pool by a white male pastor, a middle-aged white woman with a stylish hat and glasses singing on stage, a middle-aged African American man speaking on stage, and a group of people standing in the middle of a group of sitting congregants praying together in a circle. The "find a location" feature on the website repeats: "We are one church that meets in many locations around the Triangle. Find a campus near you!" As of 2024, their many locations number twelve, including a downtown Durham location that is the historic Carolina Theatre, the only remaining, independent, non-profit cinema in the city. Like the Beastie Boy look-alike opening the website, the Carolina Theatre gives Summit Church a sheen of cool.

"The Carolina" as locals refer to the theater shares a square and brick walls with the Durham Arts Council and the Durham Convention Center. It is the center of the mainstream, downtown Durham. The Carolina Theatre website describes their history in this way: "the Carolina Theatre continues to be a source of civic pride; an important marker of historic change; a valuable touchstone for the community; a crucial resource for education through the arts, and a beacon attracting visitors to its city's vibrant downtown."[85] In 2024, the Carolina Theatre hosted the OUTSOUTH Queer Film Festival, and it has served as the hub for the Full Frame Documentary Film Festival, an internationally celebrated festival running since 1998. The Carolina partners with the local Durham Arts Council, with Durham Public Schools, and with the University of North Carolina, Carolina Public Humanities, Carolina K-12 program. The Durham Arts Council and the Carolina Theatre overlap in promotions and efforts. If a reader has heard of Durham and "Arts" they may have heard of Full Frame, but they likely have not heard of the Durham Arts Council unless they have family here.[86]

The Arts Council is one of two local arts centers, the other being the also celebrated Hayti Heritage Center, which has been flourishing since 1975 in Durham. The Center describes itself as "a cultural enrichment and arts education facility that promotes cultural understanding through diverse events, activities and programs that preserve the heritage and embrace the experiences of Americans of African descent."[87] I do not know whether leadership at Summit Church requested to hold services adjacent to the Hayti

Heritage Center. There are many large, predominately African American Baptist churches in Durham. They are members of Baptist associations other than the Southern Baptist Convention.

The location association most theatergoing, concert-seeking customers who did not grow up in Durham have with the city of Durham is the "DPAC," a venue that seats thousands and hosts *Mama Mia* and *The Lion King*. The Durham Performing Arts Center opened with a price tag of $48 million. In 2016, WRAL news reported "For the past six years, DPAC has ranked among the top five most attended theaters in the country."[88] It is part of a relatively recent Duke-related development to attract tourists to Durham, right off the Durham highway that rendered in concrete a split between downtown Durham and the African American Hayti neighborhood in 1970.[89] In the 2019 article for the *IndyWeek* "A Half-Century Ago, Durham Separated Hayti from Downtown. Now, the Neighborhood's Leaders Want to Reconnect It to the City's Core," Erin Williams quotes director Angela Lee on a plan to reconnect Hayti with downtown through other walkways. "It will get people reenergized about their community to feel like they are not being rejected or disregarded by the city," Lee says. "That has been a prevailing attitude because, well, we have been."

The DPAC is part of the American Tobacco Historic District, which also includes the Durham Bulls ballpark. The website for the conglomerate is cheerful: "Working together, local government and private sector leaders re-made the former American Tobacco factory, developed the Durham Bulls Athletic Park and opened the stunning Durham Performing Arts Center … rejuvenating this unique city and setting a new live-work-play standard."[90]

In 2011, a former student working for the evangelical parachurch organization Young Life wrote to me to recommend I attend an event at the DPAC. "Tickets are $35—quite pricey. Maybe you can use $$ money research budget (??) to go." He added "[Tim] Keller's not necessarily the enemy, for lack of a better word, but [Mark] Driscoll lovers, like I said, will be there." The event was May 4, 2011.[91]

Using the internet archive, the description on the Durham Cares website reads: "Join us for an evening of celebration, fellowship and inspiration in a benefit fundraiser for the DurhamCares partners. Neighbors and congregations from across the city are invited as we explore what it means to Love Your Neighbor as seen in the Bible and ask what our next step might be to bless our city."[92] The invitation highlights again the numbers approach to success in describing Tim Keller: "Over the past 20 years, the church has grown to five services at three sites, with a weekly attendance of over 5,000. Named one of the Top 25 Most Influential Churches in America, Keller's ministry is notable not only for winning over New Yorkers who are skeptical to faith … " The event featured a 3-minute video on the giant screen at the DPAC with talking heads of numerous clergymen and one clergywoman. It is entitled "Love Your Neighbor Film."[93] The description below the film on YouTube, posted by DurhamCares, reads: "Durham-area pastors relay the Good Samaritan parable in the context of loving your Durham neighbor. Music by local Durham musician David McKnight." The group of clergy includes prominently Summit Church's J. D. Greear and then Dean of Duke Chapel Sam Wells. They are each wearing professional clothing and reading the words of the story, with emphasis on "your Durham neighbor."

The opening is large letters: "WHO IS YOUR NEIGHBOR?" and then moves to show David McKnight sitting on a stool, looking up at the filmmaker. The filmmakers then go on to contrast the talking faces of clergy with David, sitting at his usual daytime spot on Durham's quirky 9th Street, playing his violin. He is depicted in the film symbolically as "the neighbor" the clergymen and one woman are recommending viewers love. The clergy are depicted alone on the camera, reading the words, as heads. David is shown from his ankles up, against the backdrop of the street. David introduces himself to the camera: "David McKnight. Out of work newspaper man. Came to work in Durham in the 1970s at the Durham *Herald-Sun* for a hundred dollars a week and I'm almost making that now in music."

David McKnight, who died in 2017, was a friend and neighbor. We talked politics and journalism regularly at Duke's Lilly Library on East Campus, near 9th street, where we were both often doing research in their online newspaper archives. I knew him as much as an always curious researcher of North Carolina politics as a musician. Whenever we'd see one another, if he was not already playing something else, and sometimes even when he was, he would play and sing Craig Fuller's 1972 song "Amie," asking "Amie, what you gonna do?" Part of what we talked about was how I was going to stay at Duke when I was so much at heart more a Durham townie than a gown-wearing scholar. After his death, a few local entrepreneurs advocated to erect a statue of him, playing his violin, on 9th street. Friends balked, saying that it would make him seem more like a mascot than a human being. One musician named him in a tribute "In Memory of David McKnight" as "the itinerant fixture of the [Durham] music scene," noting that this "consummate musician" also played every week at the Durham Farmer's Market at Central Park, Durham.[94] The *Charlotte Observer* ran his obituary with the headline: "David McKnight, street fiddler who walked across NC in political bid, dies of brain tumor."[95] The use of David's music, his face, his body, his presence, as a symbol of "the neighbor" who a "good Samaritan" is to love runs alongside the faces of twelve clergymen, and one clergywoman, with website addresses linking to each church's website.

The event in 2011 was ostensibly to bring people across the city together to consider how best to love one's neighbor. There were no reflections on the loss of local journalism, on the divides of gentrification and the local governmental regulations that could provide structural solutions to lack of affordable housing, on the defunding of public schools initiated with the hostile takeover of the state government. The emphasis in Tim Keller's speech to Durham about love of neighbor was on contributing congregational money to non-profit efforts like DurhamCares. J. D. Greear hosted the question-and-answer section. It was more a lovefest for hosting congregations, and a lovefest for bestselling evangelical patriarch Tim Keller, than it was a convening for collaboration across diverse congregations in Durham for the sake of the city.[96] It was not localism. It was not Durham Arts Council or Carolina Theatre, much less was it Hayti Community Center.

Again, with the loss of local journalism, coverage of super-marketed churches in an area shrinks, and is sometimes funneled. A key strategy of this neo-Calvinist brand of evangelicalism is to present the lead pastor as with-it, as cooler than the lead pastor at a city's First Baptist Church. This is the angle the *IndyWeek* presented to readers in 2018. Episcopalians sent me the link to the article. Secular Jewish friends sent me the link to the article. People who did not know anything about the backstory of Acts 29 and the supermarket of muscular ministries took the article at face value, including

J. D. Greear's welcoming, smiling face. His visage is featured twice, once on page 3 and again across the full page of the main article, which is the first full article of the issue.[97] "Summit Church's J.D. Greear Wants to Take the Southern Baptist Convention Into the Twenty-First Century. The Old Guard Would Rather He Not."[98]

In what sense is this multi-site network of people bringing the Southern Baptist Convention into the twenty-first century? Readers might ask, is Summit Church collaborating with labor union efforts in the state? Or perhaps Greear is leading the charge to accept that women may be qualified to teach men? Maybe he is bringing the Convention into the twenty-first century through the full acceptance of gay people as people? People who sent me the article knew I was writing on masculinity and mainstream evangelicalism. All of them sent me a note that ran along the lines of "this guy seems to be good, right?"

The cover of the June 6, 2018, issue of *IndyWeek* celebrates their ongoing "Best Of The Triangle" awards. Local establishments from hair salons to plumbing services display an award given framed in person and on their websites. The yearly issue is as important as their regular voting guides in deciding local elections. The cover illustration by Christopher Williams shows a line of people drawn in various hues, one interracial couple with the dad holding the baby in a sling on his chest, a person in a construction hat reading the issue of the *IndyWeek* on which he is appearing, same with a dark bearded man in a linen suit. Another African American man is looking at his phone, indicating the "Best Of" can also be found online. Above the people are cutely drawn birds perched on the straight lines of the stylized, bright pink star that is the emblem of the "Best Of" awards.

The Durham *Herald-Sun* having been bought by the megapolis and downsized to nearly nothing, the *IndyWeek* became in the last decade the main, local news outlet for people in Durham who consider themselves progressive. White progressives carry their endorsements for local candidates with them on their cell phones when voting at the beautiful new Main Library downtown during early voting. The University of North Carolina library archives describe the *Independent Weekly* newspaper as being "best known for its coverage of local music, film, visual arts, theater, dance, and pop culture, as well as for its strong focus on progressive politics and social activism."[99]

Amanda Abrams wrote the 2018 piece on Greear. It reads similarly to the article in *Oprah Magazine* selling the Rob Bell brand to readers in 2014. She begins with a contrast between the local Baptist church from which Greear launched Summit and the current church of many campuses. "Twenty years ago, Homestead Heights was a traditional, red-brick Baptist church located off of Duke Street in northern Durham" she writes. She depicts the church as having dwindled to "only about 350 people." A congregation of 350 people is sizeable for a normal, mainstream Baptist church in Durham, but she depicts the congregation as failing, until Greear came to save it. The church was part of "a decline in church attendance besetting the country." She immediately moves to the numbers-success story. "But today, it boasts ten thousand worshipers on Sundays." The "it" is ostensibly the previous congregation of 350 members, only now the "it" is a network of "campuses throughout the region." Abrams continues, "Summit is one of the largest churches in the Triangle and one of the fastest-growing congregations in the country. Far from teetering on the edge of obsolescence, its pews are packed with enthusiastic young people." From the "edge of obsolescence" to "packed" with "enthusiastic young people." She characterizes Summit's success with "young professionals and millennials" due to "theological orthodoxy paired with informality and openness, a commitment to service, and an unstinting focus on bringing the gospel to all corners of the earth." Abrams announces that Greear has been "a resounding success in the Triangle" and that he will "take that formula national."

Abrams is an experienced journalist. Her home page has as one of her specializations "Faith in Action."[100] She acknowledges that the "packed with enthusiastic young people" situation has involved "smart strategizing by longtime church staff" but then attributes the change to "the dynamism of its pastor, JD Greear." The piece highlights his impending election as head of the Southern Baptist Convention and contrasts Greear with "longtime leader Paige Patterson" who had been in the news for overt sexism. Greear, for his part, is "easygoing, eminently relatable 'regular guy' albeit one who knows the Bible and can easily dissect its finer points." For *IndyWeek* readers, Abrams accentuates Summit's influence on the city, the region, and international relations:

> In a way, that sums up Summit's focus, adhering closely to a traditional interpretation of the Bible's teachings, while simultaneously exhorting worshipers to get involved in their communities and in missions abroad. Summit has done that well. The church has established, or "planted," in Christian parlance, more than two hundred churches overseas and another forty in the United States. Of the forty-six thousand churches that are part of the Southern Baptist Convention, Summit has by far sent the most missionaries into the field.

One of the qualifications Abrams highlights is Greear's Ph.D. For readers who have no sense of Southern Baptist politics, it would have been helpful to note that Southeastern Baptist Theological Seminary decades prior had purged faculty who supported women's ordination. All faculty members must sign several documents on biblical inerrancy. The social principles in one of the required documents does include care for the vulnerable, and that care is set within a very particular understanding of sexuality, gender, and sin.[101] The leadership of the school affirmed in 2004 a commitment to the Danvers Statement on gender and sexuality. That statement includes these beliefs, beliefs that continue to define who is and is not congruent with the Southern Baptist Convention: "Distinctions in masculine and feminine roles are ordained by God as part of the created order and should find an echo in every human heart"; and "Adam's headship in marriage was established by God before the Fall and was not a result of sin" and "In the family, husbands should forsake harsh or selfish leadership and grow in love and care for their wives; wives should forsake resistance to their husbands' leadership." These "principles" are fundamental to the plan to "save" a city: "We are convinced that a denial or neglect of these principles will lead to increasingly destructive consequences in our families, our churches and the culture at large."[102]

Abrams quotes from a Summit member who considers herself "feminist." She notes that Greear keeps to the basics of the Southern Baptist Convention on women's ordination and homosexuality, but ultimately, she characterizes the (brief) challenge to his leadership of the Southern Baptist Church as one of stodgy old people versus young, enthusiastic, open-minded people. "At heart, the question of who supports Greear (and why) is about how an aging denomination, one whose churches were once very similar, responds to change and modernization."

In this "Best Of The Triangle" issue, read by people at diners and barber shops across the Triangle, J. D. Greear's photo is at the top of page 3, next to the table of contents. He is shown sitting on a set of stairs, from his ankles to above his head, smiling, wearing jeans and a short-sleeved blue plaid shirt, tanned, muscular arms shown to full effect, a large watch on his wrist.[103] Underneath the photo the description reads "J. D. Greear has turned Summit Church into one of the fastest-growing congregations in the country." The article about him appears on page 7 of the issue, the first named article in the table of contents. "The Indy's annual comprehensive guide to everything awesome in the Triangle" is listed in the table of contents as "Center." The words appear on the same linear plane as Greear's chest. The cumulative, rhetorical effect of the coverage, from text to photographs to the choice of the June 6, 2018, issue is that Summit Church has won the award for "Best Congregation in the Triangle."

Political scientists refer to the effect of Donald Trump on political discourse in many ways, but one common theme is a shift to what seems "good" given the reactionary gender politics of the Make America Great Again, or MAGA, brand. I am sure I am not the only writer to call this the "Trumpian Overton Window."[104] The "Overton Window" is a shorthand term, drawing on a concept described by a twentieth-century political scientist named Joseph Overton. The *OED* gives as the definition: "In political contexts: the spectrum of ideas on public policy and social issues considered acceptable or viable by the general public at a given time."[105] Abrams uses this contrast between Trump supporters and people who have not overtly supported Donald Trump in her piece on Greear. She characterizes the network's growth among "young Christians who have been disgusted by the hypocrisy that they see in the Religious Right," naming in particular how "fellow evangelicals have supported Donald Trump." The brief challenge for Greear's role as head of the Southern

Baptist Convention was, she notes "endorsed by Robert Jeffress, the Dallas preacher who has become a close associate of Trump's." The *Indy Week's* showcasing of Summit worked in the Triangle to help Summit appear mainstream. Look, the messaging goes, here is a patriarchal or brotherly or avuncular Christian figure who is not wearing a red hat or bragging about his sexual conquests or calling overtly for the expelling of Muslims from the U.S. In this, the call to sovereignty and submission becomes mainstream.

Office Space

The last Acts 29 church I visited for this research was Renovation Church in the greater Atlanta area. The building is technically in Marietta, Georgia. The website for the congregation describes it as "A multiethnic church in Atlanta" and "A church that strives to look and act like Jesus." The website in 2023 also featured "testimonials." Kenechi, who is Black and young, appears in her testimonial image dressed modestly, hair pulled back. The text alongside her image and name reads "Being at Renovation has given me the ability to be with people who are working towards the same goals. The community has been amazing to be a part of." Chris & Lauren are a white couple. She is wearing a yellow beanie, and he is wearing a black baseball cap and sunglasses. Their words read "The vulnerability, honesty, and overall realness from leadership and members cultivates a true safe space for anyone of any culture at any point in their walk to feel welcome and wanted." Immanuel also appears. He is Black and wears a church staff lanyard. He is young, wearing a zip-up jacket and a baseball hat. Immanuel's testimony reads: "The authenticity of people and leadership helped me to be more vulnerable and honest about my journey with Jesus. You truly have the freedom to work on your spiritual growth."

Renovation Church shares a series of roads through an office park with a high school, the national headquarters of the Hooters restaurant chain, and the national headquarters for Freshens yoghurt.

My adult daughter and I drove the non-highway route from Decatur, Georgia (where she was a student) and the Renovation campus. What she and I both noticed along the way was passing through remarkably wealthy neighborhoods with private schools, including one with a stable of horses. We passed several church structures that looked like giant castles up above the main roadway. These included Church of the Apostles, a towering "one campus" church that describes itself as "an evangelical, Bible-believing church in Atlanta, Georgia, declaring the whole counsel of God, as evidenced through our Statement of Faith." Another church we passed that is the size of a cathedral is Mt. Paran, a Church of God congregation that had hired traffic officers to control the flow of cars up the hill to the campus. By the time we drove into the parking lot for Renovation Church, both of us were noting that the church looked nothing like the sections of the greater Atlanta area through which we had passed. The vehicles in the parking lot were basic, the people walking into the building dressed like normal people we would have seen if we had stopped at Walmart on our way in. My daughter had never attended a church in this network. She grew up attending plain vanilla Methodism in Durham. She is multi-racial herself, with piercings and long, dark curly hair. We had both noted separately that the Renovation church seemed to be marketing to someone exactly like her.

Like many other Acts 29 churches, Renovation is in a repurposed building, this time in an office park. They describe their plans for continuing the work of the campus, with "an outdoor space for the community around us, and our church family, to have a place to gather and play" and add that "The outdoor space will provide two soccer fields, a basketball field, and a playground, for the use and flourishing of our neighbors." Several facets of the experience struck my daughter. First, that the building felt more to her like a cinema than a church. From the basic lobby to the coffee section downstairs to the auditorium worship space, it struck her as a performance venue. Also, people did not seem to know one another. There were groups of teenagers talking to one another, but the choreography of the morning involved people walking alone and in families into the auditorium, sitting for the service, then leaving. And, during the service, there was minimal interaction across the aisles and from the stage to the auditorium seating. I had become accustomed to the noise level of these services, remembering to bring earplugs after my first time years ago. Renovation Church, along with other such congregations, hands out infant and child size noise cancelling headphones so people who prefer not to drop their children off at the childcare facilities onsite can do so without harming their children's future hearing. The music in churches following this style is so loud you literally cannot hear your own voice. The phrase "you cannot hear yourself think" rings true. And, as at so many other churches in this style, the preacher appeared on the stage, in person, with two giant screens on either side of him. So, he appeared large, above the congregation, and in triplicate. The congregation was the most racially mixed congregation of any kind I have visited in my years as a person, not just as a researcher. The preacher's message was, however, point for point what I would have expected from a Southern Baptist congregation in the South. Repent, be saved. Be in the actual world—a theme throughout the Renovation church messaging—but be a witness to a different reality.

Our visit to Renovation was four days after the Economic Policy Institute issued a report titled "Rooted in racism and economic exploitation: The failed Southern economic development model."[106] The Economic Policy Institute describes itself as "an independent, nonprofit think tank that researches the impact of economic trends and policies on working people in the United States. EPI's research helps policymakers, opinion leaders, advocates, journalists, and the public understand the bread-and-butter issues affecting ordinary Americans." The summary of the report reads "Southern politicians claim that 'business-friendly' policies lead to an abundance of jobs and economic prosperity for all Southerners. The data actually show a grim economic reality." The "key findings" include the facts that, in most Southern states, "prime-age workers" who are employed are "lower than the national average." "Median earnings in nine Southern states are among the lowest in the nation, even after adjusting for lower cost of living." "The child poverty rate in the South is 20.9%—higher than in any other region." The overall assessment of the report is clear in the title of the study, but the author reiterates: "These statistics reflect an anti-worker economic model whose signature policies are low wages, low taxes, few regulations on businesses, few labor protections, a weak safety net, and vicious opposition to unions." The summary continues: "A long history of anti-worker policies in the South—rooted in a racist agenda—has had devastating consequences for its residents. Business interests and the wealthy have stoked racial divisions to maintain power and ensure access to cheap labor—at the expense of working people." They give as prescription: "We must begin to reverse 150 years of anti-worker policymaking in the South—starting with raising minimum wages and protecting workers' right to organize. We also need to enforce appropriate regulations on business practices, reform a broken tax structure, and strengthen the safety net for Southerners."

In the Atlanta area of the early to mid-2020s, the city includes the largest international airport in the world, a highway structure that people regularly refer to as akin to something from a Mad Max apocalyptic hellscape, and neighborhoods mere miles from downtown sequestered for cozy walkways, dog parks, and crosswalks. The economic disparity in the city is not subtle, as the 1996 post-Olympics-hosting reality has become only more so, dividing the service working poor from struggling middle-class to new professionals moving into the area in the tech industry. The city, repeatedly called "the City too busy to hate" by African American and white leaders in Atlanta since the 1960s, could benefit from churches committed to thinking together about how to advocate for, in the words of the EPI report "working people."

A consistent thread throughout this line of research was the importance of attracting young professional people newly transplanted to cities like Atlanta, the Metroplex in Texas, and the Triangle in North Carolina. Again, the network started in Seattle, with the face of the brand being a no-nonsense advocate for more fist fights for Jesus. From Mark Driscoll in the 1990s to J. D. Greear in the 2020s, this formula for success is meant to appeal to young adults trying to find a place to connect with one another. Through slick marketing, book production schemes to promote an author as a "bestseller," and other well-funded promotions, these Christians are ostensibly about reaching young men, and those around them, who are otherwise alienated by modern life. I have detailed here why I find this success-driven, marketing-driven setup to be emasculating to the poster men designated to be the icons of avatar masculinity. At least Mr. Whitesnake (whose name is David Coverdale) does not have to pretend also to be Mr. Whitesnake, holy husband of Mrs. Whitesnake, appearing regularly with their properly friendly, well-behaved children. I suggest here, again as in the last chapter, that there are other resources for reaching the target demographic. Even if the goal is something less constructively useful than the basic changes needed in these cities to make the cities logistically livable for young adults, the brand could at least draw from better pop culture suitable for the task of recruitment.

For congregations meeting in repurposed office parks and similar, Mike Judge's 1999 comedy *Office Space* would be at least as useful as yet another predictable praise band rendition of "He is Holy! He is Mighty!" The film was shot in Dallas and Austin and serves decades later as a cult favorite for the Acts 29 and Summit Church target market. Mick LaSalle wrote a review of the movie for the *San Francisco Chronicle* entitled "Workers' Souls Lost in 'Space.'"[107] "Judge presents a corporate culture that is the enemy of kindness, individuality and any other human value." Writing for *USA Today*, film critic S. Wloszczyna describes Judge as a "cheesy doodler" who nevertheless "possesses an eye for the uncensored truths of our daily lives." His "knack elevates this humble ode to the unsung corporate drones of high-tech America into a kind of Norma Rae for the cubicle dwellers."[108] "The humor—which rarely resorts to cheap shots, easy targets or toilet gags—is in the profanity-laced details, and Judge is obviously someone who has been there, done that, kicked a jammed copier or two in his time. From morning traffic jams to passive-aggressive bosses who justify their existence by making yours miserable, Space gets it right," Wloszczyna writes.

A more incisive, less charitable way to characterize many of these neo-Calvinist efforts is that this is the pastoral equivalent of ambulance chasing. Recognizing the real pain of alienation and atomization of a city, chase the unchurched to build a multi-campus network of men and women who will shape the politics of a city such that they do not advocate for their own dignity at work but instead continue the anti-labor policies of the Southern Baptist Church, even sending that message across other parts of the nation and, as so many of these churches insist, through overseas missions. What Mike Judge's humor requires is a recognition that this economy under which human beings are living is grisly, dehumanizing, and wrong. A film writer in San Francisco was able to note that workplaces lead to the "Souls Lost in Space," but the formula for these churches involves no such recognition. What this brand of mainstream Protestantism advocates is a submission to authority running counter to any such overarching, systemic criticism of the mess or even a setting in which men could talk together about how they must stand up for themselves in their workplaces. Hierarchy between male and female, boss to worker, government to citizen is not a sign of the fall for these networks. It is a sign of God's providence, bringing a "gospel" friendly to global capitalism from Reno to Raleigh.

4

Mill Town Cathedrals

Mr. Rockefeller appeals both to evolution and to divine sanction. "The growth of a large business," he is reported as declaring in one of his Sunday school addresses, "is merely a survival of the fittest... The American Beauty rose can be produced in the splendor and fragrance which bring cheer to its beholder only by sacrificing the early buds which grow up around it. This is not an evil tendency in business. It is merely the working out of a law of nature and a law of God."

WILLIAM J. GHENT, *OUR BENEVOLENT FEUDALISM* (1902)[1]

When Kevin Michael Kruse wrote succinctly on the social media platform BlueSky in July 2025 that the Supreme Court might as well simply "issue a ruling" that was "go fuck yourselves, peasants!" he was able to do so because the trope of rulers versus peasants connects to an abiding Americanist tradition of resistance against such distinctions. This chapter on pulpits erected to undergird that distinction relates to my decision to go to "Rewired" in Oklahoma rather than to the New Canaan Society gathering of "Marketplace Men" in 2013. While the Southern Baptists of Oklahoma gave me my own "Man Card," I doubt the New Canaan Society would have let me in the door. In these last two chapters, I declare myself amongst the peasants.

Donald Trump became President for a second time as I was completing the edits on this book. That spring, facing federal cuts, the President of Duke University declared the need to "prune" employees for the sake of a more "vigorous" future. He sounded like a Victorian eugenicist, or a Rockefeller patriarch.

Early in this research, I was asked to present my work to my (mostly male) colleagues. I put onto the presentation screen images from Acts 29 churches, explaining the influence of neo-Calvinism, and images from an effort by conservative celebrity Eric Metaxas called "Socrates in the City." Metaxas holds a B.A. from Yale. His websites were, and still are, polished. He is straight out of Lisa Birnbach's 1980 satirical *Preppy Handbook*. One older Calvinist colleague, a mentor in my field, pointed out that there was a divide between someone like Mark Driscoll of Acts 29 infamy and Eric Metaxas, a Yale graduate bringing the language of "virtue" and "wisdom" to New York City. He suggested I was maligning Eric Metaxas by likening him to Mark Driscoll. This was a turning point. If I did not write about my own setting, I would be, as the youngsters name it, "punching down." This book must include an account of the posher conceits of Christianity. "Muscular Christianity" involves not only "Fight Club Church," or Moody Bible Institute, but also edifices built to impress and legitimize an intertwining of hierarchical power, traditional manhood, and education.

A high steeple setting like Duke Chapel or Riverside Church works architecturally to showcase a successful "gospel," presenting a different kind of power and awe than a musical dial turned up to eleven. There are other buildings on which I could focus. I work in the shadow of Duke Chapel, and I teach Christian Ethics in a world shaped by Rockefeller money, where "survival of the fittest" is a Sunday School lesson on the "law of God." These two chapters name what I have been privy to know teaching Christian Ethics at a top-tier university. I knew how to spell oil when I arrived at Yale in 1990. Then I moved to North Carolina and learned how to spell tobacco.

When Oral Roberts announced in 1980 that none other than a 900-foot Jesus had told him to continue building his campus in Tulsa, he opened himself up to a world of derision and public failure. He was only tapping into tradition.[2] Harry Emerson Fosdick, the senior minister for whom John D. Rockefeller, Jr. built Riverside Church, and Franklin S. Hickman, the first preacher to the University and the first dean of Duke Chapel, were situated visually as agents of divine providence. The architecture of each structure promoted ministerial legitimacy during a time of economic turmoil. The gothic grandeur of Riverside leant an air of authority and tradition to Fosdick's anti-fundamentalist, progressive evangelicalism. From Duke Chapel's tower to its towering pulpit, the Duke endeavor helped a regional, newly rich campus appear older and wiser than if it had been built in the style of a one-story Quaker Friends Meeting House. This is a basic, architectural observation, but such historic structures and their storied past reinforce notions of "Leadership" or "Gravitas." To worship inside of or in the shadow of such a structure is to worship in a particular way, through awe. It was not impossible for spirited populism to break out inside Riverside Church or Duke Chapel, but the architecture suited to help congregants and neighbors sense their place within an orderly structure, rather than to activate participants prophetically to challenge the order of things. Vaulted pulpits, up marble stairs, into which a preacher must fit—these make Muscular Christianity concrete.

The stories behind the creation of Riverside Church and Duke Chapel each represent a partnership between industrial wealth and Protestant Christianity, to baptize and legitimate the scene of wealth's creation. Construction of each began within a few years of one another (Riverside, 1927; Duke Chapel, 1930). Each building was inaugurated to impress during the Great Depression. Duke Chapel is at the center of Duke and was built to be seen from trade routes into Durham. The official history page of Duke Chapel features a highlighted quotation from James Buchanan Duke: "I want the central building to be a great towering church which will dominate all of the surrounding buildings, because such an edifice would be bound to have a profound influence on the spiritual life of the young men and women who come here."[3] Riverside Church in New York was erected at the highest point of that New York City borough of Morningside Heights and remains the tallest church building in the U.S.

The term that best suits both structures is the British word "folly." A folly is a structure built as a serious whimsy—a mixture of earnest intent and profligate fantasy. A clever contributor added this on the Wikipedia site regarding an architect known for follies: "[a folly] represent[s] both the potential of colossal industrial wealth and the desire to escape the scene of that wealth's creation."[4] The *OED* offers from 1773—"(A name for) an ornamental structure or building, such as a tower, temple, or artificial ruin, that is placed in a large garden or grounds and is primarily decorative rather than functional."[5] Both Riverside and Duke Chapel function decorously.

Liston Pope's 1942 *Millhands and Preachers* focused on the erection of churches near the mill towns in Gaston County, North Carolina, using local knowledge from the 1910s and 1930s; architectural plans and financing; and local, state, and national media coverage to document a shift that drew people who worked in mills toward small church buildings within a concentric circle near the mills at which they worked. Duke Chapel and Riverside Church were erected as large-scale mill town cathedrals. The Rockefeller reach traveled from New York to California by way of national newspapers. The Duke reach was newer and ranged from New York to Georgia.

Pope described the role of churches and the language of Protestantism in the aftermath of the 1929 strike at the Loray Mill in his chapter entitled "Cultural Reintegration." "The mill management," Pope explains, "attempted through publicity to convince its workers of its good will toward them." "The Golden Anniversary Edition of the *Gastonia Gazette*," for example, "published a year after the strike had ended" featured the mill with "a full-page advertisement" reading: "LORAY The Mill With a Purpose, Where the Boss Is the Worker's Friend." He continues "in answer to the question, 'What Makes the Spirit of Progress?'" the advertisement gave the reply: " … the full co-operation of one man with another; of one organization with another; of one community with another … builds the great finished fabric known as modern civilization … in accord with the Golden Rule."[6] Concurrently, "the mill sponsored an essay contest on the subject, 'Why I Enjoy Working at the Loray.'"[7] Pope quotes the conclusion of the Loray promoting leaflet, "Last but not least are the churches of the town. One can hardly get from under the shadow of their towering spires. It can be truly said that Gastonia is a church-going city." The history of the 1929 strike and the role that cash plus Christianity played matters for understanding the "New South." The erecting of pulpits in mill towns was strategic.

The history of the erecting of Duke Chapel and Riverside Church during a time of economic disaster for large segments of the population matters for understanding how cash plus Christianity helped to control people in each region related to, as the Moody Bible poster named it, "the gospel." With

Duke, the association to regional industries was obvious. The donation of Duke money to Trinity College required that the institution be newly named "Duke." "Trinity," a reference to the Western Christian understanding of the divine, remained as a sidenote to the name "Duke." With Riverside Church, the association of the Rockefeller Family was also obvious, even if the church did not have ROCKEFELLER emblazoned across the marble.

Liston Pope's study of the people who preached and the people who worked their hands at the mill is not forgotten. It was through North Carolina families and labor organizers that I learned of the book in the first place. And, through much effort, the Loray Mill Historic District was added to the U.S. Park Service National Register of Historic Places in 2001.[8] These are efforts to remember and to learn.

Monuments

Donald Trump will predictably be recalled as the President of the United States who has most sought to undermine the most beloved legacy of Teddy Roosevelt—the creation of national parks. The National Park Service features a podcast series through the National Center for Preservation Technology and Training, their description being "Preserving Our Past for the Future."[9] Episode 147 is "Communities of Ludlow." Fawn-Amber Montoya and Karin Larkin edited *Communities of Ludlow: Collaborative Stewardship and the Ludlow Centennial Commemoration Commission.*[10] The collaboration included "the various communities that rallied together to keep this history alive and show its relevance, including lineal descendants, members of the United Mine Workers of America, historians, archaeologists, scholars, artists, interpreters, authors, playwrights, and politicians." Larkin explains that "the Ludlow Massacre was the culmination of one of the most violent events in US labor history," yet "very few people know about it." The massacre "happened over a century ago in 1913 and 1914 when southern Colorado coal miners went on strike to fight for better living conditions, safer working conditions, and fair wages." The event involved "thousands of miners and their families [who] went on strike." Eventually "they were kicked out of their company owned housing

[and] moved into tent colonies [and] suffered through one of the coldest and snowiest winters on record." Ludlow was one of these tent groupings, the largest. Larkin relates: "April the 20th, 1914, bullets flew through the Ludlow tent colony … four women and 11 children went and hid … the militia and the National Guard came through, and they lit the tent colony on fire."

Montoya tells listeners why she sought to study this history: "When I was growing up, we lived outside of Trinidad in a small town called Hoehne, Colorado," she explains, "and it was my first field trip for third grade." She also relates a memory from a family reunion, during which her great-uncle, a former coal miner, visited the site on the morning of the reunion, "Ludlow was as important to him as it was to his family." Larkin says, "I honestly had never heard of the Ludlow Massacre or the site before I became involved with the archeological project to excavate it." Her work became personal. "And then I started doing the actual archeology, and I became deeply involved and really touched by what we were recovering during the archeological excavations." "We were finding things that you would expect … children's toys and parts of baby bottles, heirloom dishes and canning jars that still had food in them."

Montoya and Larkin also name the intentionally public, civic, and regional nature of their book project. Montoya explains that their book is "for the people that were in community with us. And I'm more concerned about what they think about the book … I'm more concerned about whether we did right by the women and children that were killed at Ludlow and less about what my historian colleagues might think about it." They conclude: "The story did not end with the cessation of the strike; instead, its aftermath and influence continues over a hundred years after the events. This longevity illustrates that Ludlow is a story of stewardship, collaborative scholarship, and social memory."[11]

Social Memory

Wendell Berry is an Appalachian author intent on giving a truthful account of the Appalachian region. Bill Moyers was a journalist who grew up in Texas and helped create Public Broadcasting in the U.S.[12] Both Wendell Berry and Bill

Moyers were born in 1934, during the Great Depression, Berry in Kentucky and Moyers in Oklahoma. Each man documents the creation and protection of wealth by two men whose fortunes survived the Great Depression—James Buchanan "Buck" Duke and John D. Rockefeller.

In 2012, Wendell Berry gave the Jefferson Lecture, hosted by the National Endowment for the Humanities. The NEH describes the position as "the federal government's highest honor for achievement in the humanities." In an interview also featured on the main website for the lecture, Berry explains that he was raised by a father who had combined farming with advocacy for federal programs to help small farmers. His father "helped draft the enabling [tobacco farming] legislation under the New Deal. The first year the program was in effect was 1941." Berry continues, "The federal tobacco program supported millions of farm people in thirteen states. The program was administered in Kentucky and four adjoining states by the Burley Tobacco Growers Cooperative Association, Burley being a variety of tobacco." He adds that "The program combined price supports with production controls. And it worked."[13]

Berry continues, noting that "a boomer is motivated by greed, the desire for money, property, and therefore power. James B. Duke was a boomer, if we can extend the definition to include pillage in absentia. He went, or sent, wherever the getting was good … " He explains his own commitment to and connection with the farm his family tended in Kentucky, then connects the lecture specifically to Duke University, telling listeners about a visit to campus:

> … by surprise, I came face-to-face with James B. Duke… He stands imperially in bronze in front of a Methodist chapel aspiring to be a cathedral. He holds between two fingers of his left hand a bronze cigar. On one side of his pedestal is the legend: INDUSTRIALIST. On the other side is another single word: PHILANTHROPIST. The man thus commemorated seemed to me terrifyingly ignorant, even terrifyingly innocent, of the connection between his industry and his philanthropy. But I did know the connection. I felt it instantly and physically. The connection was my grandparents and thousands of others more or less like them. If you can appropriate for little or nothing the work and hope of enough such farmers, then you may dispense the grand charity of "philanthropy."[14]

Berry's meaning depends on reading the words alongside one another. At the center of this contrast between "boomers" and "stickers" is a sense of "imagination" and a sense of "affection." He connects imagination with "contact," with "tangible connection." Through "imagination" people may be able to "recognize with sympathy the fellow members, human and nonhuman, with whom we share our place."

James B. Duke failed in a sense of "affection" for the region, for his neighbors, and for the land. As Berry describes it, he "came from a rural family in the tobacco country of North Carolina" and, as a young man, Duke "would have known men such as my grandfather." With "his rise as an industrialist, the life of a small tobacco grower would have been to him a negligible detail incidental to an opportunity for large profits." Berry brings this into the present day throughout the lecture. By the reckoning of "'captains of industry,' then and now, the people of the land economies have been reduced to statistical numerals." This failure of affection led to the agribusiness of today, Berry explains.

> It may seem plausible to suppose that the head of the American Tobacco Company would have imagined at least that a dependable supply of raw material to his industry would depend upon a stable, reasonably thriving population of farmers and upon the continuing fertility of their farms. But he imagined no such thing. In this he was like apparently all agribusiness executives. They don't imagine farms or farmers. They imagine perhaps nothing at all, their minds being filled to capacity by numbers leading to the bottom line.

Berry's conclusion is a combination of sober realism and a summons to solidarity. "No amount of fiddling with capitalism to regulate and humanize it, no pointless rhetoric on the virtues of capitalism or socialism, no billions or trillions spent on 'defense' of the 'American dream,' can for long disguise this failure." He notes that it is likely that the "greatest success" of this form of capitalism "is an astounding increase in the destructiveness, and therefore the profitability, of war." Berry also describes throughout the lecture the absurdity of using "mobility" to name as virtue what has been decades of "displacement and scattering" of people who have "lost their hold on the land." While he does not name it explicitly here, he has elsewhere. The "displacement and scattering" that was "the West"—the destruction of peoples and ecosystems—has shaped land use and people use, and the use of non-human animals since. Berry's last words in his lecture cause in me, as a reader, a profound sadness and a determination to continue teaching "Christian Ethics" underneath the "Methodist chapel aspiring to be a cathedral," as Berry describes it. I have, myself, grown a deep affection for the region and for my neighbors. And, as Berry ends his Jefferson lecture: "We do not have to live as if we are alone."

Journalist Bill Moyers helped to bring attention to the human cost of oligarchic capitalism throughout his career as a visual journalist. Wendell Berry conscientiously kept himself from reels of film. He is a written word person. These two pedagogical methods employed by two white men born the same year, each working against the grain, matter for memory and for resistance to the fictions of "Muscular Christianity."

Moyers's series "A Walk Through the 20th Century" ran from 1982–1984. The description reads: "Countless observers have attempted to make sense of the last century—a time of rampant technological change, wild economic fluctuations, two world wars, two remarkable Roosevelts, and at least two homicidal dictators bent on world domination."[15] "The Image Makers" ran in 1983.[16] Moyers introduces the episode referencing his present of the 1980s, "every government department, every major corporation, every organization with a mission employs experts in public relations whose job is to get their message across in the best possible light." Looking into the camera straight at the viewers, Moyers teaches that "Public relations has become a major industry of the 20th century, product and symbol in a way of our age."[17]

"The Image Makers" narrates "the growth of mass communication and the birth of the concept of public relations." Moyers begins by contrasting before and after the work of two men considered to be the fathers of "public relations," Edward Bernays and Ivy Lee. "A century ago, a reporter asked the railroad tycoon William Vanderbilt how the cancellation of his trains would affect the public," Moyers narrates, "Vanderbilt replied, 'the public be damned.'" Moyers has a poetic way with words, and I have added italics to note his diction in the audio: "You could get away with such *contempt* in those days if you were rich and powerful and *audacious* enough. *Plundering potentates* like Jay

Gould and Jim Fisk built their *vast fortunes through fair means and foul and cared not a fig what anyone thought of them.*" The change, as Moyers tells the story, came when "America moved into the new century [and] business had to contend with the public opinion made possible by the new media of mass communications." This led to "the pseudo event … contrived news created for a purpose. The news conference, the press release, the staged event, all became part of a constant drama of persuasion. Offstage, the public relations experts were writing the script and directing the actors." He then focuses on "one moment when public relations, as we know it, began to come into its own as a 20th century phenomenon … a meeting in 1914 between Ivy Lee and his most famous client, a man whose very name embodied the whole capitalist system."

The man whose name "embodied the whole capitalist system" was John D. Rockefeller. To borrow Moyers's musical alliteration, the "Image Makers" made it their business to cover over, distract, and put fig leaves over foul means. Moyers uses the word "contempt," a term requiring a worldview in which it is plausible for a member of the aspiring aristocracy to mistreat someone that is economically below them. Moyers presents a worldview that allows for a member of the American aristocracy to be in error if they treat other citizens as commoners rather than as neighbors. The eldest Vanderbilt consigned people in "the public" in the early twentieth century to hell. They may "be damned." In the twentieth century, "the new century," men in charge of big businesses could not continue to be openly contemptuous. If the masses could no longer be damned, then that same medium, "mass communications" could be used to manipulate the masses, to shape perspectives of people from one coast of the U.S. to the other.

Moyers explains that, for "the generation before the first World War, Rockefeller was the rapacious Midas, a billion dollar tyrant who would crush anyone in his way," adding that "bodyguards had to surround him when he went to church." The documentary shows political cartoons of Rockefeller prior to Ivy Lee's public relations magic. Rockefeller "was their one man rogues gallery of barnyard images, as greedy as a pig, as slippery as an eel, as vile as a vulture preying on the public." So, "What in the world happened?" and "What transformed the ogre into the grandfatherly choir master of the news reels?"

He describes "the turning point" as "a strike by the miners of the Colorado Fuel and Iron company in which the Rockefellers were principal shareholders … In 1914, the problems centered on the town of Ludlow, Colorado, a scene of violent confrontation. They called it a Bloody Ludlow."

Ivy Lee, second only to Edward Bernays in their field, had turned the scandal of the Ludlow Massacre into a challenge for public relations. The documentary features the late South Dakota Senator George McGovern, who had written his dissertation on the Ludlow Massacre. McGovern explains the conditions of "company towns," "where everything was owned by the company, the stores where they bought their groceries and supplies, the churches, the schools, even the courts were more or less controlled by the companies in that period." He calls the situation "appalling" and "very dangerous," where "it was not unusual for 100 or 200 miners to be killed in a single year." Men "worked at subsistence wages without any union representation." McGovern continues, characterizing the mainstream media's perspective on striking men at the time. "A striker did not have a very high standing in the eyes of the American public when the strike began in 1913." Striking workers were viewed as "unappreciative," "undisciplined," and depicted as "under the control of sinister foreign influences." Men on strike had been cast as disloyal, "and therefore, every resource of the police power or private corporate power could be directed at breaking a strike was generally accepted." Things shifted significantly after nationwide coverage of "Bloody Ludlow." "For the first time, public opinion sympathized with the strikers. Rockefeller was condemned as the man behind the guns, the murderer of women and children," Moyers explains.

McGovern names the effort as "the first time in any American labor struggle where you had an organized effort to use what has become modern public relations to sell one side of the strike to the American people, in this case, the Rockefeller or the management side." "It was a total public relations campaign," McGovern says, including "a series of fact sheets that he published to give the mine operator's side of the strike." First, Lee fueled disgust with the miners. "Everything was done to discredit the strikers morally and to paint them as substandard citizens," McGovern explains. Then, Lee "engaged the services of prominent people to sign articles that gave the mine operator's side of the story." The documentary presents a journal aimed at the effort: "The Struggle in Colorado for Industrial Freedom."[18] The preface, signed by three heads of the coal mining companies, states "It is to be hoped that a knowledge by the American people of the facts may promote permanent and healthy industrial peace throughout the United States." The "bulletins" run from June to August, 1914 with an acceleration of tone in titles like "What a Small Coal Mine Owner Suffered"; "No 'Massacre' of Women and Children in Colorado Strike"; and "Not Union Labor—But Organized Tyranny, the Issue in Colorado."

"Industrial Freedom" and "Industrial Peace" are precisely wrought words. Ivy Lee orchestrated a solid return to the pre-massacre depiction of the striking workers. He used his acumen in how mass media worked to boomerang the story. Sympathy in mainstream settings was open to such manipulation. This is during the same decade when there was much emphasis on the importance of "fit" boys and men for the sake of national progress. Teddy Roosevelt's speech praising "the man who does not shrink from danger, from hardship, or from bitter toil, and who out of these wins the splendid ultimate triumph" from fifteen years prior was fresh in the public memory. By one perspective, the men working in the mines had been publicly emasculated, having failed to protect their women and children in the most basic of ways. Lee used this sense of failure to turn the sympathy of newspaper readers and local and national leaders away from the faces of men who had ordered their massacre. This, Lee combined with the depiction of John D. Rockefeller, Jr. as an everyday man, willing to roll up his sleeves and pick up a pick.

One highlighted article reads "John D. Jr. and Miners Meet Man to Man" and carries the byline "Drainage, hygiene, and rent problems considered, rather than production statistics." Another reads, in bold print "ROCKEFELLER IN OVERALLS, WORKS WITH PICK IN MINE." Yet another reads "Rockefeller Jr. Turns Hate of Miners to Love" with "Magnate's Mixing of Joys and Sorrows of His Workers." Lee arranged "publicized trips by Mr. Rockefeller to Colorado" McGovern explains, including "pictures of him visiting with strike organizers, talking with the miners and their families, asking the mothers about the conditions in the homes, asking the miners about the conditions under ground." No mercenaries to see here. No "Massacre."

McGovern calls all of this "a snow job for the mine operators" manufactured to "discredit the union in every possible way." He puts it in the matter of dollars and cents. "It's a lot cheaper for Rockefeller and his colleagues to pay Ivy Lee $1,000 a month to give them a new face than it would be to address the grievances of pay that was too low, hours that were too long, mines that were unsafe, housing that was substandard … " This method of managing "industrial disputes" began, he states, in 1914 "with the Rockefeller-Ivy Lee marriage and has continued from that day until the present." Moyers notes that, while some "working conditions improved" the "principal demand" for recognition of the United Mine Workers Union "was averted." Casting the struggle as "Organized Tyranny," shifting the scenes to Rockefeller, Jr. smiling and meeting "Man to Man" as well as Magnate alongside Mining Mothers, the owners of the industry achieved the defeat of meaningful recognition.

Lee managed the brand from thereon out. The Rockefeller family "commissioned him to undertake a full-scale renovation of the Rockefeller name," Moyers explains. Lee persuaded the family "it was better to be seen as a philanthropist and take the credit than to leave the public only the critic's side of the story." Ivy Lee "became the man between the family and the press." The filmmakers show a 1937 Pathe News produced newsreel that announces in bold lettering: "Rockefeller Dead at 97! John D. Sr., Founder of Oil Dynasty, Passes Away." "Deeply interested in his fellow men, Rockefeller was particularly fond of little children," the newsreel narrator intones. "And in recent years, became famous for giving them dimes on every occasion. Rockefeller had the real Christmas spirit of giving and loved to present gifts to as many friends and to the children he always was delighted to have around him." The producers then show the church with the narration "Riverside Church with its world-famous Laura Spelman Rockefeller carillon is an imposing monument to his faith. And Rockefeller Center, the greatest development of modern times stands as a tribute to the man who devoted his fortune to the progress of humanity."[19] This connects with Harry Emerson Fosdick (1878–1969) and his brother Raymond (1883–1972), two Protestants keen to be leaders for a new era of such "progress."

"Modern Times"

In 1936, John D. Rockefeller Sr. entered his ninth decade. As the newsreel notes, he was one of the wealthiest patriarchs on planet earth. That same year, in 1936, filmmaker Charles Chaplin put to the newsreel watching public a movie called "Modern Times." The best-known image is of Chaplin in a work uniform, signature black mustache, and accentuated astonished eyes, winding through the gears of a giant factory clock.

The Museum of Modern Art in New York City held a series of events in 1989 to celebrate Charles Chaplin's life and work, "to pay tribute to the singular genius of Charles Chaplin" "on the one-hundredth anniversary of his birth." Their press release opens with a quotation from Charles Silver, supervisor of the Film Study Center and author of the accompanying volume *Charles Chaplin: An Appreciation*: "Chaplin elevated the most basic human needs and vulnerabilities to the highest levels of art. In the process, he touched more people, more deeply, than any artist in human history, and he is touching us still." [20] The release describes Chaplin as "one of the indisputable geniuses of the cinema. Its first complete auteur—actor, writer, director, producer, composer— he established precedents in the film industry for stardom, financial reward, and artistic independence." [21]

Riverside Church and Duke Chapel were erected during the Great Depression to mark onto their local geography a formal evocation of awe. To borrow from the newsreel boosting Rockefeller, Sr., each building was constructed as "an imposing monument" to the faith of the benefactor. As Duke Chapel's website states, the building was built "to be a great towering church which will dominate all of the surrounding buildings." [22] Chaplin used his own power as a commercially successful artist to construct differently. Chaplin was also a leading man. Chaplin had, in a sense, a pulpit. Ivy Lee constructed a set of stories to depict the Rockefellers as "folks," men willing to take up a pickax, men giving dimes to children, and passing out gifts to their grandchildren at Christmas. The public relations effort included both "imposing" and a false sense of leveling. The Rockefellers and Dukes are somehow like us, but also exponentially better. Charlie Chaplin communicated in a different language altogether.

Modern Times is a different "folly," "a foolish action, error, idea, practice, etc.; a ridiculous thing, an absurdity."[23] In Joan Mellen's 2006 volume on the film for the British Film Institute, she situates Chaplin's break from the expectations in the Hollywood market. "Until the end of the decade, Hollywood for the most part avoided even mentioning the Depression. An overwhelming number of the films produced during the 30s were comedies featuring socialites in furs and jewels sipping highballs in elegantly appointed apartments." She continues, "*Modern Times*, with its persistent description of how ordinary people were faring during the Depression, would be an act of enormous political courage, and Chaplin knew it."[24] His brilliance was put to the work of "folly," of exposing the "absurdity" of his time. Silver writes of Chaplin's 1914 creation of "the tramp," calling him "a messiah for the modern age." The Tramp was "a figure of shabby elegance and decidedly dubious dignity, a denizen of the slums … a bum … [s]crambling for survival against uneven odds and frequently giving the representatives of authority a forceful kick in the butt." He "attracted the allegiance of that mass of humanity for which the twentieth century offered a threatening present and a potentially dire future."[25] Joan Mellen writes "Out of the juggling, cycling, dancing, stilt walking, magic and other specialty acts, out of the stock characters of the late nineteenth-century music halls, the Drunkard, the Pest, the Rowdy and, indeed, the Bum, Chaplin created the utterly unique figure of his Tramp."[26]

Given I cannot reproduce through words what truly does require seeing, I offer Silver's storytelling: "Charlie does not resent the dehumanizing work itself, but rather the little indignities imposed on his person. The boss spies on him in the toilet, and there is no time to scratch an itch." "Dubious dignity" is a perfect term, as "Chaplin risks crudeness with a reminder that we are all bodies and not just souls. Appropriately, even the most fundamental of physical functions, eating, is threatened when he is used as a guinea pig to demonstrate a feeding machine." Silver calls the scene "one of the most inspired comic sequences ever put on film," as "Charlie is reduced to a helpless cipher by this merciless figment of industrial imagination, symbolically [violated] by a manic corncob and a mechanical mouth wiper in a fit of fastidious frenzy." Chaplin chose to use his voice in another key scene: "poverty forces the tramp to succumb to the role of singing waiter, and Chaplin's voice is heard for the first time … The tramp is left to sing in gibberish, a final defiant comment on the lack of saliency of language for, in spite of his incoherence, or because of it, Charlie is a great hit." He invites viewers to recognize themselves as deserving of time to go to the toilet alone and to eat without being timed for efficiency. *Modern Times* evokes an antonym of "awe." The leveling accentuates the difference between what Silver calls "wage slaves" and those assigned to imagine industrious absurdities like the time clock and the feeding machine. The Tramp's "amok" response is "balletic," human, "incoherent" and "gibberish." All of this made "the Tramp" a hero viewers could recognize as a sane response to the insanity of "Industrial Freedom" and "Industrial Peace" (from the Committee of Coal Mine Managers, 1914) then and the "merciless figment of industrial imagination" to this day.

"The Only Road to Salvation"

The project to construct progress went on in earnest during the era covered by historian Lily E. Kay in her 1993 book *The Molecular Vision of Life: Caltech, The Rockefeller Foundation, and the Rise of the New Biology*. Kay describes how an evangelical Protestant zeal for shaping human existence toward order served as a motor for the movement: "Animated by a potent conjunction of Protestant values and technocratic visions, the [Rockefeller] Foundation's civic missions were formulated within the dominant cultural categories of race, class, and gender, as well as within a socioeconomic framework that defined norm and deviance for individuals and groups." Rockefeller money "cultivated scientific and managerial elites in order to address the root causes of social dysfunction: culturally specific and historically contingent forms of maladjustment. Their projects aimed to restructure human relations and to develop social technologies commensurate with the material and ideological imperatives of industrial capitalism."[27]

Lily E. Kay describes how men of industry and men determined to be at the top of new academic institutions conspired to construct languages as girders for industrial capitalism. The "motivation behind the enormous investment in the new agenda was to develop the human sciences as a comprehensive explanatory and applied framework of social control grounded in the natural, medical, and social sciences." She continues,

> the new agenda [of the 1920s] was articulated in terms of the contemporary technocratic discourse of human engineering, aiming toward an endpoint of restructuring human relations in congruence with the social framework of industrial capitalism … the new biology (originally named "psychobiology") was erected on the bedrock of the physical sciences in order to rigorously explain and eventually control the fundamental mechanisms governing human behavior … [28]

The development of a sizeable network of scholarly projects with related goals was the result neither of cosmic kismet nor of spontaneous, collective effervescence: "the rise of the new biology was an expression of the systemic cooperative efforts of America's scientific establishment—scientists and their patrons—to direct the study of animate phenomena along selected paths toward a shared vision of science and society."[29] The donors and their employees "aimed to transcend disciplinary boundaries and employ whatever tools the problem at hand demanded." A reader must understand that the "commitment to social reform" involved "two interconnected levels of commensurability: the economic and the ideological." By this, Kay means that the "social reform" efforts that revolved around the name and money of "Rockefeller" included both "materialistic and utilitarian" considerations and, in terms of "ideology," the efforts were to "combat vice, raise moral standards and improve human conduct." She summarizes: "The life of labor, the practice of self-control, and the drive for prosperity formed the essential elements along the spiritual-material continuum of a social intervention project based on Protestantism, republican principles, and industrial capitalism."[30]

Harry Emerson Fosdick's preaching, from Rockefeller's Riverside Church pulpit, was one form of "social technology" that allowed for the "conjunction of Protestant values" and "industrial capitalism." A key figure on which Kay focuses her research is Harry's younger brother Raymond. "No single figure exemplified this synergy of Christian values and science-based social mission better than Raymond B. Fosdick, Rockefeller trustee, counselor to J. D.

Rockefeller, Jr., and later president of the Foundation." She explains the two Fosdick brothers, were brought up "in a home devoted to Protestantism"; "Raymond Fosdick and his prominent brother Harry Emerson Fosdick (Rockefeller trustee and pastor of Riverside Church) were suffused with the Calvinist ethos." Their "extreme evangelical training" shifted, but their mindset involved "the deep sense of calling, duty, and predestination" in what Kay calls "a modernized form, accommodating both science and social action." "Harry fulfilled his calling through the social gospel of the ministry, reaching millions throughout America," and "Raymond ministered to society through law and social science."

The elder Fosdick is best known for his sermon "Shall the Fundamentalists Win," which he preached in 1922. It was first published in *The Christian Century* and *The Christian Work* in June 1922.[31] The National Endowment for the Humanities U.S. Oratory Project "Voices of Democracy" includes the sermon as one of twelve addresses under "Religion and Morality in Public Life."[32] Among the "Classroom Activities," the NEH editors pose this question: Fosdick "emphasized progress, to the point of suggesting that God works in the world progressively … that God's revelation came … over time, and that the return of Christ was occurring gradually every day. How do you think this viewpoint fit within the political and social context of the early twentieth century?"[33] They also recommend looking up "other characters" in what they call a "little drama." The first two they name are Ivy Lee and John D. Rockefeller, Jr. The site also offers an accompanying "Interpretive Essay" by Eric C. Miller. Miller begins "On the morning of May 21, 1922, from the pulpit of the First Presbyterian Church of New York City, the Reverend Dr. Harry Emerson Fosdick delivered one of the most provocative sermons of the twentieth century." Miller then explains the subsequent segment of the drama: "By all accounts," he writes, "'Shall the Fundamentalists Win?' was well-received at the First Presbyterian Church, raising few hackles within that liberal body. Had the sermon remained confined to the sanctuary, it may well have passed quietly into history." How did Fosdick and his sermon become a cause célèbre? "Thanks to the efforts of Ivy Lee, a First Presbyterian member and influential advertising executive, Fosdick's message spread much further than that. Lee acquired, lightly edited, and distributed the text of the sermon in pamphlet form, prompting its subsequent publication in both the *Christian Century* and *Christian Work* magazines."

"Shall the Fundamentalists Win?" cost Fosdick his position at First Presbyterian, but gained him a cathedral. As Miller recounts, Fosdick left First Presbyterian as part of Ivy Lee's "efforts." The industrial strategist orchestrated the distribution of Fosdick's 1922 sermon "Shall the Fundamentalists Win?" in pamphlet form to Protestant clergy across the U.S., and the subsequent publication of the sermon in two significant outlets for mainstream evangelical and progressive readers across the U.S.

> Due to his national reputation as an orator—and in no small part because of his close connections to members of the New York elite—the pastor had his pick of new pulpits and opportunities. Especially attractive was an offer made by his good friend John D. Rockefeller, Jr. to finance the construction of a new gothic cathedral specifically tailored to Fosdick's preaching.

Ultimately, "Fosdick occupied his new pulpit on October 5, 1930. He would preach there—in unapologetically liberal style—for the next sixteen years."[34]

Harry Emerson's younger brother Raymond was a chief advisor to the Rockefeller family during the 1920s and the President of the Rockefeller Foundation from 1936–1948. The collaboration of the two as Rockefeller funded social entrepreneurs encouraged educated, mainstream Protestants to perceive themselves as living through a crisis, in fact, an *unprecedented* crisis that called for "leadership." The elder Fosdick's role convening speakers of industry at Riverside Church gives an adjacent, related model of marketing "the gospel" from the previous chapter on mega-churches and forward to the next chapter on "leadership." An emphasis that links these forms of Muscular Christianity is the sense of holy husbandry, as Kay describes it "a deep sense of calling, duty, and predestination" among leading men to forge the future of humankind. Already in the 1922 sermon made famous by Ivy Lee, Fosdick avowed a God who works through the ingenuity and industry of progressive men.

Fosdick's form of liberalism allowed for a pro-business arrangement of Christianity to eliminate impracticalities facing men who ran corporations like Rockefeller's Standard Oil and General Electric. To name one example, Owen

D. Young, head of General Electric and member of the board of the Rockefeller Foundation, preached from Riverside's pulpit on the importance of a nimble faith capable of serving and not alienating the chief industrialists who were financing the new future. Young's "What Is Right In Business" appears in a collection of his speeches published in 1930 by the General Electric Company, "delivered from the pulpit of Dr. Fosdick's church in New York on January 20, 1929."[35] Comparing the spread and growth of intercontinental corporations with the bumpy but fortuitous spread of automobiles, Young announced: "big business has not justified the fears of our people. Exploiters no longer own the big concerns. Bankers no longer own them. Their shares, like motor cars, are spread from one end of the country to the other in every city and village." This was, he announced from "the pulpit of Dr. Fosdick's church," a blessing: "broadly speaking, the vast organizations are in skilled hands and the road is reasonably safe." Riverside christened a form of business that described "The Golden Rule," as rightly "applied by men of great understanding and knowledge, as well as conscience." Owen continues, such men must be "technicians in the sense of making the connecting link between the golden rule on the one side and the most complicated business transaction on the other."

Harry Emerson Fosdick had a kindred spirit with Bruce Fairchild Barton, author of the abidingly popular handbook for aspiring and arrived Christian capitalists in the U.S., *The Man Nobody Knows: A Discovery of the Real Jesus* (1925). The chapter titles include: "The Executive"; "The Outdoor Man"; "The Sociable Man"; "His Method"; "His Advertisements"; "The Founder of Modern Business"; and "The Master." The epigraph reads: "Wist ye not that I must be about my Father's business?" Here Barton makes a literary leap so absurd it would be charming if directed by Chaplin. But Barton is dead serious: "what interests us most in this one recorded incident of [Jesus's] boyhood is the fact that for the first time he defined the purpose of his career." Jesus "did not say, 'Wist ye not that I must practise preaching?' or 'Wist ye not that I must get ready to meet the arguments of men like these?' The language was quite different, and well worth remembering. 'Wist ye not that I must be about my father's business?' he said." Jesus, "thought of his life as business."[36]

Harry Emerson Fosdick's *The Power to See It Through* (a 1935 collection of sermons) and his *The Secret of Victorious Living* (1934) read today as more consonant than discordant with the piety of *The Man Nobody Knows*. Fosdick and Barton were pitched to different audiences, but both messages were essentially pro-corporate providentialism and pro-capitalist holy husbandry. Fosdick's references in his sermons to Shakespeare and Keats signal his distance from the striving-upper-middle-managerial style of an advertising executive like Barton's Jesus. But the Fosdick brothers recreated Protestant notions of "the Promised Land" to layer over a narrative of capitalist progress. Raymond Fosdick oversaw an interdisciplinary program in the biological and social sciences to explain the rationality of hierarchy and social design. The world of their time demanded grand strategists to sort and direct toward an end, or else (the case goes) the machinery of industrialism would crush humanity. The "leaders" who were destined to serve as ecclesial alchemists, market cartographers, or well-funded socializing scientists were to take as their guide a form of ethics that was more about vapidly individualized integrity than about questioning the larger system they saw themselves destined by God and evolutionary science to direct.

One way to discern Raymond Fosdick's contribution to the endeavor that was the "New Biology" is through his collection of essays *The Old Savage in the New Civilization*, published in 1928. The collection is made up of college addresses across the country. The "supreme question" facing inter-war America, the world, was whether "humanity" would find the resolve to overcome both inertia and fear to forge an organized scheme for progress: "Here lies the hope of the future. With such high-visioned and creative leadership we can conquer the most powerful creatures with which man has ever had to contend—creatures which he himself fashioned and set free: his own machines."[37] He uses a rhetorical method throughout. Industrialization is a man-made force now let loose on the world, something like Godzilla plus Frankenstein. As he describes this turn, Fosdick makes the shift ineluctable, as if the rise of industrialization, while a result of human engineering, was inevitable, ineluctable—a naturally occurring, social-evolutionary shift upward in complexity and size. Machines "have risen like living things to dominate our entire civilization. They have called into being hundreds of millions of people who otherwise would not have been born."[38] Was anyone sufficiently evolved, sufficiently "high-visioned" to take in the scope of the monster and steer it?

His epigraph to the collection reads: "a naked Polynesian parading in a top hat and spats." "People" in general are of little use. In his myriad descriptions of "the" human predicament, he casts the average set of workers like faceless extras in a monster movie—making their way without individual distinction through meaningless lives. What is needed, he insists, is "a new Aristotle" to give answers to the leaders so that they may provide direction for the masses, his sixth essay being "Wanted: An Aristotle."

He addresses graduates during a *singular* moment in time. "Since the days of Assyria and Babylon—indeed since the days of our Neolithic forefathers—nothing has occurred which has so completely and in so short a time changed the method and manner of living of the human race, as the mechanical revolution of the Nineteenth Century."[39] He repeats, "We are living in a world that is utterly different from any world that has existed before. Modern science has suddenly compressed the planet we occupy—jamming together into a single community widely diverse peoples and civilizations." Humans are "suddenly armed to the teeth … asked to live in peace, crowded together with neighbours whom he never knew before and for whom he has no particular liking."[40] Humanity has outstripped itself, Fosdick exclaims, as the machinery of progress has led to more human beings than is humane. The predicament requires a sober reckoning with the capacity of "the people" to do anything beyond grinding: "Civilization has, in fact, become a great machine, the wheels of which must be kept turning or the people starve. For millions of human beings it is a vast treadmill, worked by weary feet to grind the corn that makes the bread that gives them strength to walk the treadmill."[41] As in the title of the collection, there is no reason to believe, Fosdick asserts, that "The human stock" is up for the task, "We cannot be dogmatically sure that there has been substantial improvement in the human stock since the old days of the Egyptians or the Greeks."[42] Given that "fate may overtake us while we are still admiring the slow processes of history," there is no allowance for aimlessness: "To drift without question of goal, or to steer our course by old reckonings which have not recently been checked, is to court a disaster perhaps without parallel."[43]

Traditionalism causes inertia. What is needed is "boldness, for a spirit of daring, for a certain scorn of the past, for a fearless facing of present facts."

All "human institutions and practices" require "reevaluation." He calls for a "fundamental reappraisal of things that have hitherto been regarded as more or less sacrosanct … " The time called for "a spirit of adventurous liberalism, an eagerness for truth wherever it may be found, a willingness to follow facts wherever they may lead."[44] He uses quite the rhetorical flourish to emphasize the stakes:

> The accepted conclusions of the social sciences are always made to run the gauntlet of tradition and prejudice. The forces of the established order are marshalled in full array against change … Whether it be in the field of eugenics in an attempt to breed a better race, or in economics in an endeavour to distribute more fairly the rewards of industry, or in law through the establishment of a new international court, the response is invariably the same.

Traditionalists "condemn the man who dares to preach a new way of life, a new method of salvation for the race." "He perverteth the people," we cry. "Crucify him!"[45]

Combining anti-populism with anti-clericalism, Fosdick calls on the enlightened listeners at Wellesley, Columbia, and Kansas to heed the harsh facts of human stock:

> There is real truth in Herbert Spencer's observation that majorities are generally wrong … It was the majority that stood behind the Spanish Inquisition … that supported the burning of witches … that upheld in election after election the institution of slavery … that rallied behind our unjust war in Mexico … that prohibited the teaching of evolution in Tennessee … Majorities are generally wrong.[46]

People may choose to "sit supinely and helplessly in this temporary lull before the approaching crash of civilizations—of populations, rather—driven by hunger, competing for the mere occupancy of the earth?" or they may bring forth the discipline "steer this biological evolution?" "Can the science of eugenics reshape a process that is tumbling with such gigantic forces? Can the power of man's intellect make this world a worthy and beautiful home to live in instead of a place to fight and freeze and starve in?"[47] Humans fit to lead must "determine where we want to go and the best methods of advance." His language is infused with Christian-ish imagery: "with the promise of the new land beckoning ahead, humanity can strike its tents and once more take up the march."[48] Within the decade, those for whom Fosdick was speaking had coordinated the Rockefeller Foundation's goals. The 1936 Annual Report, written by Raymond Fosdick reads: "While, necessarily, the old classifications are employed, such as medical science, natural science, and social science, an endeavor is being made to think of the objective in coordinated and synthetic terms and to shape the program toward what has been called the science of man."[49]

"Modern Times" required, in sum, men fit to direct the machines and conduct the unflinching task of "the science of man." The language of Raymond Fosdick coheres with the form of modernism in the architecture of Riverside Church, crafted to be a beacon to progressive Christianity. The grammar of this collaboration is of science, reverence for the men courageous enough to wield it, and the gratitude toward such men by the economic class of people eager to avoid the "crash of civilizations" and the tyranny of the "majority." "There is no royal road to the millennium, no short cut to the Promised Land," Fosdick had warned listeners in his 1928 tour. As Harry Emerson Fosdick had written in his 1922 sermon, "Man's architecture has developed from the crude huts of primitive men until our cathedrals and business buildings reveal alike an incalculable advance and an unimaginable future."

Legacies

Paul Krause was a graduate student in history at Duke when the magazine *Tobacco Road* published his article "Buck Duke's Legacy."[50] *Tobacco Road* was produced at Duke, "an experimental magazine funded by the Undergraduate Publications Board," running from 1978 to 2003.[51] In 1982, they ran a piece tied to the raging controversy around the proposed Nixon Presidential Library. *Duke Magazine* ran an article in 2011 about the controversy giving the basics.[52] Robert J. Bliwise summarizes the story as "Duke lost the opportunity for—or the burden of—the library. That outcome was largely a consequence of lingering criticism of Nixon, the only U.S. President to have resigned his office, who by then had embarked on a sort of rehabilitation campaign." The rejection "reflected the work of a vocal group of professors [who] resented being peripheral players in a process that, as they saw it, might have changed the physical—and intellectual—face of the campus."

With this background in mind, consider the publication of "Buck Duke's Legacy" in a Duke student-run paper from that time. Krause concludes that a corporate-interest, moneyed version of university governance was par for the course, given how "Buck" Duke had financed Duke and how he described the purpose of a regional university. If a regional university was set up to favor the many Duke-owned financial endeavors, then was it shocking that the Duke of 1982 would consider it reasonable to house the Nixon library? Krause begins his article with a vignette from 1925, the year after Buck Duke secured the change in name of then Trinity College to Duke. Krause told the story: "One evening in June, 1925, about four months prior to his death, James Buchanan Duke entertained some of his business advisors at a house that looked out upon a Piedmont lake. Also present was Ben Dixon MacNeill, who covered the electric power industry in North Carolina for the *News and Observer* of Raleigh." Krause describes the paper, "published by self-proclaimed progressive Josephus Daniels," who "engaged 'Buck' Duke in many rhetorical skirmishes rising from the growth of his many business interests. The interests—notably, the American Tobacco and Southern Power companies."

Krause quotes from a 1929 article from *The American Mercury* by North Carolina journalist Ben Dixon MacNeill.[53] The 1929 article was entitled "Duke."[54] As Wendell Berry narrates in his 2012 lecture on boomers and stickers, the Duke name was about booming. MacNeill had related to readers of *The American Mercury* in 1929 how the Piedmont Region of the Carolinas worked in the industrial age of tobacco. "James Buchanan Duke went to South Carolina and bought the river," MacNeill wrote. "When he was told that it extended across the line into North Carolina and up into the Blue Ridge Mountains, he bought the remainder of it." MacNeill explains Duke Power was "the first of the great hydro-electric power corporations of America," and that into that corporation "Duke poured all the power of his American Tobacco Company wealth."

The investment was worthwhile. "On an evening in June, before Buck died, another company of men were gathered in a house designed for masculine pleasure," MacNeill reports, "Its wide porches looked out upon a long, smooth lake encompassed by the profitable damming of the river. Assembled were gentlemen of consequence in engineering, legal and financial matters, come together to discuss problems having to do with big industry." This is the quote Krause then highlighted in 1982.

> "What I mean is that I've got 'em fixed now so there won't be any more meddling with it by legislatures and courts and newspapers like I've been bothered with all my life. But I've got 'em now and it's going on making profits. Not even Joe Dan'els will cuss me now." "How do you mean, Mr. Duke?" asked the lawyer patiently.

> His meaning was not without its simplicity. Public thinking and public attitudes toward private business, he explained, are determined primarily by lawyers who dominate government; by preachers who dominate religion; by doctors who dominate life and death. Duke University would have the outstanding medical school of the South, and hard by would be a great school of theology and another of the law. It was simple enough. Here were the sources of public opinion. The university would take care of them.[55]

Today Duke Chapel's own history aligns: "I want the central building to be a great towering church which will dominate all of the surrounding buildings, because such an edifice would be bound to have a profound influence on the spiritual life of the young men and women who come here."[56] Lawyers, preachers, and doctors—people trained at a campus with a great towering church to "dominate" all other edifices assembled beneath—these would "take care of" the public. Duke did not have to hire Ivy Lee.

5

Leadership

Any leader who adopts the posture of seeing himself on the stage of history is a glory to himself and a menace to all whom he must lead.

David Bromwich in his 2013 film review "How Close to Lincoln?" for *New York Review of Books*

I attended the 2013 National Prayer Breakfast, with sessions for days before and after. In this chapter, cowboy capitalism is in my crosshairs. The *OED* links the terms "cowboy diplomacy" and "cowboy capitalism,"—"designating an approach to politics, finance, etc., which is risky, reckless, aggressive, or characterized by unethical or illegal practices, as in cowboy capitalism, cowboy diplomacy, etc."[1] In the 1964 movie *Dr. Strangelove or: How I Learned to Stop Worrying and Love the Bomb*, the man assigned the cartoonish task of riding the bomb was Louis Burton Lindley Jr., aka Slim Pickens. Slim Pickens brandished a cowboy hat while riding the weapon set to destroy the earth, shouting "WAAAHOOOO!" His *New York Times* obituary gave his credentials, "Mr. Pickens came naturally by his ability to play saddle tramps and range bums, for before he got his first Hollywood role he had spent 20 years as a rodeo bronco buster, trick rider and clown."[2] The backdrop of *Dr. Strangelove* is earth-destroying insanity. To focus on the men and women drawn to Western themed ministries is to mistake the saddle tramps and rodeo clowns as a source of menace. The cowboys in this chapter do not brandish hats and shout "WAAAHOOOO!" To quote one Christian CEO who had a genuine epiphany, they are "plunderers." This chapter is about posturing leaders, plunderers, and their apologists.

Vikings

Abraham Vereide is the man credited with beginning the network known today as "The Family." *Modern Viking: The Story of Abraham Vereide, Pioneer in Christian Leadership* is a biography of sorts, compiled from letters and accounts by and about Abraham Vereide by Norman Percy Grubb. It was published by Zondervan Publishing House, Grand Rapids, Michigan in 1961 and in multiple editions after.[3] On page 203 of my copy, the cover photo description reads: "Abraham Vereide with President Kennedy, Sen. Carlson, Billy Graham, and Vice President Lyndon Johnson." It is included as "Epilogue, The 1961 Breakfast" with "President Kennedy and the 1961 Breakfast" as the heading.

Grubb offers as the "Prologue" the opening story: "President Eisenhower walked through a crowded breakfast room in the Ballroom of the Mayflower Hotel in Washington. The date was February 1960." Nine hundred people there included "secretaries of state, senators and congressmen, chiefs of staff, judges of the Supreme Court and foreign ambassadors of various nations." He describes "a broad-shouldered, upright, white-haired man, with ruddy countenance, striking features, and blue eyes" who accompanied Eisenhower out of that breakfast, the "Modern Viking" himself, a Norwegian-American Methodist layman. From the beginning, this network assembled power across veins of the body politic, from Norway to the U.K. to the U.S., to remind each successive President of the United States of America that they could convene such a group. "Overstaying his time by twenty minutes, although he was due at a Security Council meeting, the President had been listening to various speakers—a newspaper owner from Los Angeles, a Metropolitan Opera singer, a British member of Parliament, a senator, and a congressman ... " What did these dignitaries have in common? They had in common "the change in their lives and the effect in their homes and in their business and political activities, since they made a personal commitment of themselves to Jesus Christ."[4]

By 1961, the networks for which Vereide was the photographed hub had developed through international conferences on "Christian Leadership," the first one in 1952. "Such men in each country need to know each other—on the same level—in order to produce global team work." Vereide's letter continues, "Those who know the Light, who know the Way, must assist those who search and want to find … where they are in international affairs." "So," Vereide explains, "we meet as International Christian Leadership for the annual meeting of the Council at The Hague—May 22–25." The first issue Vereide names in his correspondence is the struggle between "Communism" and "the idea of free democracy."

The historiography of the National Prayer Breakfast tells a story. It is important to read how different mainstream Protestant constituencies handled Jeff Sharlet's scrupulously researched journalism about the network, beginning in 2003. His reporting was sidelined, dismissed, and covered over. Sharlet was cast as delusional and mean-spirited. Prayer. Leadership. Faith. Wouldn't any reasonable citizen cheer on a celebration of these, particularly given that the gathering is "bipartisan" and features Bono?

Diane Winston is a scholar of religion and media studies at the University of Southern California. She covered the National Prayer Breakfast for "The Conversation" in 2017 under the title "National Prayer Breakfast: What does its history reveal?"[5] "On the morning of February 2, 2017, more than 3,500 political leaders, military chiefs and corporate moguls met for eggs, sausage, muffins—and prayer," Winston offers. "The Washington, D.C. gathering, the 65th National Prayer Breakfast, is an opportunity for new friends and old associates, from 50 states and 140 countries, to break bread and forge fellowship in Jesus' name," she tells readers. The tone is cozy. There were "moguls," and they "met." There were muffins and prayer. The event is a "gathering," an "opportunity," for "friends" to "forge fellowship." The term "break bread" is, the *OED* explains, "sacramental," particularly when paired with, as Winston puts it, "in Jesus' name."[6] The meaning of the meeting is more than mere muffins, and that meaning is connected, in Winson's description, to something holy. Winston describes her interest in the history of the National Prayer Breakfast: "As a scholar of American religious history, I am intrigued by how presidents negotiate the intricacies of church/state relationships versus religion/politics entanglements … That's why the prayer breakfast is noteworthy—it is an opportunity for leaders to appear as Christ's servants rather than formidable heads of state." Opportunity, connected to "Christ's servants," gives the meeting a particular setting of scene. Leaders who otherwise must "negotiate" as brokers of power become, while breaking bread, "servants."

The Prayer Breakfast is not primarily "noteworthy" because it allows "leaders to appear as Christ's servants," unless the emphasis is on "appear." By 2017, Jeff Sharlet's book about the network the Fellowship or Family, entitled *The Family: The Secret Fundamentalism at the Heart of American Power* had been out for almost a decade. Sharlet had been interviewed for National Public Radio multiple times for his reporting on the network.[7] As of 2024, NPR features an excerpt from Sharlet's book introducing the network: "'We desire to see a leadership led by God,' reads a confidential mission statement … Another principle expanded upon is stealthiness; members are instructed to pursue political jujitsu by making use of secular leaders 'in the work of advancing His kingdom.'" Sharlet explains that members are "to avoid whenever possible the label Christian itself, lest they alert enemies to that advance." The network runs on "prayer groups, or 'cells' as they're often called," and they "have met in the Pentagon and at the Department of Defense." Sharlet's reporting revealed that "the Family has traditionally fostered strong ties with businessmen in the oil and aerospace industries."[8]

In his 2003 essay for *Harper's Magazine* "Jesus Plus Nothing: Undercover among America's Secret Theocrats," Sharlet had reflected on his time with a group of young men who called themselves "brothers" while living in a house called "Ivanwald."[9] Ivanwald "sits at the end of Twenty-fourth Street North in Arlington, Virginia," Sharlet explained, and "is known only to its residents and to the members and friends of the organization that sponsors it, a group of believers who refer to themselves as 'the Family.'" It "has operated under many guises, some active, some defunct: National Committee for Christian Leadership, International Christian Leadership, the National Leadership Council, Fellowship House, the Fellowship Foundation, the National Fellowship Council, the International Foundation." These organizations "are intended to draw attention away from the Family, and to prevent it from becoming, in the words of one of the Family's leaders, 'a target for misunderstanding.'"[10] He quotes a *Los Angeles Times* article from September 2003: "the Fellowship Foundation alone has an annual budget of $10 million, but that represents only a fraction of the Family's finances. Each of the Family's organizations raises funds independently." He continues, "Ivanwald, for example, is financed at least in part by an entity called the Wilberforce Foundation. Other projects are financed by individual 'friends': wealthy businessmen, foreign governments, church congregations, or mainstream foundations that may be unaware of the scope of the Family's activities."

For her part, Winston calls the establishment of the National Prayer Breakfast "a signature achievement" facilitated by Billy Graham—"Graham interceded, Hilton offered his hotel and the rest is history." She draws a contrast between the National Prayer Breakfast with Donald Trump and before Donald Trump, offering the reassurance that, in 2017, "There are Muslims and Jews as well as Christians of all stripes. The Fellowship Foundation, an organization started by Vereide that sponsors the breakfast, considers the National Prayer Breakfast as an inclusive event. Hillary Clinton has attended, as has Tony Blair, Senator Joseph Lieberman and musician Alison Krauss." The first featured photograph in her 2017 article, under the heading "Faith First" is "President Dwight D. Eisenhower in a personal chat with Rev. Dr. Billy Graham in Gettysburg on Sept. 8, 1961."

When assigning someone to review Sharlet's *The Family*, *The Christian Century* chose James L. Guth, "who teaches political science at Furman University, Greenville, South Carolina, and is coeditor of the forthcoming *Oxford Handbook of Religion and American Politics*." Thus credentialed, Guth then dismissed Sharlet as a "conspiracy theorist." Guth wrote "great conspiracies have great histories, of course, and the story of how the Family got where it is today constitutes much of Sharlet's meandering narrative." Guth concludes, "books such as Sharlet's suggest answers that are far too easy—and too alarmist." *Christian Century* readers were to allow the fad to pass: "Although these qualities will probably win this volume the same fleeting popularity enjoyed by many previous exposés of the Christian right, they do little to advance our understanding of the role of conservative religion in American public life and institutions."[11]

In 2011, *Sojourners* highlighted: "The secretive, elitist Capitol Hill organization has cozied up to despots and, in my case, done genuine good."[12] For readers of this purportedly progressive, evangelical periodical, Lucy Bryan Green served as a cheerful, female counterpart to Jeff Sharlet. Sharlet had been friends with associates of Ivanwald and present at Ivanwald during the early 2000s. Lucy Bryan Green was at the Cedars, the large house to which Ivanwald is adjacent, during this same period. Green writes that in June 2002, "the summer after my freshman year of college, I arrived at the Cedars, the Family's colonial mansion in Arlington, Virginia, and got my first taste of Family theology." Her narrative tracks with Sharlet's depiction of the gender expectations of the network. "A former congressman spoke to the small group that had gathered for lunch," she writes, "including me and a friend who had come to serve on the Cedars' all-female, all-volunteer maid staff." Green found the theology "revolutionary," in a good way. "Raised in an Episcopal church attended by the country club crowd, I jumped ship at age 16, opting out of a liturgy I considered stuffy and lifeless." She moved from there to "a charismatic community church, where I gyrated for Jesus to rock music every Sunday, wept frequently for my sinfulness, and tried my best to 'win the souls' of my non-Christian friends." What the Family offered her was a third, sweeping alternative, specifically the removal of "the overwhelming burden of converting every heathen I encountered … All I had to do was love them, and God would do the rest." The Family is neither "stuffy and lifeless" nor focused on converting heathen, but characterized by "love."

The timing of the *Sojourners* piece matters. Green begins by referencing Sharlet's research on the Family's connections to conservativism in Uganda. Students who were part of the network sent me articles about the draconian anti-gay legislation in Uganda. The Duke Divinity Center for Reconciliation had a "Great Lakes Initiative" set in that region since 2005, attracting young evangelical, charismatic, and Pentecostal students with ties to World Vision, an evangelical organization with deep roots there.[13] Green wrote: "When last September's issue of *Harper's* landed on my coffee table, I hardly expected to find my past within its glossy pages—least of all in an article about Uganda's persecution of gays and lesbians. But right there, in Jeff Sharlet's 'Straight Man's Burden,' was an indictment of the organization that had shaped my college years: the Family." Her essay is a first-person, narrative book review that reassures a relatively liberal-leaning, relatively young, mainstream evangelical readership that, while Jeff Sharlet may have his facts straight about the Family's influence domestically and internationally, he got the *feel* all wrong. Green ultimately concludes, "for all its failings, I believe the Family's influence on my life was unequivocally positive." While living with Alexandria-based members of the Family, she had learned "open-mindedness, loving others, accepting differences, and servanthood." She names "a talk about reconciliation" that leads her to find a different way than what she reads as Sharlet's "black and white" depiction of the world. Her time with the network helped her "not to draw lines in the sand, not to see the world in terms of 'us' and 'them.'"

She does offer a bracing story about the network's use of "Africa." During a Family funded training on "Leadership," she writes, "one of Sudan's 'Lost Boys' took the microphone during John Ashcroft's speech and said, 'I just want to know if there is anyone who knows if there is a world court that can help my people. Is there anyone who can help us? Please!'" There was only "an awkward silence." Green was at the Cedars the summer of 2002. The International Criminal Court was ratified and instituted in the summer of 2002.[14] Her story tracks. Many students from evangelical mainstream circles participated in misguided, simplistic media blitzes like the Oprah endorsed "Kony 2012" (purportedly focusing on Uganda) but were largely unacquainted with any forms of international law.[15] Those who were acquainted had been taught that international, legal accountability structures are un-Christian, the Nuremberg Trials, for example, being more "retributive" than "reconciling."

Sojourners became a brand through a vapid, bi-partisan bumper sticker message associated with two senior evangelicals in the U.S., messaging along the lines of "God is not Republican or Democrat." Or, "God Has No Party, Democrat or Republican." One is Jim Wallis, a senior evangelical strategist and the founder of *Sojourners*. The other is Tony Campolo, a senior evangelical professor of sociology. Jim Wallis is the author of a highly promoted book for a young, evangelical readership in 2006 called *God's Politics: Why the Right Gets It Wrong and the Left Doesn't Get It*. Tony Campolo had published *Is Jesus a Democrat or a Republican* in 1995, making him a household name in book-purchasing, white evangelical households.[16] *Sojourners* ran a follow-up article to Green's, written by Campolo, who calls the network "the Fellowship." Campolo avers: "Imitating Jesus is what the Fellowship is all about, and Sharlet fails to understand that what he sees as a kind of political triumphalism is not what the Fellowship is all about. Instead, the Fellowship calls for the triumph of the loving lifestyle that Jesus prescribed in the Sermon on the Mount."[17] He advises: "I do hope that [Green] did not take what Sharlet had to say about the Fellowship too seriously because he misinterprets the motivations of the many good folks who work along with Doug Coe, and the book is marked by a host of distortions of the reality." After all, Campolo tells readers, "at their big annual event, you will find people on the political left as well as those on the political right. You are as likely to find George W. Bush as Barack Obama in attendance." Even "Hillary Clinton is a regular attendee." From "Jim Wallis, Bono, and dictators from Asia and Africa," the network "does not make judgments about who are sinners and who are righteous." Do not worry, he reassured readers, "There is no need to get upset over the fact that a homophobic president of Uganda is as likely to be in attendance as someone like Mother Teresa."

The two Protestant periodicals most read by mainstream clergy and laity in the U.S, *Christian Century* and *Sojourners*, ran a scholarly review so negative it cast Sharlet as a fad-seeking nutjob, a testimony by a female peer whose "love" made Sharlet seem surly, and an appeal from an avuncular patriarch to see the network as "good folks" bridging "the political left" and "the political right." Jeff Sharlet and Kathryn Jones explained in their 2007 piece for *Mother Jones*. "That's how it works," they summarized, "[t]he Fellowship isn't out to turn liberals into conservatives; rather, it convinces politicians they can transcend left and right with an ecumenical faith that rises above politics." Yet the results are clear; "the faith is always evangelical, and the politics always move rightward."[18] The network is about "love," and rightward politics.

Agape

There are two distinct entries for "agape" in the *OED*. The second is the biblical word for "love" in evangelical circles. Agape is a Greek word transliterated to English. The first definition is "adverb and adjective," "So as to be gaping or wide open; in a gaping fashion; spec. with the mouth open in an attitude or state of astonishment, anticipation, wonder, or incomprehension." Under "proverbial usages" there is "She will gape like a Pig on a Spit." This section involves my being agape "like a pig on a spit" at one donor's influence on my field: the Alonzo McDonald Agape Foundation.

During the 2005–2006 academic year, I was invited to apply for an inaugural, endowed chair at Harvard University Divinity School, the Alonzo L. McDonald Family Professor of Evangelical Theological Studies. I was on a short list, and my interview involved a public lecture on campus, as well as meetings with students and faculty from across the university. One of the young men at Duke, related to mainstream evangelicalism and considerable money in Washington, D.C., met with me in my office beforehand and told me, with some urgency, that, should I be chosen for the McDonald chair, the position would come with power to "do good." I prepared my interview lecture on Charles Kingsley, "Holy Husbandry," and eugenics. But I knew one thing. I did not "like Billy Graham." Was I sufficiently "evangelical" to win a chair in "Evangelical Theological Studies" with a capital "E"? Definitely not. It was an instructive experience, as people who know these circles explained the history and implications of a chair in "Evangelical Theological Studies" at Harvard University.

Harvard Divinity News reported the progression of funding in the announcement of McDonald's passing. He had "established the Alonzo L. McDonald Family Scholarship for HDS students in 1989, and endowed the Alonzo L. McDonald Family Professorship of Evangelical Theological Studies as a visiting professorship in 1996 and later as a full professorship in 2004."[19] The dean of Harvard Divinity during the initial negotiations was Ronald Thiemann (1986–1998), a scholar of political theology who resigned as dean. The Harvard obituary for Thiemann in 2012 worded the situation in this way: "His resignation came soon after a national controversy over pornographic downloads on his University-owned computer."[20] William A. Graham was dean during the search for the full, permanent professorship, and he renegotiated the terms to which Thiemann had agreed. Harvard hired a historian *of* evangelicalism. "Going forward," Dean Graham stated "we shall now have the collegial presence and gifted teaching of a noted historian of Methodism and evangelical pietism in Britain, Ireland, and North America."[21] Rather than hire a scholar with an "Evangelical" theology, Graham used the McDonald funding to hire a historian focusing *on* evangelicalism.[22]

Four years later, *New York Times* religion reporter Mark Oppenheimer wrote about Alonzo McDonald's influence on the field of "Theology." Oppenheimer wrote "in 1989 Mr. McDonald put his wealth into the McDonald Agape Foundation, a family-run philanthropy." Oppenheimer quoted from the McDonald philanthropy's website in 2010: "We work only with a small, selected group of distinguished universities and within them their most influential faculty members." He added that "Mr. McDonald is by no means an ecumenical seeker. He helped found the Trinity Forum, an evangelical leadership institute, and he has given money to the Fellowship, also known as the Family, the secretive Christian association." He also reported Alonzo McDonald's description of intent: "We have focused on the great universities that have gone predominantly secular." Oppenheimer connected the dots. The McDonald Agape Foundation gives to schools whose prevailing ethos they disagree with. Oppenheimer uses the word "redeem" to characterize how Alonzo McDonald described the purpose of these donations, "The foundation gives between half a million and a million dollars a year, occasionally more, Mr. McDonald said." "That is not a lot of money," Oppenheimer explained, but "divinity schools tend to be poor and small, so one or two traditional Christians on the faculty make a big impact. Especially at schools where liberal religion dominates."

The foundation works with a "small, selected group of distinguished universities," with "their most influential faculty members," focusing on "great universities" that have become "secular," with the aim of shifting a great, secular university. A Divinity School in a top-tier university, "poor and small" in comparison to other parts of a university, can serve as a fulcrum to shift other aspects of a university. With enough money, funding may secure "influential faculty members" to exert their influence. This process did not occur seamlessly at Harvard. Oppenheimer reported that "efforts to prescribe how his money got spent at Harvard led one dean to insist that the terms of the gift be rewritten … Mr. McDonald has very particular ideas, and universities are reluctant to give donors too much power." Oppenheimer had put on his gumshoes:

"It took about 10 years before we negotiated the chair at Harvard," Mr. McDonald said. "And another 10 years before I got the chair I wanted at

Emory on the life and teachings of Jesus. I had three Methodist bishops" – Emory's Candler School of Theology is Methodist – "who said, 'We don't want a chair on Jesus.'"

The dean of Harvard Divinity School, William Graham, praised Mr. McDonald's generosity and said the donor did not meddle with the search for the Alonzo McDonald Family Professor of Evangelical Theological Studies. (The historian David N. Hempton got the job.) But when I asked about Mr. McDonald's comments that the gift was tough to negotiate, Mr. Graham offered some specifics.

"I didn't feel we could activate the professorship under the original terms," said Mr. Graham, whose predecessor, Ronald Thiemann, first agreed to accept the money. "There was some inadvertent ambiguity in the description of the chair in 'evangelical' Christianity that might have been construed as requiring that the incumbent be himself or herself an evangelical Christian, and that would not be either legally or academically acceptable." Mr. Graham said that Harvard's lawyers and Mr. McDonald's agreed to change the terms of the gift.[23]

Oppenheimer implicitly posed a question for administrators at major research universities with established divinity schools. Which "poor and small" divinity school would be able sufficiently to reassure Alonzo McDonald that they would shift the university away from a "liberal" or "secular" identity?

Two years after I had been on a short list for that chair, a newly arrived senior colleague told me that he was the "point person" at Duke for "the McDonald funding." He stated this loudly in a quiet restaurant. This tall and irascible man told me my questions about conservative donor agendas were idiosyncratic and pristine. "Do you think you are better than Mother Teresa?" he asked, noting that she famously took funding from the Italian mafia to fund her projects. He also averred boisterously over boutique enchiladas that he would be "happy to take money from Hitler." Even through my annoyance with his tactics, I worried that people eating lunch at a quiet restaurant near campus now knew that my departmental chair would be "happy to take money from Hitler." I met with the dean of Duke Divinity, noting my concerns. His reaction was instructive. The dean was incensed that our colleague had claimed to be the point person for the McDonald funding. "He is not the point person for the McDonald funding!" the dean insisted, "I am the point person for the McDonald funding!"

In summer 2024, the website for the McDonald Centre at Oxford featured on their "About" section this note: "Based at the Faculty of Theology & Religion in the University of Oxford, the Centre is generously supported by the McDonald Agape Foundation." The link to the Faculty of Theology and Religion in the University of Oxford opened with this announcement: "The Faculty of Theology and Religion is delighted to announce that His Majesty The King has approved the appointment of two new Regius Professorships." Luke Bretherton was approved by The King to serve as "Canon and Regius Professor of Moral and Pastoral Theology at Christ Church, Oxford, in succession to The Reverend Canon Professor Nigel Biggar C.B.E." Bretherton now serves as the new Director of the McDonald Centre for Ethics. Luke Bretherton had moved his family from England to Durham, North Carolina in 2012, hired at Duke by a search committee chaired (and, from my perspective, commandeered) by the man who was, it turns out, the "point person" for the McDonald funding at Duke.[24]

The setting at Oxford immediately prior to the opening of the Alonzo McDonald Centre for Ethics is important context to understand how, as Oppenheimer reported in the *New York Times*, a few conservative scholars, well-placed, may serve to "redeem" a university toward the purposes of a conservative donor. In May 2007, the *Guardian* reported, "Unholy row at Oxford's college for clergy amid staff exodus and claims of bullying." "One of England's most respected theological colleges is facing claims that staff feel bullied and intimidated as the institution becomes increasingly conservative," the piece reported. "The discontent at Wycliffe Hall … has seen several resignations [as] the college has been accused of becoming more theologically conservative, more hostile to women's ordination and more homophobic," Stephen Bates explained.[25] In September 2007, the BBC ran a letter by faculty with context. "To date," William Crawley reported, "more than a third of the staff of Wycliffe Hall, Oxford, have resigned since the appointment of the Hall's new principal." Wycliffe is "one of Oxford University's permanent private halls and an evangelical theological college which provides clergy-training for the Church of England."[26] Crawley called this "Evangelicalism's internecine war." The distinctions faculty made within "evangelicalism" were confusing to British journalists and to the secular adjudicators of the "internecine war."[27] But one fact was clear, and widely reported. Elaine Storkey, the most public-facing scholar on faculty, a senior woman who is both feminist and evangelical, was fired mid-year in November 2007. Storkey had served as a columnist for *The Independent* and a contributor to the BBC's *Thought for the Day*."[28] Within a year of the launch of the McDonald Centre for Ethics the diversely "evangelical" school at Oxford had been gutted, and their senior female scholar had been summarily fired for standing up to the administration doing the gutting.

Between Luke Bretherton's arrival at Duke in 2012 and his return to England in 2024 to head up the Centre, the McDonald effort was much in the news. In December 2017, four faculty members at Oxford penned a letter addressing a project hosted by the McDonald Centre and promoted by Nigel Biggar. They noted that Biggar's status had linked Oxford's name to a defense of "colonial history." The fact that Oxford was highlighting and hosting a defense of "Ethics and Empire" meant that this position could be "misconstrued as representative of Oxford scholarship," which, the letter-writers explained, could shape the lives and perspectives of their students and prospective students. The showcasing of Biggar's perspective could "reinforce a pervasive sense that contemporary inequalities in access to and experience at our university are underpinned by a complacent, even celebratory, attitude towards its imperial past."[29] News coverage in the U.K. from this period suggests that McDonald received his money's worth. *The Daily Mail* reported, "Oxford University last night stood by the professor, saying he was 'entirely suitable' and an 'internationally-recognised authority on the ethics of empire.'" Biggar had not been an "internationally-recognized authority" on any particular subject prior to the creation of the Centre. "Christian Ethics" is a relatively obscure field of nerds. But Biggar became a scholar about whom Oxford would announce as an "internationally-recognized authority on the ethics of empire."[30]

The *Guardian* assigned their "Education Editor" Richard Adams to the story. Adams wrote "Oxford University accused of backing apologists of British colonialism—Letter signed by more than 170 international academics opposes Ethics and Empire project investigating rights and wrongs of imperialism." He continued, "signatories to the letter say they are dismayed at the project's aims, which they say seek to 'test the ethical critiques of empire against the historical facts of empire' and develop a 'Christian ethic of empire.'" Then the *Guardian* ran a piece by Ian Jack, a journalist *The Independent* described as having "few peers as a long-form writer" and as "an excellent reporter, ferreting researcher and beautiful writer."[31] Jack wrote about Biggar's initial opinion piece that prompted news coverage. Biggar's piece appeared in *The Times*: "Don't feel guilty about our colonial history: Apologising for empire is now compulsory but shame can stop us tackling the world's problems."[32] Jack explained, "What alarmed Biggar's detractors wasn't so much the *Times* piece itself … their concern arose out of what the *Times* piece alerted them to … a project called Ethics and Empire, which according to its website would scrutinise the proposition, common to 'most reaches of academic discourse', that 'imperialism is wicked; and empire is therefore unethical.'" Jack reported "the project will run over five years and is held under the auspices of Oxford's McDonald Centre, endowed by an American foundation, the McDonald Agape, whose rubric is 'Encouraging distinguished scholars for Christ.'" Jack reported that the project's "main objective is to develop 'a nuanced and historically intelligent Christian ethic of empire.'" Jack added, "though when I spoke to him this week, Biggar said he wondered if the word 'Christian' was helpful." The chief concern of scholars at Oxford and scholars who had trained there was that the McDonald Centre was establishing a "Christian Ethic of Empire" at Oxford. Which it has, in the name of love.

An Infomercial from Yale

When I showed a friend *Doing Virtuous Business*, a 2010 PBS documentary, she called it an "infomercial."[33] The word is dated, but accurate. The *OED* times the use from 1981, related to "Broadcasting (originally and chiefly U.S.) … An advertisement (esp. one shown on television) which promotes a product, service, etc., in an informative and purportedly objective style."[34]

Combine "documentary" and "infomercial" and you have "documercial," an item connected to a respected television outlet, like PBS, known for their "purportedly objective style" but that is, in fact, an advertisement. *Doing Virtuous Business* is an infomercial posing as a documentary—a documercial.

As a Yale alumna, I receive updates about goings on at Yale Divinity and related to the Graduate School of Arts and Sciences. In 2013, I received "16 Reasons to Celebrate: New Titles by YDS Faculty," describing "the mark of academic excellence we have here at Yale Divinity School." "Rounding out the night were publications by Miroslav Volf and Ted Malloch." Ted Malloch was heralded by YDS for his 2013 Wiley published book *The End of Ethics and a Way Back: How to Fix a Fundamentally Broken Global Financial System* with alumni told that the book accomplishes "what its title so fittingly promises." Yale Divinity School News and Media announced that Malloch had, with his book, fixed a fundamentally broken global financial system.[35] His publicists at the time referred to "Ted" as "Theodore Roosevelt Malloch," who was serving "as Professor and Fellow of the Practice of Management at Saïd Business School, The University of Oxford" and as "a Research Professor for the Spiritual Capital Initiative at Yale University."[36]

In 2017, the *Financial Times* ran an article "Oxford distances itself from Trump favourite Ted Malloch. Academic said to be in line for EU post accused of falsely claiming college fellowships." "Oxford university has distanced itself from the political scientist who wants to be Donald Trump's ambassador in Brussels, accusing him of falsely claiming to be a fellow at two of its colleges," the article reads. "Ted Malloch, who has compared the EU to the Soviet Union, taught at Oxford's Saïd Business School until last year. He has appeared regularly on British television since the US election in November, often billed as a likely Trump appointee."[37] Malloch "has built his credibility on associations with a wide variety of well-regarded institutions, from Yale University to the World Economic Forum. However, many of his roles have ended after two years or less." They also report from the Saïd Business School. The administration "declined to specify whether it had done due diligence before appointing Mr. Malloch, stating it had received references from Yale, where he was a research professor, and that he 'gave no reason for suspicion' during his time in Oxford."[38] Theodore Roosevelt Malloch is also the author of

Doing Virtuous Business: The Remarkable Success of Spiritual Enterprise (2011), the book connected to PBS's *Doing Virtuous Business*.[39]

On October 19, 2010, Yale Divinity School announced, "At the Divinity School: The upside of 'Doing Virtuous Business.'" "A document titled "Doing Virtuous Business"—based on the book "Spiritual Enterprise" by Theodore Malloch, senior research scholar at the Yale Divinity School (YDS)—will be screened at 5:30 p.m. on Wednesday, Oct. 30, in the school's Niebuhr Hall, 490 Prospect St." The announcement continues. "The film, which features many YDS faculty, explores the concept of 'values-based' management strategies that can both improve the bottom line and strengthen a company's relationships with customers, employees, vendors, the environment, and the world at large."[40]

The effort was well-timed. The conclusion of the documercial cites a 2002 *Harvard Business Review* article called "The Virtue Matrix." The full title is "The Virtue Matrix: Calculating the Return on Corporate Responsibility." Roger L. Martin begins with a note on this period in North American history and "business ethics": "The images from recent meetings concerning globalization in Seattle, Davos, and Genoa might seem to suggest that only the unwashed and the unruly are pressuring business to show a greater sense of social and environmental responsibility." Yet, Martin reports, "calls are coming from mainstream quarters of society as well."[41] By "recent meetings concerning globalization" he means large, international gatherings of global corporate leaders at which "the unwashed and unruly" protested. Coverage in the U.S. of protests at the World Trade Organization's Ministerial Conference in 1999 in Seattle was significant both in depth and reach, emboldening "unwashed and unruly" people like Roman Catholic women religious, American Indian activists, Mennonite pastors, and lawyers advocating for the unhoused. As Colette Shade recalled in her article on the 25th anniversary of "The Battle in Seattle," World Trade attendees "were met by at least 40,000 organized protesters from all over the world, including anti-sweatshop activists, unions, environmental organizations, anarchists, Indigenous rights groups, artists, students, farmers, and progressive religious leaders."[42]

The documercial counters an award winning documentary. *The Corporation* was, in 2003, the most watched and celebrated documentary in Canadian history.[43] Common Sense Media describes the film as "detailing the past and present of corporate power and influence and its effects on societies, the environment, and individuals. There are many disturbing images: a child with no eyes due to birth defects, mass graves during the Holocaust, battles between police and protestors, and the bloodied body of a teen boy slain by police during protests in Bolivia." The family-friendly assessors also warn "An economics professor abruptly yells, 'Bulls–t!'" but recommend "this Oscar-winning documentary" for teaching about "how the same amendment that ended slavery after the Civil War also declared corporations to be 'people' in the 19th century and how, if corporations are indeed people, they most closely resemble psychotics … "[44]

The "economics professor" who "abruptly yells, 'Bulls—t!'" is Ira Jackson, then the Director, Center for Business and Government, Kennedy School, Harvard University. Jackson speaks to the interviewer about a metaphor for a "principled company." He says with a straight face, "The eagle. Soaring, clear-eyed, competitive, prepared to strike, but not a vulture. Noble, visionary, majestic, that people can believe in and be inspired by, that creates such a lift, that it soars. I could see that being a good logo for the principled company." He then looks disgusted and takes off his lapel mic, "Okay guys, enough bullshit."

Doing Virtuous Business camouflages the bullshit and psychoses of global, corporate capitalism with Yale blue. The opening music is anodyne, featuring serious yet vaguely hopeful tones. The narrator announces that the film has been provided by "Major funding from the Templeton Foundation." "Additional funding," the narrator tells the Public Broadcasting viewer was provided by "The Lilly Foundation, Inc., the Ford Foundation, and the Ecophilos Foundation." Theodore Roosevelt Malloch is listed as the Executive Producer. Todd Gould is listed as the Writer/Producer. "Doing Virtuous Business" is narrated by Wendell Ray, an African American man with a baritone voice.[45] The filmmakers secured a narrator who sounds like God.

The Lilly Foundation is the funding source that a senior colleague quipped should be the focus of a book, but that such a book would be the last book the author published. He was making a joke, but he was also being serious. Lilly helped create the "Fit for Ministry?" era of theological education at Yale Divinity, Chicago Divinity, and Duke Divinity in the last thirty years.[46] The Templeton Foundation has worked alongside to shape perceptions of "Science and Religion" with massive donations across the U.S., the U.K., and Europe. Lilly is funded by major pharmaceutical money, Eli Lilly Incorporated, as of this edit number 127 of the Fortune 500 worldwide, headquartered in Indianapolis.[47] The Templeton Foundation is part of a consortium of reactionary donors, including the Ahmanson, Coors, and DeVos families. These donors created a common sense answer to a vanilla flavored question: Who among the PBS viewership in Indiana would not wish for more virtuous businesses? One need not be part of the "unwashed and unruly" to have some concerns.

The narrator states with *gravitas*: "From the classroom to the board room, virtue ethics will be explored within the framework of 14 business success stories." "An in-depth look with *unprecedented* access to many of the world's *top* CEOs and corporate leaders who each explore *this core question*: Can corporations create wealth by *virtuous* means?" The viewer hears these words while watching people making tortillas, stocking grocery store shelves, imprinting steel for oil valves, as well as the intent, thoughtful visages of "the world's top CEO's."[48] The opening visuals feature computer-generated images of white columns. The narrator continues "Unfortunately, this aggressive chase [of business] has at times led to questionable practices, schemes, and scandals that have ruined careers, bankrupted companies, and contributed to a devastating, worldwide financial crisis." Miroslav Volf then appears sitting amongst bookshelves, described as "Founding Director Center for Faith and Culture. Yale Divinity School." Volf says, "How do businesses contribute to an authentically flourishing human life? Is it simply by increasing the bottom line? Or must we think about businesses as contributing to human flourishing?" After the introduction, the narrator continues, with a background of more white columns and another image of "Aristotle." "Aristotle, known as the founder of virtue ethics, along with other great minds throughout history, identified 14 qualities they believed would allow one to live a virtuous life." Then Theodore Roosevelt Malloch is walking on the Yale campus, a flowering tulip magnolia behind him. The words beneath read: "Dr. Theodore Roosevelt Malloch, Research Professor, Yale University, Author of *Spiritual Enterprise*." "Recent research has shown," Malloch intones, "that corporate leaders who commit themselves to a core mission that is more wholistic and steeped in spiritual capital often succeed in righting wrongs and creating genuine personal and social progress while also succeeding and generating strong profits."

The viewer of "Doing Virtuous Business" is then acquainted with the 14 "classical" virtues, along with the corporation to which the virtue is tied. Among these are "Leadership. To guide and inspire others. Our word is our bond. Cargill." "Justice. Equitable. Moral rightness. Miller's social agenda. Cummins Inc." "Gratitude. Grateful. Filled with thanks. Closed on Sunday. Chick-fil-A Restaurants Inc." "Forgiveness. To Grant Pardon. Free of Resentment. Spirit in the Workplace. Tyson Foods Inc." "Patience. Quiet, even-tempered perseverance. Forming a sustainable, social business. Dannon Foods International." "Faith. Supreme trust. The soul of the firm. ServiceMaster Inc." "Perseverance. Steadfast persistence. Creating Conscious Capitalism. Whole Foods." "Honesty. Truthful. Fair. Sincere. Managing by the golden rule. Four Seasons Hotels and Resorts."

In the introduction to "Doing Virtuous Business," Harold Attridge, listed as "Dean, Yale Divinity School" speaks a set of words that do not make sense except perhaps as an answer to a question along the lines of, "What are we doing here?" Attridge says to the camera: "It's developed over the last couple of years with the economic … uh downturn, and the events that led to it that's raised consciousness about the importance of fundamental values." John E. Hare, Noah Porter Professor of Philosophical Theology also says these words: "The moral demand is that we care about all of the people affected by what we do, and we have to make their purposes our purposes."[49]

Around the middle mark of the documercial, at 18:29, the focus is on Tyson Foods and the character marker of "Forgiveness." The words on the screen read: "FORGIVENESS" "TO GRANT PARDON" "FREE OF RESENTMENT" "Spirit in the Workplace" "Tyson Foods, Inc."

A man in a managerial Tyson Foods uniform, labeled as "Rick McKinnie, Director, Chaplain Services, Tyson Foods" explains that chaplains provide a "ministry of wandering," going down hallways and "just saying, 'are you having a good day?'" The narrator explains that at the headquarters for Tyson Foods, workplace chaplains are an integral part and are a "growing trend in business today." Chaplain Rick explains that they are a "faith friendly" program, and that they want to reach out to people of different religions. The images show a woman working an assembly line of chopped chicken, another a set of hands packaging tortillas. The earnest but uplifting music plays behind the words of Rick McKinnie, and the narrator, along with various executives at Tyson Foods.

The narrator then informs viewers: "The first record of chaplains in the American workplace dates back to the Massachusetts Bay Colony in the early 1600s." The background for these words is a series of three paintings, shown in plain greyscale: "Embarkation of the Pilgrims" by Robert Walter Weir, "The First Thanksgiving at Plymouth" by Jennie A. Brownscombe, and an image from Pilgrim Stock Photos. Many businesses are recognizing "the importance of having a corporate counselor available to support the spiritual side of the American workplace," to be the "eyes and ears" of the company. The narrator cites a "recent *New York Times* article" on the growing practice of workplace chaplaincy. The words and images are to convey that workplace chaplaincy is both as old as the pilgrims and as innovative as virtuous business.

There is a slight change of tone, a more somber sense of music, and the narrator tells viewers "The ascent of Tyson as a giant in the food industry has not been without controversy." Viewers see an image of a *Wall Street Journal* headline, date blurry, "Tyson Face Arkansas Class Action," and a *New York Times* headline "U.S. Files Complaint vs. Tyson." There is also an image of the heading of a Security and Exchange Commission filing. "In the past," the narrator elaborates, there have been "published reports about aggressive business practices, lawsuits, and battles with regulators." But, with a change in musical tone, "today, corporate leaders believe that innovations such as the Tyson Chaplaincy Program can help the company place a greater emphasis on the virtue of forgiveness and cultivate a greater spirit of goodwill." "Forgiveness," "To Grant Pardon." "Free of Resentment," the text reads.

Beginning minute 35:20, the heading "PERSEVERANCE" appears, with the words "Steadfast persistence" underneath. The text announces, "Creating Conscious Capitalism" and "Whole Foods." The music playing during the headings is somber and serious. The music shifts as soon as the footage turns to John Mackey, sitting at a desk, dressed in a casual buttoned shirt.

Viewers now hear a bright, spring-like set of stringed instruments. The music continues throughout the segment on Whole Foods. The color tones in the footage are complementary shades of green, periodically interspersed with bright colors worn by people "all over the world" credited with creating items sold at Whole Foods. John Mackey speaks indirectly, adjacent to the camera: "Conscious capitalism rejects the idea that business is merely to maximize profits and shareholder value, and that the shareholder is the only stakeholder that matters so the conscious business has discovered or created its deeper purpose when a business taps into its deeper purpose it tends to inspire and motivate the employees it releases more creative energy." The narrator announces: "These notions of conscious capitalism have transformed Whole Foods into a vast Fortune 500 supermarket empire. The unlikely success story of a company is a lesson in sheer perseverance, more than 30 years in the making." Viewers see the hero of "PERSEVERANCE" on the PBS screen with the narrator's voice: "John Mackey was a 25-year-old college dropout who, along with his 21-year-old girlfriend, opened a natural food store in Austin, Texas … the couple struggled early in their careers … " Then Mackey speaks, "We are continuing to discover deeper purpose in Whole Foods … " The documercial continues using the voice of Wendell Ray: "Mackey's perseverance helped turn Whole Foods into an international leader in marketing natural food products, an organization that works with suppliers all over the world through the Whole Planet Foundation to help develop small family farms into international suppliers as well." Mackey "helped to create the Conscious Capitalism Foundation, an organization founded on many Buddhist principles, a group that attracts fellow leaders committed to building corporate value."

The viewer at Yale and the viewer via Indianapolis Public Broadcasting were to be reassured that the C.E.O. of Whole Foods, of Tyson Foods, and other captains of industry are virtuous. They were, as the Rockefeller funded Riverside Pulpit had assured similar readers and viewers in an earlier era, following something like "the Golden Rule," this time also with "many Buddhist principles."

Rulers Make Bad Lovers

In April 2020, a month into the COVID-19 pandemic, *Business Insider*'s Hayley Peterson wrote "Amazon-owned Whole Foods is quietly tracking its employees with a heat map tool that ranks which stores are most at risk of unionizing."[50] The basics require an extended quotation, given the particular elements that go into such a "heat map tool" for a company like Whole Foods. "Whole Foods is keeping an eye on stores at risk of unionizing through an interactive heat map … risk scores are calculated from more than two dozen metrics, including employee 'loyalty,' turnover, and racial diversity," Peterson wrote. "The map also tracks local economic and demographic factors such as the unemployment rate in a store's location and the percentage of families in the area living below the poverty line." Whole Foods was on trend. "Overall, US companies spent at least $100 million on consulting services for anti-union campaigns between 2014 and 2017, according to data from the Economic Policy Institute based on disclosure forms filed with the US Department of Labor," Peterson reported, "Walmart, for example, hired an intelligence-gathering service from Lockheed Martin and ranked stores by labor activity when it faced protests eight years ago."

"Doing Virtuous Business" presents John Mackey as guided by "many Buddhist principles." Mackey had made clear his own values in a 2009 *Wall Street Journal* opinion essay, which he then reiterated in 2022. *Business Insider* ran a piece by Grace Kay entitled "Whole Foods CEO says 'socialists are taking over' in the US and young people in liberal cities 'don't seem like they want to work.'"[51] Kay quotes from a 2022 podcast episode.[52] The "they" here are "socialists." "They're taking over everything," Kay reports from Mackey's interview. "It looks like they've taken over a lot of the corporations. It looks like they've taken over the military. And it's just continuing. You know, I'm a capitalist at heart, and I believe in liberty and capitalism," he said. "Those are my twin values. And I feel like, you know, with the way freedom of speech is today, the movement on gun control, a lot of the liberties that I've taken for granted most of my life, I think, are under threat."

It is possible to create a documentary on the "Virtues" related to "Business" in the U.S. that connects those "Virtues" to "Spiritual Enterprise," to use

Theodore Roosevelt Malloch's phrase. But that would require a less sprightly, spring-like set of tones. Mackey's "twin values," which are not unusual for a CEO of a multinational corporation, are "liberty and capitalism."[53] Mackey had written his 2009 opinion essay without the imprimatur of Yale blue and the gauze of Whole Foods green.[54] Mackey opens with a quotation from Margaret Thatcher: "The problem with socialism is that eventually you run out of other people's money." A core part of his argument in 2009 is that there is no "right" to health care in the U.S. "Many promoters of health-care reform believe that people have an intrinsic ethical right to health care—to equal access to doctors, medicines and hospitals," Mackey wrote. "While all of us empathize with those who are sick, how can we say that all people have more of an intrinsic right to health care than they have to food or shelter?" he asked. "Health care is a service that we all need, but just like food and shelter it is best provided through voluntary and mutually beneficial market exchanges," Mackey instructed his readers. His conclusion is stark: "A careful reading of both the Declaration of Independence and the Constitution will not reveal any intrinsic right to health care, food or shelter. That's because there isn't any. This 'right' has never existed in America." With proper "lifestyle choices," "we" "should be able to live largely disease-free lives until we are well into our 90s and even past 100 years of age," Mackey explains.[55]

Mackey's use of "We" is significant. Who is "we?" Consider for contrast a 2011 essay by Obie Award-winning playwright and actor Wallace Shawn called, with matching candor, "Why I Call Myself a Socialist," which originally appeared on *Tom Dispatch*, an online news source created in 2001 by Guggenheim winning editor Thomas M. Englehardt.[56] The *Nation* editors who reran the essay chose as the accompanying photo Wallace Shawn, in black and white, looking down at the camera with a characteristic, quizzical look.[57] Shawn has won awards for his plays, including, from 1985, "Aunt Dan and Lemon," which the Royal Court Theatre describes as: "Aunt Dan and Lemon explores the frightening pathways of influence, the glamour of cruelty and the shadow side of nostalgia."[58] But what he is best known for is the 1987 nostalgic romp *The Princess Bride*.[59]

Shawn starts with an invitation to imagine. Live, community theater is something about which people in "reasonably large towns" will have some acquaintance. One of the aspects of life that the existence of live theater means is that "in various quiet neighborhoods in these towns, you can usually also find some rather quiet individuals, the actors who work regularly in that theater … who surprisingly at night put on the robes of kings and wizards, witches and queens, and for their particular community temporarily embody the darkest needs and loftiest hopes of the human species."[60] "Businessmen, for example, don't take their clothes off or cry in front of strangers in the course of their work," Shawn points out, whereas that is exactly the feat expected of an actor. People who spend time on the craft that is acting "understand the infinite vastness hiding inside each human being, the characters not played, the characteristics not revealed." He then traces a series of branches to this realization. "Schoolteachers can see every day that, given the chance, the sullen pupil in the back row can sing, dance, juggle, do mathematics, paint, and think."

In a section entitled "Sorting Babies on the Global Market," Shawn notes that among the "4,000,000 babies" who are "born on earth each day," there are those who live as "casualties of the conditions in which their mothers lived—malnutrition, polluted water, mysterious chemicals that sneak into the body and warp the genes." What is "much more tragic," Shawn writes, "is that most of these babies are born "ready to become a person who wakes up happily in the morning because they know they're going to spend the day doing work they find fascinating, work that they love." "Wiggling beside their mothers," he writes, "they have no idea what's going to be done to them." What is done, he writes is a "sorting" of "the global market."

Shawn is a socialist because the form of capitalism in which he and I live is lacking in creativity and imagination. He asks his readers, many of whom will know his own adaptability to his craft as well as his love for the theater, to adjust our vision to see that "the play we're watching is an illusion." Consider that "the baby who now wears the costume of the hustler in fact had the capacity to become a biologist or a doctor, a circus performer or a poet or a scholar of ancient Greek." With this opened perspective on the world as it currently is, "the division of labor, as now practiced" may appear newly, and "inherently immoral." "The costumes are wrong," Wallace Shawn concludes. "They have to be discarded. We have to start out naked again and go from there."

Consider these two different appeals to a reader's imagination. There are uses of the words "we" and "us" in the rhetoric of Mackey in the *Wall Street Journal* and the rhetoric of Shawn in *Tom Dispatch*. Mackey writes to his readers that "all of *us* empathize with those who are sick" but "how can *we* say that all people" have a "right" to "health care" or "food or shelter" "*our* health-care problems are self-inflicted" and with the correct "choices" "*we* should be able to live" "disease-free" "into our 90s and even past 100 years of age." Mackey assumes of his readers that we are currently "well." He also has as his imagined reader a person who is not currently fighting for adequate health care and wages sufficient to secure food and livable shelter. His "we" shifts to include both "we" and "them" who are fighting for "health care" as a human right. Those people, if they would make better "lifestyle choices," would recognize that "our" health-care system works for people who are not so pathological as to "choose" to live in ways that are "self-inflicting." Mackey's summons is for those without health and/or health care to look at themselves in the mirror and see themselves as failing and as capable of fixing themselves and, thereby "our health-care problems" in the U.S. By eliding "we" and the implied "them," the "us" who "empathize" may have "our" myopia corrected. "Our" problems as a country are a matter of individual choice. Shawn's "we" is also an appeal to a readership that is basically secure, but Shawn asks "us" to imagine this world as an immorally arranged fiction. Shawn suggests his readers consider the eugenic nihilism of corporate capitalism as "an illusion," not to be taken as an ineluctable fact of nature.

In early May 2020, The *New York Times* offered a teaching guide, linked to an April article by Karen Weise and Kate Conger, with an opening photo of a woman named Tonya Ramsey standing with colleagues outside a warehouse in Romulus, Michigan. Tonya Ramsey looks like she might be only recently out of high school herself, with a blonde and blue ponytail and a determined look on her face. Tonya Ramsey is holding a sign that reads: "We fear coming to work. We're anxious and uneasy when working and we're afraid to go home and infect our loved ones. Bezos close DTW1 down for cleaning and show you care about safety!" The author's note in 2024 reads "Nicole Daniels has been a staff editor with *The Learning Network* since 2019. She was previously a classroom teacher, museum educator and curriculum writer." Nicole Daniels's lesson published May 8, 2020, has this concise description of the learning objectives:

> In this lesson, we look at a fleet of workers who ensure we can stay home and still receive groceries, puzzles and pizza delivered straight to our front doors. You will learn about essential workers at big companies, like Amazon and Domino's, who are fighting for health and safety measures at work along with paid time off—something that many Americans take for granted.[61]

The accompanying video is three minutes long, and it begins in a simple hotel room, with one man speaking in Spanish to the camera. The documentary ends: "Does it really take a strike for companies to do what's right?" The effort of Nicole Daniels to teach online during the pandemic, and to engage teachers across the country who were turning to the *New York Times* for resources deserves close attention. The efforts of the families to stand up for their own safety and dignity during this time deserve close attention. The short video is entitled: "Domino's is raking in money. What about its employees?" Viewers see a Latino man with grey hair and a blue medical mask. He is speaking directly in Spanish to the camera. "Two weeks ago, I was told I have Coronavirus." He continues, with a sense of pride in his eyes, as they lighten to the words of what he does. "I work for Domino's. I deliver pizzas, pasta, salads." When he says the word for salad, he lights up beneath the mask. "This job is important because I earn little, but it's to support my family." "I'm staying at a hotel." As he says these words, the camera focuses closely on a book. It is a Bible, and it is clearly not the hotel Bible, because it is thumbed and has a buckled leather cover. This is what my grandmother would call a "really read Bible." He continues, "I've been quarantined for 10 days." At this point, he is obviously distressed. This was early in the pandemic, when people knew next to nothing about how and why people were dying so quickly. "Domino's the company needs to pay for my medical bills and the hotel bills." The person on film is crying, visibly weeping with a form of desperation that is mixed with shame. "They don't care about people just money."

On the screen, the words read, in *New York Times* script, white on black background: "On April 7 (2020) workers at Domino's franchise went on strike demanding basic worker protections after their coworker tested positive for Coronavirus for almost a month. The store refused to budge." The documentary then shows news footage from Fox News and other outlets noting that, in the first weeks of the 2020 pandemic, "Domino's sales are significantly up." The editors show news from Domino's franchise owners, speaking about their success and commitment. Then the screen goes to Felix Lopez Barbosa. His name is listed on the screen, again in *New York Times* font, "Delivery driver; Domino's Pizza; Los Angeles California." "I'm a delivery driver, but right now we're on strike. Here is one of my colleagues." The camera shows footage of "Fast Food Workers Strike" by "Eyewitness News ABC7." Barbosa continues speaking. "There's five that have already tested positive for Coronavirus and another nine that have symptoms. Nobody told us anything. We kept working. They don't think about that, they just want us to go back to work. You had to buy your own gloves and masks. Domino's, all we're asking for is PPE like masks, gloves and sanitizer." Mr. Lopez Barbosa continues, "We're also asking for hazard pay and that you tell us when a worker is infected so we don't infect ourselves our families, or our customers." "The CDC says that the employer needs to let employees know when there's a possible contagion and Domino's hasn't done any of that," he explains, "This problem goes far beyond Domino's." There is footage of police officers standing and visiting outside of a McDonald's hamburgers location, a woman inside a car with a handwritten sign reading "No hold your burgers hold your fries worker here risking their lives … unions."

The film ends with "On May 1 (2020) after six workers tested positive, the franchise conceded. It offered the workers proper PPE, a deep cleaning, and sick pay. The workers felt safe enough to return." The words on the screen continue "But other demands remain unmet, including hazard pay and reimbursements for medical and hotel costs." It ends with a basic question. "The workers continue to fight for their remaining demands while working. This was just one franchise nationwide. There are millions of workers who aren't getting basic protections or fair pay. Does it really take a strike for companies to do what's right?"[62]

"Marketplace Men"

The New Canaan Society describes itself as "Young Life for Marketplace Men."[63] It is the network of professional men's groups across the country that held the 2013 annual conference I forewent in favor of Rewired, the Southern Baptist men's conference in Oklahoma. Doug Coe, the designated public face of the Fellowship Family from 1969 until his death in 2017, is named as a founding "team member" of the organization.[64] Public moralist and University of Virginia professor James Davison Hunter launched his book *To Change the World* at the 2010 New Canaan Society Retreat and is repeatedly featured on the organization's website, including as a "team member."[65] Os Guinness named in a 2000 *Christianity Today* interview "The Case for Converting Kings" that his own barnacle on the network, the Trinity Forum, was set up in 1991 to shape the future by reaching elite men: "Our aim is to bring about the transformation of society through the transformation of leaders."[66] As Oppenheimer had reported, Alonzo McDonald was also on the team to create Trinity Forum. James Davison Hunter served for decades at U.V.A. as a beachhead scholar of religion and sociology, making the term "Culture Wars" into a diagnosis and a strategy.

In her "How Right-Wing Billionaires Infiltrated Higher Education," Jane Mayer explains a strategy donors call a "beachhead theory." Mayer quotes conservative strategist James Piereson. The goal is to "establish conservative cells," or "beachheads," at "the most influential schools in order to gain the greatest leverage." James Davison Hunter led one such beachhead, mainstreaming the idea that war is the best way to make "sense of the battles over the family, art, education, law, and politics," as the cover of his 1991 bestselling book asserts. As the *Wall Street Journal* names it, Hunter "coined the phrase 'Culture Wars' in 1991, a year ahead of Pat Buchanan."[67]

The New Canaan Society boasts of serving "Marketplace Men." The form of "the gospel" this version of the Moody Bible poster from 1920 represents is not for the men on the poster or the men they were to mollify but for the potential donors to whom the mollification was to appeal. The New Canaan Society was set up to attract wealthy men of various circles of influence, coming together for fellowship, to read books together, and support one another. A male colleague from Yale who has served on the Gold Coast of Connecticut explained that these men do not generally attend a conventional church. They are, he explained, above anything so local as a "church." They consider themselves, he said, "masters of the universe," referring to the 1987 film *Wall Street*. The network is made up of men taught to see themselves like Larry Osborne's creative narration of Joseph of Arimathea at the Advance 13 event at the Duke Energy Center for the Performing Arts in Raleigh. Hearing from young men brought up to succeed in these circles, I came to doubt that anyone offered them a non-utilitarian version of "the gospel." They are raised to be foot soldiers in a "culture war" and, as Hunter put it "To Change the World." My first ministry position after Yale Divinity School was in New Canaan, Connecticut, where the New Canaan Society was founded, so I have long been pastorally interested in this connection. The network creates a malleably vague form of Christianity, smoothing over bumps like the story of the rich young ruler and Jesus.

In my second year teaching bioethics at Duke, I received a summons from a dean of a free-standing, mainstream evangelical seminary to a private, ethics consultation with a major donor to the school. About a dozen scholars sat together for hours over the course of two days to discuss embryonic stem cell research. This man had a house underneath his house. We met at his residence in northern Virginia, and he explained he had built the large complex to facilitate gatherings of leaders from across the world. The under-house struck me as a Christian catacomb arranged by Howard Johnson, with a phone line to Istanbul. I was the only woman invited, or at least the only one who accepted the invitation.

The setting was disorienting. What troubled me most was the man's blend of Jesus language I associate with my grandmother's *Guideposts Magazine*, and a matter-of-fact expediency about ethics—from missile defense to torture to embryonic stem cell research. There was a disconnect between his vaguely evangelical-ish words related to Jesus and his amoralism. He described his war profiteering with no sense of remorse or even an edge of irony. It became clear that he was determined that embryonic research proceed apace because he thought the research would save his beloved. Having been able so well to master much in the universe, he was now facing the mortality of a family member. One of the older Christian ethicists at the gathering finally said out loud words I was trying to summon the courage to speak. "Even if this research moves forward apace," he explained, "it is not going to save her life." She was, eventually, going to die. "Oh, I don't know about that!" our host said, "the last doctor's report indicated otherwise!" This man with a house under his house had lost his Jesus, and he did not know where to find him.

With the help of a friend connected to the Fellowship Family, I attended the 61st National Prayer Breakfast on Thursday, February 7, 2013, in the International Ballroom of the Hilton Washington in Washington, D.C. As I walked into the lobby, I was struck by the masculinist, moneyed power. I expected a pretense of piety. There was no piety. There was also no pretense of gallantry. From the revolving doors onward, men walked over me, requiring me to step out of their way. Men in groups dropped doors in my face. Jeff Sharlet had explained that the event "is regarded by the Family as merely a tool in a larger purpose: to recruit the powerful attendees into smaller, more frequent prayer meetings, where they can 'meet Jesus man to man.'"[68] The three-day assembly was the most unabashedly utilitarian Christian-adjacent gathering of which I have been privy. It was both harrowing and aesthetically gross.

"Jesus" functions as a geopolitical lubricant. The title of Sharlet's 2003 essay is "Jesus Plus Nothing." Sharlet reports hearing Doug Coe associate the Family with the tactics of totalitarian leaders. Coe's words at the headquarters for the parachurch organization "the Navigators" have been on YouTube since around 2010, described by the editor of the video as "Sermon given by Douglas Coe to the Navigators on January 16, 1989."[69] A former student who had personal acquaintance with the network sent me the link, reminding me also that I had been there at the headquarters around 2008–2009 when I was a guest speaker in Colorado Springs, Colorado for the conservative parachurch organization "Focus on the Family." Sharlet reported

Coe listed other men who had changed the world through the strength of the covenants they had forged with their "brothers": "Look at Hitler," he said. "Lenin, Ho Chi Minh, Bin Laden." The Family, of course, possessed a weapon those leaders lacked: the "total Jesus" of a brotherhood in Christ. "*That*'s what you get with a covenant," said Coe. "Jesus plus nothing."

The goals involve using human beings as tools to broker forms of power. The machinery of the network requires submission to a "total Jesus," "covenant," and the lubrication of the machinery is "Jesus." Whenever I have asked someone where they attend church, and they tell me they are a "Jesus follower," or a "follower of Jesus," I have pulled out my mental notebook. These are the people who float above the fray of actual congregations.

The aesthetics of the National Prayer Breakfast reminded me of the Lawrence Welk Show, a stridently wholesome variety show that aired from 1951 to 1971 and that ran as reruns for decades after at off-peak times on every Texas PBS station during my childhood. But unlike the Lawrence Welk Show, the number of men to women was not matched to allow for predictable coupling. Every woman there, and we were vastly outnumbered, was accompanied by either a powerful woman or a retinue of other women dressed similarly. The only exception among the women I met was a Western European woman representing the interests of an aristocratic, political family from South Asia. The form of business attire was noticeably predictable along gender lines, and middle-class Midwestern. I did not expect people to be wearing motorcycle jackets and combat boots, but I was struck by the uniform aesthetic of muted jewel tones and lack of adornment.

Five women have been the sole, main speaker at the National Prayer Breakfast as of 2024: Barbara Jordan in 1984, Elizabeth Dole in 1987, Anjezë Gonxhe Bojaxhiu (Mother Teresa) in 1994, Condoleezza Rice in 2003, and Hillary Rodham Clinton in 2010. In 2016, Roma Downey spoke alongside her husband Mark Burnett about their evangelical influence on mainstream television, as producers. And, after the restructuring of the event in 2023, the version of the Prayer Breakfast not directly associated with the Family featured Jim Cymbala (Pastor) and Vashti Murphy McKenzie (Bishop). From 1953 to 2023, seven women have addressed the Breakfast. Billy Graham was the main speaker seven times. Ben Carson was the main speaker twice. Seven women have served as co-chair or chair of the event over the seventy years.[70] The most reported speech by a woman to the National Prayer Breakfast was Anjezë Gonxhe Bojaxhiu's address while standing next to two sitting Clintons. Mother Teresa's speech was covered widely in the U.S., U.K., and Western Europe, as she lectured the Clintons for their support of contraception and abortion rights. The most widely covered female speaker at the National Prayer Breakfast in its seventy years of existence was a woman who did not use her given name, wore clerical clothing such that one could only see her face and her hands, and spoke as an asexual prophet against female reproductive liberty.

The morning before the actual breakfast day there was an invitation only session for women. Due to the connections of my host, I was among those invited. The event opened with a recognition of the wives of politicians who were present in the gathering, with then U.S. Congresswoman from California Janice Hahn as one of the hosts. The wives of two different politicians, one Democrat and the other Republican, emphasized that through "faith in Jesus" people could form "friendships." "Anything is possible" one explained, if people focus on "Jesus and his word." The recognition of wives from across the two parties concluded with a prayer of gratitude "for wonderful Christian spouses who encourage their husbands." Then Ambassador Tony Hall's wife Janet Sue introduced Kathy Keller, known to this group as Tim Keller's supportive wife. Keller presented an exquisitely crafted, precisely Calvinist lecture. She spoke on the "value added" when Christians perceive suffering with adherence to a doctrine of absolute divine sovereignty. When asked about sexual abuse, she related a story about how a knife in the hand of an assailant can become a "syringe" of healing from God as it travels through a protective outer-bubble that God creates around his chosen.

Another way to describe conference events around the National Prayer Breakfast in D.C. is related to the books featured. Some readers will have attended an academic meeting in North America or elsewhere that is a giant circus of books, authors, publishers, and readers. At the National Prayer Breakfast, there were no book tables and exhibits as at a gathering like the Modern Language Association. The level of discourse about books was homogenized. Conversations going on about books revealed an upstream funneling. These sessions highlighted books and authors that were already bestsellers or were already on their way to becoming bestsellers. The network functions to catapult serviceable authors into the publishing stream, and then authors are expected to pull up other compatible authors into that stream with blurbs and reviews not only in populist venues but in academic and "cosmopolitan" media. One of the co-creators of the "Veggie Tales" series for children, Eric Metaxas, for example, emcees the New Canaan Society events, appeared on the cover of *The Ivy League Christian Observer* Spring 2010 under the heading "Changing the World," and then became the most celebrated biographer of Dietrich Bonhoeffer, a figure as crucial to Christianity in the twentieth century as any pope. Metaxas's 2010 *Bonhoeffer: Pastor, Martyr, Prophet, Spy* became a *New York Times* bestseller in spite of the fact that scholars of twentieth century German theology took the time to detail the book's factual errors.[71] Between *Christianity Today* and Fox News, Metaxas's work on Bonhoeffer was practically all Duke Divinity students connected to Young Life had read in 2011. Metaxas had been made into such a figure of holy masculinity to many of my students that to question him was to question the unique musical brilliance of Bono.

In 2008, the *New York Times* declared "Christian Novel is Surprise Best Seller." The abstract for the article about *The Shack* reads, "*The Shack* is the most compelling recent example of how a word-of-mouth phenomenon can explode into a blockbuster when the momentum hits chain bookstores." For the unacquainted, the *New York Times* describes *The Shack* as "a slim paperback novel by an unknown author about a grieving father who meets God in the form of a jolly African American woman … " The *New York Times* reported: "Everybody that I know has bought at least 10 copies," Mr. Nowak said. "There's definitely something about the book." "Just over a year after it was originally published as a paperback, *The Shack* had its debut at No. 1 on the *New York Times* trade paperback fiction best-seller list on June 8 and has stayed there ever since," the piece informs.[72]

Oprah Inc. continues to feature *Shack* author Paul Young in several forms, including on the "Super Soul Sunday" series.[73] The brand also features bestselling author Richard Rohr, whose collaboration with Young intersects on their websites.[74] In her essay on Rohr for *America Magazine*, devotional author Sonja Livingston writes "I am not alone. Bono is a fan. So is Oprah. Father Rohr has written countless books and was profiled last year in *The New*

Yorker. His most recent book, *The Universal Christ,* was a *New York Times* best seller."[75] Writing for the mainstream evangelical journal *Mockingbird,* Todd Brewer writes of Rohr "With a book blurb from Bono and interviews with Oprah, it's fair to say that Richard Rohr is something of a Christian superstar."[76] The superstardom of mainstream evangelicalism overlaps as predictably as horror publishing connects through Stephen King. The family who owns Hobby Lobby has been an obvious target for media attention since 2010. From purchasing artifacts stolen during war to funding overtly reactionary political schemes, the name itself—"Hobby Lobby"—allows for notice and derision. The Green family's hobby is a museum of fundamentalism in Washington, D.C.[77] What Rohr, Bono, and *The Shack* share, besides Oprah, is that they each offer emulsifying spirituality.

Consider a contrast. Martin Luther King, Jr. and Abraham Joshua Heschel recommended during their own time a form of "maladjustment." By 1966, King repeatedly named the need for something akin to an "International Association for the Advancement of Creative Maladjustment."[78] Heschel taught and wrote throughout his life about the prophetic vision as requiring what he called in 1962 a prophetic "moral maladjustment." "The prophet is a person who suffers from a profound maladjustment to the spirit of society" and may be named as living with "moral madness." Heschel continues "While his mode of perception may differ sharply from the perceptions of all other human beings, the ideas [the prophet] brings back to reality become a source of illumination of supreme significance to all other human beings."[79] Given their friendship, consider their use of this term as a collaborative summons. Then consider what it means that Richard Rohr is a bestselling mainstream source of illumination, that Bono became the face of rock Christian progressivism, and that *The Shack* became a bestselling … well, *a bestselling anything*.

The pieces of paper distributed at the 2013 National Prayer Breakfast were as simplistic as other forms of "ambient evangelicalism," only shinier. The opening page is a series of two quotes, on cream colored paper with blue typescript. First, "We hold these truths to be self-evident; that all men are created equal, that they are endowed by their Creator with certain inalienable rights, that among these are life, liberty and the pursuit of happiness; that to secure these rights, governments are instituted among men … " with a note that this is from the "Declaration of Independence." The second quote is "George Washington's Prayer for the United States of America," dated June 8, 1783. "Almighty God; We make our earnest prayer that Thou wilt keep the United States in Thy Holy protection; and Thou wilt incline the hearts of the citizens to cultivate a spirit of subordination and obedience to government; and entertain a brotherly affection and love for one another and for their fellow citizens of the United States at large." The prayer continues, ending with a commendation to emulate the "Divine Author of our blessed religion, and without a humble imitation of whose example in these things we can never hope to be a happy nation. Grant our supplication, we beseech Thee, through Jesus Christ our Lord. Amen."

The last two pages of the five-page program are, facing one another, two pages of quotes. The first are three quotes from the bible, translation not listed, and the facing page includes five quotations from past U.S. Presidents. The bible quotations are not listed as such. They are listed with a title and then the traditionally attributed author of the quotation. The use of biblical words in these documents read to me then and still reads like a fork hitting a pie pan, with no rhythm. To call the use of bible words in these documents shallow is to use the wrong metaphor, because shallow implies there could be, with more words, depth. To call the words discordant suggests that, with better tuning, there could be harmony. Out of context, they are scattered on a page to lend legitimacy to the claim of biblicism. The excerpts accentuate dependence on and submission to God, and the words of Jesus sufficiently shorn of specifics. Thousands of people sat obediently, listened to prayers said in the name of Jesus, heard "Ave Maria," and watched while the President of the United States sat through Ben Carson's jokes about being a "Black man who can tell jokes." Carson excoriated "political correctness" as "putting a muzzle on people," insisted that public education had "dumbed things down," and recommended to the entire room "a solution" to the problems he had been naming, that is, the Ben Carson Scholarship Fund.[80]

Presidents must spend time listening to, even smiling along with, words that ring false. That is politics in a country that does not silence dissent. After Abraham Vereide's team had done their work on President Eisenhower, the National Prayer Breakfast became a spectacle of submission for thousands to see. The ritual involves a pretense that Jesus of Nazareth has blessed the event, that someone with as complicated a relationship to Christianity as Thomas Jefferson would approve, and that it is perfectly normal for people to pay to pray. If my judgment of faces and body language in the room that morning is any indication, many of the people at the "National Prayer Breakfast" bowed their heads in "prayer" as performance. This detail alone should trouble any Baptist.

Still, maybe there is an opportunity at such an event for prophetic truth? Mostly not. The deciders for the 1994 keynote chose Anjezë Gonxhe Bojaxhiu to speak to President Clinton. The *Washington Post* reported, "Mother Teresa yesterday condemned abortion and contraception at the annual National Prayer Breakfast that included President Clinton, Vice President Gore and a host of congressional leaders."[81] So, yes, if that prophetic truth is against reproductive choice. Paul David Hewson (Bono) was chosen in 2006 during the U.S. wars in Iraq and Afghanistan. Hewson detailed the successful shift toward funding for HIV/AIDS in Africa, specifically naming then Republican Senate Majority Leader Bill Frist's work in Uganda.[82] He called on "folks" to support the then newly established (as of 2004) "One Campaign," saying: "One percent is a new partnership with Africa, not paternalism towards Africa; a new partnership with Africa, where increased assistance flows toward improved governance and initiatives with proven track records and away from the boondoggles and white elephants that we've seen before."[83] The speech went over well, by all media accounts. His only reference to the wars was to call A.I.D.S. the "greatest W.M.D. of them all."

For this research, I watched every episode of *Veep* and *West Wing*. The only series set in D.C. to acknowledge "the Family" is *Alpha House* (2013–2014). Jeff Sharlet's 2010 follow-up book to *The Family, C Street: The Fundamentalist Threat to American Democracy* garnered more media coverage due to publicity about the brutal anti-gay legislation in Uganda. Peter J. Boyer wrote "Frat House for Jesus," for the *New Yorker* in September 2010, preempting the release of Sharlet's book. "Frat House" sets a tone. Are these men at the center of the story, two Republicans and two Democrats, bumbling and over-sexed? Aw shucks. Yes. Boyer writes "A picture began to emerge of a boys-gone-wild house of pleasure. The men of C Street, pledged to silence, declined to respond to press inquiries, which only heightened interest."[84] Boyer goes on, "One view of the Fellowship, with some popularity on the secular left, is of a sort of theocratic Blackwater, advancing a conservative agenda … Secretary of State Hillary Clinton, a friend of the Fellowship, might dispute that view—if she spoke about the group, which she does not." Boyer repeats for *New Yorker* readers the argument Campolo offered in *Sojourners*: "The Fellowship's participants (there is no official membership) describe themselves simply as followers of Jesus … They are assertively nondoctrinal (eschewing even the term 'Christian') and nonecclesiastical." He reports, "although the core figures are evangelicals, they do not believe in proselytizing. I have spoken to Buddhists, Muslims, and Jews who consider themselves part of this network." The network serves men in power who are struggling with personal crises, as Boyer explained to readers, linking story after story of Doug Coe ministering to powerful men in need.

The premise of *Alpha House* is that four men holding office in Washington, D.C. care about one another sufficiently to speak to one another confidentially, off the record, and without expectation of gain. In the official histories of the network, written and spoken, two words that arise repeatedly are "relationship" and "friendship." But the forms of "relationships" and "friendships" among the men who are connected are about use.

A former student whose wife was a key strategist for Young Life asked me whether I understood what is morally wrong with their model. He stressed that the model of recruitment and connection—of "friendship" and "relationship"—depends on what a person offers for future recruitment? Are they particularly athletic? Charismatic, as in carrying a noticeably attractive form of charisma? Do they have theatrical abilities? The Young Life model trades on attributes that make a chapter attractive to different sectors in a demographic at a targeted school and region. The form of "friendship" is about using people. What does this mean, he asked, when/if a person becomes less useful? What if the young person turns out to be gay (and thus precluded from leadership in Young Life)? What if the athlete tears a key ligament and is unable to continue their role as the organization's conduit to athletes? What if the charismatic leader of the smoking section is arrested for possession of cocaine? If "the gospel" is embedded within this logic of usefulness, is this good news?

These group dynamics also involve the practice of lay, peer "accountability" and lay, peer "confession." In formal, clerical practices of confession, clergy are disallowed from sharing with others the confession of a person under their care. From the United Methodist Guidelines: "All clergy of The United Methodist Church are charged to maintain all confidences inviolate, including confessional confidences, except in the cases of suspected child abuse or neglect or in cases where mandatory reporting is required by civil law."[85] From the Episcopalian Church: "The content of a confession is not normally a matter of subsequent discussion. The secrecy of a confession is morally absolute for the confessor and must under no circumstances be broken."[86] But within parachurch organizations, members are encouraged to share their struggles with one another without confidentiality. Pulitzer Prize-winning journalist Lawrence Wright's reporting on religious cults seeks often to explain how people can become caught in a snarl of religiosity, secrets, and shame. In an essay for _The Mayborn_ about Wright's investigative process, Joanna Cattanach noted that "Wright's own religious youth in Dallas in the 1960s was formative. His family belonged to the First United Methodist Church Dallas, where he joined Young Life," which evangelizes and then continually connects youth from high school through college to young adulthood and into adult networks.[87] On "Here's The Thing," a podcast hosted by actor Alec Baldwin, Wright detailed how it was in Young Life that he learned "you can bend yourself into the shape of the organization in the way it wants you to be," and "the more pious you are, the higher you climb."[88] Wright's book _Going Clear: Scientology, Hollywood, and the Prison of Belief_ documents, among other strategies, ways that a cult combines a hierarchical structure—whereby someone climbs by assimilating—and a tactic of procuring secrets. As Cattanach summarizes, "Wright's books and essays today often explore religious belief as well as themes of shame, humiliation and conversion that are common among believers of all faiths … 'I'm fascinated,' Wright says, 'by how you can take idealistic good people and have them believing things they never thought they'd believe and doing things they'd never thought they'd do.'"

Another former student connected to the Family sent me C.S. Lewis's 1944 essay "The Inner Ring." Calling himself a "middle-aged moralist," Lewis tells the young men that, rather than tell them how to play their role in "post-war reconstruction," he is "going to do something more old-fashioned than you perhaps expected." He explains he is "going to give advice. I am going to issue warnings. Advice and warnings about things which are so perennial that no one calls them 'current affairs.'"[89] Using a story from *War and Peace*, Lewis describes "two different systems or hierarchies." One system is according to rules "printed" and "constant." And "the other is not printed anywhere. Nor is it even a formally organised secret society with officers and rules which you would be told after you had been admitted. You are never formally and explicitly admitted by anyone … It has no fixed name." Lewis explains that "personal friendship" from within a workplace is neutral. What is not neutral is the pressure toward a shift that makes a man a "scoundrel." "Of all the passions … the passion for the Inner Ring is most skillful in making a man who is not yet a very bad man do very bad things." And: "Exclusion is no accident; it is the essence."

On Your Knees

In the last episode of the documentary *The Family*, filmmaker Jesse Moss asks Jeff Sharlet: "When you left Ivanwald and you wrote your book, had you thought to yourself, maybe like, I got it wrong, or did you ever think like, I mean, I'm sure people accused you of being conspiracy theorist." Sharlet responds simply, "Yeah." "Did you ever question yourself?" Sharlet replies, "You know it's funny because I wrote two books about them, and I tried to give them both happy endings. They weren't happy experiences, reporting these books, you know to encounter a power that is much greater than you understood, really maybe the darkest expression of religious life that I encountered in 20 years of writing."[90] The Netflix series ends with the Family's remarkable capacity to shift "Jesus" into a serviceable tool for obedience.

The filmmakers secured an audio recording for the 2018 Prayer Breakfast. The audio records Jesse Moss arriving as Doug Burleigh explains, "we do our best work invisibly." The scene then goes to "National Prayer Breakfast Information Session, 2018." Viewers hear Burleigh, listed as "Prayer Breakfast Organizer." Then Burleigh asks, "Your name, sir, where are you from?" "It's Ayric Peyton, from Portland, Oregon."[91] Ayric Peyton asks Burleigh: "What do you say to the person who says that you don't want to say that there's leadership, because to do that would mean you'd have to take ownership of what we're actually doing?" Burleigh's response is: "So, we are sinners. We'll sure admit to that. But a lot of other things, talking about how we were involved in these conspiracies around the world and so on, they're giving us a lot of credit we don't deserve." Viewers then hear Moss as he follows Ayric. "What, what's your name?" Moss asks. "Ayric." Moss continues: "I'm Jesse." Ayric responds "Jesse, nice to meet you, Jesse." Moss follows up with a question. "Just an interesting question you asked; how did you first come here?" "I belong to a group, a Friday morning group where we don't pull any punches. We don't exchange the niceties." Moss responds, "Okay, yeah, where is that?" "Portland," Peyton answers.

The heading appears: "Portland, Oregon May 2018" with the explanation: "The Portland men's group invited the filmmakers to visit their weekly meeting." The main speakers in the circle are African American. Larry Anderson is the leader. "We're talking David, the greatest man of war," he says, with emphasis. "Bathsheba, with a look, brings him down to his knees, where that no conquering army could defeat him, but he ran from his own family!" There is laughter and scattered applause as two of the African American men in the circle do a fist bump. Viewers then learn that "the group agreed to be filmed under one condition. That Moss participate." Moss speaks, "What really struck me about, what really struck me about meeting some members of this group at the National Prayer Breakfast … pause … You stood out to me in your honest questions and, and you know, your honest conversation drew me in." Anderson says, "I think we existed for so long, it is because we don't expose ourselves to media." Anderson continues "They think that's all that this is about." He continues to describe how "they" see the group:

You know, fools down there. Black dudes hollering at the white dudes. The white dudes trying to justify themselves to the Black dudes. That's what they think, that's what's going on. And of course if you come here initially and see one of those, that is what's happening. But underneath that is a powerful work that God is doing, that's actually changing men's lives.

Anderson continues, talking at Moss: "What I would ask you. Something to think about while you're sitting here." "What are the lies that you have been telling yourself?"

Two white men sitting next to him are smirking. Anderson continues "Which one of those lies have you come to believe"? Moss responds, slowly, respectfully, but also with visible caution. "Well, I can tell you one big lie is recognizing that I can't hide behind the camera." A white man in the group speaks. He is the only white man in the group who speaks during the segment, though half are white. The man looks like he's in his early seventies, and he is holding his chin, looking earnestly, pointedly, with eyebrows furrowed. He looks at Moss and says point blank "So why is your crew all white." He says this with clear aimed, rhetorically sharp judgment and looks across at the cameramen behind Jesse Moss. Moss answers, "Yeah that's a great question." The older white man says again "Why is it?" Moss says cautiously, "yeah well I think I think that because we are, we're not doing enough to make sure that there's diverse representation in our industry." "And," he continues, "and I think that leadership has to start from the top doesn't it; there's more to it than that I mean I can say that it's it's both structural and personal."

The white man pursues with a satisfied look. "The answer is it's personal and it's you who pick the guys who are here?" His sentence is a declaration. Moss then says "that's right. I picked some of them." Anderson is shown then smiling, participating in the "gotcha" on camera. While Moss continues "I, you know, I'll say, you know, we try. We hire women. There's a, you know, it's a male dominated industry, documentary less so than other aspects of filmmaking." The white man speaks again, with a continued sense of satisfaction, "So I didn't ask you about women.I asked you about Black people." Anderson takes up the inquisition of Moss. "So you see how you struggled? See how hard of a struggle it was to answer that question?" "But you see how you struggled to answer the question?" Moss answers, "yeah." Anderson replies, "Because we see that. We see the results. All the time, this is what we deal with. All the time here in this group. THIS [he says with emphasis] is how you get stripped down in this group."

Anderson then links his Portland cell of the Family back to Doug Coe. "We're connected to Washington DC because one of the founders, Coe, is from Salem, Oregon. Doug Coe, when I first met him, asked me if I was the next revolutionary," Anderson states. "And so he opened the door and allowed people unlike himself, people very different than himself in all manners."

> It's a change of heart and a renunciation on a daily basis. You can't just repent and then run off and never have to deal with it again. A repentance is an indication that you have changed, so when you are confronted by the circumstances you have to renounce how you behaved previously. Repentance is as you renounce the old nature daily.

The camera shifts and Anderson talks straight to Moss. "You really wanna know what's going on?" Although off camera, apparently Moss has indicated that, yes, he wants to know "what is going on." "You should let me show you how you can talk to the right dude." "That's gonna require a little knee work." Anderson gestures to the ground. "Get on your knees."

Anderson prays over the group and names the presence of the guests with the cameras: "Bless these that have come to visit us today be with them in a real way. Make yourself known to them in a way that shows love and kindness favor." After the prayer and hugs, Anderson says to Moss and, by extension, the other filmmakers, "Live the experience, the whole experience, not part of the experience, the whole experience." Moss asks "How should I do that?" Andersen replies, "Surrender. Surrender. You know how you surrender? Ask God to DEFEAT you." Anderson clearly emphasizes the word DEFEAT. "And we'll pray and be in agreement about that. We say 'God we hear Jesse's prayer, and we want you to absolutely totally defeat him. Bring him to his knees. Create a desperation for him that only you can meet.'"

The young people who created the "Worship Song Song" revealed this formula. Abby Gilbert sings "I'm a rich blonde female, singing about how I fail, things are bad again, I am struggling, I'm a total mess, my life's a train wreck, I'm pure garbage [pause] I need him again!"

No Hero

Students in my Divinity courses have sought heroes. Some men and women who have trusted me with their words will want a story of heroism. I understand. I do too. Here is a story.

 Ira Jackson said at the beginning of *The Corporation* "Okay guys, enough bullshit." Ray Anderson, the CEO of Interface Inc., is featured also on *The Corporation* talking about what he had turned away from, and what he then called people toward.

> For 21 years I never gave a thought to what we were taking from the earth or doing to the earth in the making of our products. And then, in the summer of 1994, we began to hear questions from our customers we've never heard before: What's your company doing for the environment? And we didn't have answers. The real answer was not very much. And it really disturbed many of our people. Not me so much as them … I didn't have an environmental vision … And at that sort of propitious moment this book landed on my desk. It was Paul Hawken's [1993] book *The Ecology of Commerce* … fairly quickly into that book I found the phrase "The Death of Birth" … and it was a point of a spear into my chest … and it became an epiphanal experience—a total change of mindset for myself, and a change of paradigm … One day early in this journey it dawned on me that the way I'd been running Interface is the way of the plunderer. Plundering something that's not mine. Something that belongs to every creature on earth. And I said to myself, my goodness, the day must come when this is illegal. When plundering is not allowed. I mean, it must come. So I said to myself my goodness, someday people like me will end up in jail.

Ray Anderson explains that he came to "visualize an organization of people committed to a purpose, and the purpose is doing no harm, I see a company that has severed the umbilical cord to earth for its raw materials. Taking raw materials that have already been extracted and using them over and over again, driving that process with renewable energy." He describes the plan as "to climb Mount Sustainability, that mountain that's higher than Everest, infinitely higher than Everest, far more difficult to scale, that point at the top, symbolizing 0 footprint." The documentary shows scenes of Ray Anderson talking with other heads of corporations about his "epiphany." The effect of the visuals and witness in the film is an epiphanic summons to what can be, when focused on the cluster of words and associations connoted with "leadership," "virtue," and "business."[92]

Ray Anderson had an epiphany, imploring his fellow "marketplace" colleagues to note that people heading up giant corporations are one small and yet catastrophically destructive part of the Earth. What if the task is to *not* change the world?

Conclusion

"The 4/14 Window"

One inheritor of Charlie Chaplin's Tramp is Paul Ruben's Pee-wee Herman, a character set to counter the austerity politics of the 1980s. In her tribute to Ruben, "Pee-wee & Nadia's Playhouse" for *Autre Magazine*, Nadia Lee Cohen writes that Ruben's character "is equally iconic and archetypal as Charlie Chaplin's Tramp." She continues, "both characters are rife with hilarious contradictions … the Tramp was a silent and prophetic emblem of the forthcoming economic devastation of two global wars," whereas "Pee-wee may as well have been a louder-than-bombs manifestation of the late-capitalistic dreamscape of the 1980s." "Playhouse, which aired on CBS and saw an average of ten million viewers per episode, was a fantasy of talking furniture in a supersaturated world that harkened back to 1950s diners and primetime dance competitions, a satirization of Post-War Americana as a frenzied pastiche," Cohen writes.[1] The show ran for only four years. Children were regularly fed instead a version of modernity serviceable for orderly work. They were told to be useful engines.

Wilbert Vere Awdry (1911–1997) was, like Chaplin, British. His cinematic legacy of work remains sufficiently tethered to Americana in the U.S. that Mattel has an entire line of toys and a dedicated webpage to characters and storylines he created, "Thomas & Friends Collection."[2] The original British television show ran from 1984 to 2021, spanning two generations. Shauna Wilton researched the series as a scholar of political science, reminding skeptical colleagues that children's television is a serious business. "Thomas"

Wilton explains, was created by a clergyman "in the 1940s for his son in an attempt to entertain, teach simple moral lessons, and romanticize a way of life." The world became "a global phenomenon that has made its way into the lives of millions of children around the world."[3] Wilton summarizes her detailed analysis after watching dozens of episodes. "The importance of teamwork and a good work ethic is constantly repeated during the series. In total, 12 episodes mention the importance of working together and 15 episodes mention the importance of being a useful engine … " and "the greatest praise that Sir Topham Hatt can give the engines is to say that they are 'very useful.'" "On Sodor, the engines and other mechanical characters never grow up. They are forever children, powerless and dependent on Sir Topham Hatt's good will. They do not have the possibility of attaining full citizenship, but children do; therefore, they need different lessons to prepare them for the roles and responsibilities of full citizenship," Wilton continues, "The engines have no say over their collective or individual futures; they have little (if any) free will. Like the children watching them, they are powerless in the face of a greater authority that sets the rules, rewards good behaviour, and punishes those that deviate." The series conveys a message "for the young citizens-in-the-making in the audience … to follow the rules, do a good job, not complain, and hope for future rewards. What is missing, in my opinion, from this vision of citizenship is the ability to be critical, to question authority, and to participate as equals in the building of the community."

Sodor does something quite different than Chaplin's revivification of souls, which gave working people the chance to kick the authority in the butt and the chance to wipe their own butts without interference from their boss. In Sodor, the "souls" of characters, with whom children are supposed to identify, have no legs to kick, no butts to wipe. They are disembodied machines.

The Dobbs v. Jackson abortion decision decided June 24, 2022, was bracketed by two decisions on religion and public education. In Carson v. Makin, the court prohibited a state from choosing *not* to finance religious schools. Justice Sotomayor noted: "Today, the Court leads us to a place where separation of church and state becomes a constitutional violation." In Kennedy v. Bremerton, the majority of the Court went in from the other door, ruling that school officials are, in Sotomayor's words, "required to allow one of its employees to incorporate a public, communicative display of the employee's personal religious beliefs into a school event." She continues, "Government neutrality toward religion is particularly important in the public-school context given the role public schools play in our society."[4] On either side of the ruling that overturned precedent on reproductive choice were two rulings that undermine the basic role public schools play in the U.S. The Supreme Court decisions in June 2022 were decades in the making.

The list of briefs in *Carson v. Makin* and *Kennedy v. Bremerton* records the investment of foundations committed to the privatization of public goods in the name of religion and the use of public funding for religious endeavors.

I arrived in Durham during the heyday of "Charitable Choice." George H. W. Bush used the literary conceit of "1,000 points of light" to provide an image of faith-based organizations across the U.S. helping their neighbors in need. For eight years, the Reagan Administration had defunded the most basic of social goods, including many that serve children. For decades following, under the guise of "Compassionate Conservatism," people in religious communities were asked to serve their neighbors with charity. Through food banks, after-school programs, before-school programs, tutoring during school programs, shelters for people without homes, interview-suitable dresses for women newly released from prison, volunteers with national and regional organizations tried to offer local light into the void. African American, white, and Asian clergy have called on volunteers in Christian congregations across the country to fill in where trained and capable service-sector professionals have been defunded out of their own vocations.

This was bolstered by funding for theological education across private and public universities. The same donors funding shenanigans like *Doing Virtuous Business* at Yale have helped to make private funding for public goods seem normal, even preferable. I was part of a "Project on Lived Theology" through the University of Virginia to assess different faith-based models for community engagement. Duke Divinity School steadily received Lilly funding to link the words "thriving," "faith," and "community." Yale Divinity School received decades of funding for various "Faith and Culture" initiatives. The Templeton Foundation has funded efforts across universities to promote the notion that religiosity itself leads to public health. Too often, these programs have burnished a reactionary argument against government regulation and public funding.

In 2023, the American Federation of Teachers ran a press release: "In an address to the National Press Club, the leader of the 1.7 million-member union urged civil society to fight for the future of public schools and help kids learn in the face of relentless attacks from the far-right intent on dismantling the schools that 90 percent of kids attend." Randi Weingarten diagnosed an escalation: "Attacks on public education are not new. The difference today is that the attacks are intended to destroy it." What she named in 2023 is part of a long and strategically thoughtful pooling of resources and networks to undermine truly integrated, well-funded public schools across the U.S. Why? One answer is "the 4/14 window."

In his foreword to *The 4/14 Window: Raising Up a New Generation to Transform the World*, Wess Stafford wrote about the importance of mobilizing children. "Every major movement in history has grasped the need to target the next generation in order to advance its agenda and secure its legacy into the future," Stafford writes. "Political movements (like Nazism and Communism) trained legions of children with the goal of carrying their agenda beyond the lifetimes of their founders," he tells readers, noting "even the Taliban places great emphasis on recruiting children."[5] Luis Bush is the author of *The 4/14 Window*. Previously, Bush had instructed evangelicals to focus on "the 10/40 window," indicating by latitude an area of the globe "where the gospel is least present." The 4/14 window is a target for training children. This involves the dismantling of public schools in favor of Christian ones, and the demolition of the barrier between church and state for remaining public schools.

James Davison Hunter used the term "Culture Wars" as both a diagnostic and prescription, elevated to common sense through repetition and funding. The Cato Institute insisted the following in the 2022 Carson v. Makin case: "Indeed, secularism in public schools has become akin to a state-established religion: the secular values that the state promotes conflict with deeply and sincerely held religious beliefs, so classroom conflicts often arise." The brief claimed that "Maine unjustly alienates religious individuals, treating them as second-class citizens in the context of school tuitioning for merely living as their faith demands."[6] They repeat note for note Hunter's argument in *The Death of Character: Moral Education in an Age Without Good or Evil* (2000). For journalists trying to understand religion and politics, Hunter offered the metaphor of embattlement. He borrowed the term from "the German *kulturkampf* of the last decades of the nineteenth century," a term, he explains, used in Germany regarding "the religious content and character of public education."[7] Public education in the U.S. became impossible, the argument goes, because the U.S. lost its character sometime around the late 1960s.

In her forthcoming book, Bethany Moreton describes Hunter's influence, "Hunter's *Culture Wars* explanation was that it deflected attention from the content of contemporary demands for change—that is, from the liberationist claims of the Black freedom, decolonial, and feminist mobilizations—and instead defined the essence of the disagreement as attitudes to change itself." Moreton explains he cast "those guided by the spirit of the age, those who accommodated the circumstances of the moment" as standing on "mere shifting sand, while tradition—the claims of white Christian patriarchy— were solid rock on which to stand."[8] Ronit Y. Stahl, writing for *Religion and Politics* in 2022, explained that the two cases bracketing Dobbs indicate "white evangelicals want both religious schools funded by the state and religion in public schools—and the Supreme Court's (Catholic) majority is eager to assist." "The goal is religion-state consolidation," Stahl writes, "the result of decades of attacks on the Establishment Clause in the service of white conservative Christian power."[9] By 2000, Hunter headed up the well-funded Institute for Advanced Studies in Culture, and he was even less subtle about the division. His *The Death of Character* was reviewed and discussed from Harvard to Stanford. Character itself had been killed, and what 2000 had ushered in was an era without good or evil.

Critical to the long game of the "4/14 Window" is an ideology that understands children as weaponry. Babies are future combatants in a struggle spanning generations. Every Christian pregnancy is a potential combatant in the protracted struggle for truth, goodness, and beauty—the fight for Western civilization. By this account, the meaning of an individual human life is set within a larger, collective effort. A pivotal scene in the 2015 film *Spotlight* illumines this mindset. Mitchell Garabedian is the lawyer representing victims of sexual violence, and he explains to muckraking journalist Michael Rezendes: "The Church thinks in centuries, Mr Rezendes." "Do you think your paper has the resources to take that on?"[10] The Church thinks in centuries. An outré form of this mindset is the Quiverfull Movement, which provided a scintillating side show on cable television. They exemplify Christian co-belligerence. Evangelical Christians may disagree with Pentecostal Christians may disagree with Roman Catholics may disagree with Fundamentalists … but when it comes to beating secularism (feminism, socialism, trade unionism) they are in this together for the long ("the Church thinks in centuries") haul. I aver that a long centuries view of children, or elders, or pastors, or any of the rest of "us" is grim. Each one of "us," deserves a life shorn of "deference." We deserve a different "Modern Times."

Also, my mother's legacy matters. Groups of young people learning together across every economic, ethnic, racial, and gender divide are as much of my heritage as my belief in Jesus. My granddaughter deserves the deal that the "radical dominionist billionaires seeking to destroy public education" (as Glenn Rogers calls them) have, out of their fear and greed, stolen. My granddaughter deserves this not because she is a potentially useful tool in anyone's project. She need not "Change the World." She need not become the face of any cause. She deserves well-funded public education as a human being. I end this book with the memory of my mother's decades teaching teenagers across West Texas, and in tenacious anticipation for my granddaughter's first year of fully funded pre-K.

Notes

Acknowledgments

1   "History of OED," Oxford English Dictionary, 2024, https://www.oed.com/ information/about-the-oed/history-of-the-oed/.

2   Randall Herbert Balmer, *Mine Eyes Have Seen the Glory: A Journey into the Evangelical Subculture in America* (New York, NY: Oxford University Press, 2014), 5, 7–8.

Introduction

1   The Saturday Review of Politics, Literature, Science, and Art, "Two Years Ago," review of *Two Years Ago*, by Charles Kingsley, *Saturday Review*, February 21, 1857, 176–177.

2   *Oxford English Dictionary*, s.v. "muscular *(adj.)*, sense 4," March 2024.

3   *Oxford English Dictionary*, s.v. "pulpit *(n.)*, sense 2.a," March 2024.

4   *Oxford English Dictionary*, s.v. "bully pulpit *(n.)*," September 2023. Quoted from Lyman Abbott, "A Review of President Roosevelt's Administration IV—Its Influence on Patriotism and Public Service," *Outlook 1893-1924*, February 27, 1909, 430, paragraph 1.

5   Daniel Silliman, "An Evangelical Is Anyone Who Likes Billy Graham: Defining Evangelicalism with Carl Henry and Networks of Trust," *Church History* 90, no. 3 (December 17, 2021): 622.

6   John Dart, "Billy Graham Recalls Help From Hearst," *Los Angeles Times*, June 7, 1997, paragraphs 1, 2, https://www.latimes.com/archives/la-xpm-1997-06-07-me-1034-story.html.

7   *Billy Graham and the Age of Anxiety* by Elliot Berger, Ph.D. dissertation, Rice University, 2017.

8   "Obama's Pastor: God Damn America, U.S. to Blame for 9/11," *ABC News*, March 13, 2008, paragraphs 5, 8, https://abcnews.go.com/Blotter/story?id=4443788.

9   Laurie Goodstein, "Falwell: Blame Abortionists, Feminists and Gays," *The Guardian*, September 19, 2001, paragraphs 10–13, https://www.theguardian.com/world/2001/sep/19/september11.usa9.

10 *Oxford English Dictionary*, s.v. "secularize *(v.)*, sense 3," December 2023.

11 See also the *New York Times* coverage of the service, held September 14 in "Bush Leads Memorial Service for Victims of Terror Attack: The Memorial," *New York Times*, September 14, 2001, https://www.nytimes.com/2001/09/14/national/bush-leads-memorial-service-for-victims-of-terror-attack.html?searchResultPosition=1.

12 Mary Frances Schjonbserg, "Trump Inaugural Events End in Prayer at National Cathedral," *Episcopal News Service*, January 21, 2017, https://episcopalnewsservice.org/2017/01/21/trump-inaugural-events-end-in-prayer-at-national-cathedral/.

13 "Inside Donald Trump's Relationship with Rev. Billy Graham," *ABC News*, March 2, 2018, paragraph 4, https://abcnews.go.com/Politics/inside-donald-trumps-relationship-rev-billy-graham/story?id=53448191.

14 Silliman, "An Evangelical Is Anyone Who Likes Billy Graham," 622.

15 Silliman, "An Evangelical Is Anyone Who Likes Billy Graham," 627–628.

16 Lamuel Nelson Bell to John Howard Pew, November 2, 1965, box 231, folder C, J. Howard Pew Personal Papers, Hagley Library and Museum. As referenced in Darren E. Grem, "*Christianity Today*, J. Howard Pew, and the Business of Conservative Evangelicalism," *Enterprise & Society* 15, no. 2 (June 2014): 337.

17 John Kreiser, "Bush: The Decider-In-Chief," *CBS News*, April 20, 2006, https://www.cbsnews.com/news/bush-the-decider-in-chief/.

18 Dan Wakefield, "Slick-Paper Christianity," *The Nation* 184, no. 3 (January 19, 1957): 56–57.

19 Alexander McConnell, William R. Moody, and Arthur Percy Fitt (Editors), "What Can We Do?," *Record of Christian Work*, October 1885, 1, paragraph 3.

20 "What Can We Do?" *Record of Christian Work*, 1, paragraph 4.

21 Timothy E. W. Gloege, "The Name You Can Trust," in *Guaranteed Pure: The Moody Bible Institute, Business, and the Making of Modern Evangelicalism* (Chapel Hill, NC: University of North Carolina Press, 2015), 219. Along the bottom of the poster the text reads "The Moody Bible Institute of Chicago Bulletin is published monthly by the Moody Bible Institute, at 153 Institute Pl., Chicago, IL." This particular version of the poster is the May issue, 1920, volume 6, number 5. Thank you to Corie Zylstra at the Crowell Library and Archives.

22 *Oxford English Dictionary*, s.v. "melting pot *(n.)*, s. 3.b," July 2023.

23 "The Melting Pot," Finborough Theatre, accessed June 26, 2024, https://finboroughtheatre.co.uk/production/the-melting-pot/?archive=2017.

24 Guy Szuberla, "Zangwill's The Melting Pot Play Chicago," *MELUS* 20, no. 11 (Autumn 1995): 3.

25 *The Moody Bible Institute of Chicago Bulletin* (Chicago, IL), May 1920 6, no. 5.

26 Carroll Van West, *Capitalism on the Frontier: Billings and the Yellowstone Valley in the Nineteenth Century* (Lincoln, Nebraska: University of Nebraska Press, 1993), 200. Jennings quoted in W. Thomas White, "Boycott: The Pullman Strike in Montana," *Montana* 29 (October 1979): 4–5. *Billings Gazette* (Montana), July 7, 1894, 5 and *Billings Daily Times*, July 7, 1894.

27 James R. Barrett, "Unionization," in *Encyclopedia of Chicago*, 2005, http://www.encyclopedia.chicagohistory.org/pages/1284.html. James R. Barrett includes the accompanying Bibliography: Derber, Milton. *Labor in Illinois: The Affluent Years, 1945–80.* 1989; Newell, Barbara. *Chicago and the Labor Movement: Metropolitan Unionism in the 1930s.* 1961; Schneirov, Richard. *Labor and Urban Politics: Class Conflict and the Origins of Modern Liberalism in Chicago, 1864–1897.* 1998.

28 Darren Dochuk, *Anointed with Oil: How Christianity and Crude Made Modern America* (New York, NY: Basic Books, Hachette Book Group, 2019), 353.

29 Liston Pope, *Millhands & Preachers: A Study of Gastonia* (New Haven, CT: Yale University Press, 1942), xi, https://archive.org/details/millhandspreache00pope_0/page/n5/mode/2up.

30 Pope, *Millhands & Preachers*, 71.

31 Patrick Huber, "Mill Mother's Lament: Ella May Wiggins and the Gastonia Textile Strike of 1929," *Southern Cultures* 15, no. 3 (Fall 2009): 81.

32 See for one example: Chuck McShane, "The Loray Mill Strike in Gastonia: Demands for Higher Pay and a 40-Hour Workweek Ignite a Furor in Gastonia in 1929," *Our State*, January 29, 2014, https://www.ourstate.com/loray-mill-strike/.

33 Huber offers multiple examples of coverage by pro-mill, mainstream periodicals from that time, and even a simple online search for the terms "communist" and "Gastonia" or "Loray Mill Strike" shows the linking of these two terms in the telling of the story.

34 Pope, *Millhands & Preachers*, 293.

35 Pope, *Millhands & Preachers*, 198.

36 Pope, *Millhands & Preachers*, 177.

37 *New Georgia Encyclopedia*, s.v. "Killers of the Dream," by John C. Inscoe, last modified March 20, 2021, https://www.georgiaencyclopedia.org/articles/arts-culture/killers-of-the-dream/.

38   "Killers of the Dream," paragraph 6.

39   Susan Faludi, *The Terror Dream: Myth and Misogyny in an Insecure America* (New York, NY: Picador USA, 2008), 5, https://www.powells.com/book/the-terror-dream-9780312428006.

40   Daniel Howard Cerone, "Full House Not Enough for ABC Pot," *Los Angeles Times*, May 23, 1995, https://www.latimes.com/archives/la-xpm-1995-05-23-ca-4995-story.html.

Chapter 1

1   Richard Slotkin, *Gunfighter Nation: The Myth of the Frontier in Twentieth Century America* (Norman, Oklahoma: University of Oklahoma Press, 1998), 175.

2   *The Muppet Christmas Carol*, Jerry Juhl and Charles Dickens (1992; Disney).

3   Victoria Lamont, *Westerns: A Women's History* (Lincoln, NE: University of Nebraska Press, 2016), 11–12.

4   *Oxford English Dictionary*, s.v. "Social Darwinism *(n.)*," March 2024.

5   For an account of the sermon contests, see Christine Rosen, "Fervent Charity," *Preaching Eugenics: Religious Leaders and the American Eugenics Movement* (New York, NY: Oxford University Press, Incorporated, 2004), 42.

6   Dwight Garner, "Cormac McCarthy, Novelist of a Darker America, Is Dead at 89," *The New York Times*, June 13, 2023, headline caption and correction statement, https://www.nytimes.com/2023/06/13/books/cormac-mccarthy-dead.html.

7   Greg Grandin, "Cormac McCarthy's Unforgiving Parables of American Empire," *The Nation*, June 21, 2023, closing paragraph, https://www.thenation.com/article/culture/cormac-mccarthy-obit-melville/.

8   *Oxford English Dictionary*, s.v. "gospel *(n.)*, s. 1.a," December 2023.

9   Jim Harrison, "Geopiety," in *West of 98: Living and Writing the New American West*, eds. Lynn Stegner and Russell Rowland (Austin, TX: University of Texas Press, 2011), 71.

10   "Values of Home," (1922), SWHP0092, Social Welfare History Archives, Youth and Life, University of Minnesota Libraries, Online Exhibits, description, https://gallery.lib.umn.edu/exhibits/show/youth_and_life/item/35.

11   "What Kind of Children?," (1922), SWHP0071, Social Welfare History Archives, Youth and Life, University of Minnesota Libraries, Online Exhibits, https://gallery.lib.umn.edu/exhibits/show/youth_and_life/item/56.

12 "The Spirited Horse and the Sex Impulse," (1922), SWHP0021, Social Welfare History Archives, Keeping Fit, University of Minnesota Libraries, Online Exhibits, https://gallery.lib.umn.edu/exhibits/show/swha_keeping_fit/item/257.

13 Sarah Handley-Cousins and Elizabeth Garner Masarik, "National Parks in America: Health Manhood, and Wilderness," May 16, 2018, in *Dig: A History Podcast*, podcast, 51:25, https://digpodcast.org/2018/05/06/national-parks-america-manhood/.

14 *Oxford English Dictionary*, s.v. "Neurasthenia *(n.)*," July 2023.

15 Barbara Will, "The Nervous Origins of the American Western," *American Literature* 70, no. 2 (June 1998): 294.

16 Will, "The Nervous Origins of the American Western," 296.

17 Will, "The Nervous Origins of the American Western," 301.

18 Will, "The Nervous Origins of the American Western," 309.

19 Edward G. White, *The Eastern Establishment and the Western Experience: The West of Frederic Remington, Theodore Roosevelt, and Owen Wister* (New Haven, CT: Yale University Press, 1968).

20 White, *The Eastern Establishment and the Western Experience*, 7.

21 "Theodore Roosevelt," (1922), SWHP0047, Keeping Fit, Social Welfare History Archives, University of Minnesota Libraries, Online Exhibits, https://gallery.lib.umn.edu/exhibits/show/swha_keeping_fit/item/237.

22 "Roosevelt Timeline," American Museum of Natural History, accessed September 16, 2024, introduction, https://www.amnh.org/exhibitions/permanent/theodore-roosevelt-memorial/hall/roosevelt-timeline.

23 Rachel F. Seidman, "This Little House of Mine," *Common Place the Journal of Early American Life*, no. 3.3 (2003), part I, paragraph 5, https://commonplace.online/article/little-house-mine/.

24 Stephanie Coontz, *The Way We Never Were: American Families and the Nostalgia Trap* (New York, NY: Basic Books, 1992), 73, https://archive.org/details/wayweneverweream00coon/page/72/mode/2up.

25 Kat Eschner, "The Little House on the Prairie Was Built on Native American Land," *The Smithsonian Magazine*, February 8, 2017, paragraphs 2, 6, https://www.smithsonianmag.com/smart-news/little-house-prairie-was-built-native-american-land-180962020/.

26 Lawrence Goodwyn, *The Populist Moment: A Short History of the Agrarian Revolt in America* (New York, NY: Oxford University Press, 1978), xxiii-xxiv.

27 Charles Kingsley, *Westward Ho! Or The Voyages and Adventures of Sir Amyas Leigh, Knight of Burrough, in the County of Devon, in the Reign of Her Most Glorious Majesty, Queen Elizabeth, Rendered into Modern English* (Germany: Leipzig B.

Tauchnitz, 1855), 1, https://archive.org/details/westwardhoorvoya02kinguoft/page/n5/mode/2up.

28   Erik Eckholm, "Boy Scouts End Longtime Ban on Openly Gay Youths," *New York Times*, May 23, 2013, https://www.nytimes.com/2013/05/24/us/boy-scouts-to-admit-openly-gay-youths-as-members.html.

29   Anthony Esolen, "A Boy's Life with Unisex Scouts," *Public Discourse*, April 23, 2013, https://www.thepublicdiscourse.com/2013/04/9970/.

30   Esolen, "A Boy's Life with Unisex Scouts," closing paragraph.

31   Max Blumenthal, "Princeton Tilts Right," *The Nation*, February 23, 2006, paragraph 15, https://www.thenation.com/article/archive/princeton-tilts-right/.

32   Deborah Yaffe, "A Conservative Think Tank with Many Princeton Ties," *Princeton Alumni Weekly*, 2008, paragraph 16, https://www.princeton.edu/~paw/web_exclusives/plus/plus_071608witherspoon.html.

33   Charles Darwin, *On the Origin of Species by Means of Natural Selection* (London: Watts, 1903), 174.

34   Charles Kingsley, The Water-Babies: Fairy Tale for a Land-Baby (London: Macmillan, 1863). In public domain.

35   Kingsley, *The Water-Babies*, 80.

36   Kingsley, *The Water-Babies*, 70.

37   Kingsley, *The Water-Babies*, 69.

38   Kingsley, *The Water-Babies*, 28.

39   Kingsley, *The Water-Babies*, 308.

40   Kingsley, *The Water-Babies*, 309–310.

41   Larry Uffelman, *Charles Kingsley* (Boston, MA: Twayne Publishers, 1979), 70–71.

42   Kingsley, *The Water-Babies*, 80.

43   David Millward, "Well-Preserved Golly Retired After 91 Years," *The Telegraph* (U.K), August 23, 2001, https://www.telegraph.co.uk/news/uknews/1338229/Well-preserved-Golly-retires-after-91-years.html.

44   Kingsley, *The Water-Babies*, 55.

45   Kingsley, *The Water-Babies*, 222.

46   Kingsley, *The Water-Babies*, 221.

47   Kingsley, *The Water-Babies*, 217–222.

48   Kingsley, *The Water-Babies*, 222.

49 "Mr. Kinsgley's Water-Babies," *The London Times*, January 26, 1864, 6, column 2, paragraph 5.

50 Kingsley, Charles, "The Natural Theology of the Future," *Macmillan's Magazine*, 1871, 23:137, 526.

51 Kingsley, "The Natural Theology of the Future," 373.

52 Kingsley, "The Natural Theology of the Future," 373.

53 Kingsley, "The Natural Theology of the Future," 374.

54 Kingsley, "The Natural Theology of the Future," 378.

55 Peter Bradshaw, "*Winter's Bone* Review: Twisted Monument to Poverty, Catastrophe and Despair," *The Guardian*, September 16, 2010, https://www.theguardian.com/film/2010/sep/16/winters-bone-review.

56 *Oxford English Dictionary*, s.v. "white trash *(n., adj.)*," accessed March 2024.

57 Theodore Roosevelt, "The Strenuous Life" (speech, April 10, 1899), Voices of Democracy, https://voicesofdemocracy.umd.edu/roosevelt-strenuous-life-1899-speech-text/.

58 Kevin D. Williamson, "Chaos in the Family, Chaos in the State: The White Working Class's Dysfunction," *National Review*, March 28, 2016, https://www.nationalreview.com/2016/03/donald-trump-white-working-class-dysfunction-real-opportunity-needed-not-trump/.

59 https://theweek.com/articles/603701/how-conservative-elites-disdain-workingclass-republicans.

60 Kevin D. Williamson, "Chaos in the Family, Chaos in the State: The White Working Class's Dysfunction," *National Review*, March 28, 2016, paragraphs 4, 1, 2, 15, 18, 23, https://www.nationalreview.com/2016/03/donald-trump-white-working-class-dysfunction-real-opportunity-needed-not-trump/.

61 Jamelle Bouie, "Poor Whites Trashed," *Slate*, March 30, 2016, paragraphs 2, 14, https://slate.com/news-and-politics/2016/03/why-conservatives-are-talking-about-poor-white-people-the-way-they-usually-talk-about-black-people.html.

62 "2012 Jefferson Lecture with Wendell Berry," National Endowment for the Humanities, April 15, 2012, paragraph 3, https://www.neh.gov/news/2012-jefferson-lecture-wendell-berry.

63 David Skinner, "Wendell E. Berry Jefferson Lecture," Lecture Text, *The Magazine of the National Endowment for the Humanities*, May/June 2012, paragraph 21, https://www.neh.gov/about/awards/jefferson-lecture/wendell-e-berry-biography.

64 Goodwyn, *The Populist Moment*, xiii.

65 "The Rise and Fall of Mars Hill," *Christianity Today*, accessed August 19, 2024, description, https://www.christianitytoday.com/ct/podcasts/rise-and-fall-of-mars-hill/.

66 Mark Oppenheimer, "A Muckraking Magazine Creates a Stir Among Evangelical Christians," *New York Times* (New York, NY), November 8, 2014, A.19, paragraphs 1, 3.

67 Goodwyn, *The Populist Moment*, x.

68 Timothy E. W. Gloege, *Guaranteed Pure: The Moody Bible Institute, Business, and the Making of Modern Evangelicalism* (Chapel Hill, NC: University of Chapel Hill Press, 2015), 41.

69 Elesha Coffman, "A Long Ride on the Mainline: 100 Years of the Christian Century," *Christianity Today*, November/December 2008, paragraphs 2, 3, https://www.booksandculture.com/articles/2008/novdec/12.20.html.

70 The Age Discrimination in Employment Act of 1967, volume 29 United States Code 621 (1967), https://www.eeoc.gov/statutes/age-discrimination-employment-act-1967.

71 Barbara Wheeler, "Fit for Ministry?," *The Christian Century*, April 11, 2001, 16–18, 22–23.

Chapter 2

1 Paul Gauntt, "History of Cowboy Church Movement," *Waxahachie Daily Light*, Saturday, April 25, 2009, hdl.handle.net/10079/3807c9ab-d8ab-4b96-b26a-142ed47eade7.

2 "Western Heritage," *Texas Baptists*, accessed August 19, 2024, description, https://www.texasbaptists.org/ministries/western-heritage. "Western Heritage Ministries exists to connect with cowboy churches and partner with Texas Baptists Cowboy Churches to encourage, inform and help them reach their ministry goals. We also assist churches in planting new cowboy churches."

3 Victoria Lamont, *Westerns: A Women's History* (Lincoln, NE: University of Nebraska Press, 2016), 5.

4 Annie Proulx, Larry McMurtry, and Diana Ossana, *Brokeback Mountain: Story to Screenplay* (New York, NY: Scribner, 2005), 29, 94.

5 Proulx, McMurtry, and Ossana, *Brokeback Mountain: Story to Screenplay*, 22.

6 Anne Proulx, "Brokeback Mountain: Cowboys and Horses and Long, Lonely Nights in the Wilderness," *The New Yorker*, October 13, 1997, 85.

7 Proulx, McMurtry, and Ossana, *Brokeback Mountain: Story to Screenplay*, 28.

8   Proulx, McMurtry, and Ossana, *Brokeback Mountain: Story to Screenplay*, 140.

9   John White, *Westerns* (New York, NY: Routledge, 2011), 153–158.

10 White, *Westerns*, 153–154.

11 Proulx, McMurtry, and Ossana, *Brokeback Mountain: Story to Screenplay*, 97.

12 Kathleen Schalch. "The Marlboro Man." *Morning Edition*, NPR, October 21, 2002, https://www.npr.org/2002/10/21/1152015/present-at-the-creation-the-marlboro-man.

13 Schalch, "The Marlboro Man," paragraphs 11–15.

14 For a Hollywood version of this, see: *Thank You for Smoking*, directed by Jason Reitman (2006; New York, NY: Fox Searchlight).

15 Paul H. Carlson, *Wool and Mohair Industry*, Handbook of Texas Online (Texas State Historical Association, 1996), paragraphs 7–8, https://www.tshaonline.org/handbook/entries/wool-and-mohair-industry.

16 John J. Miller, "He Created a New Kind of Western," *The Wall Street Journal*, November 24, 2009, paragraphs 15–16, https://www.wsj.com/articles/SB10001424052748704013004574517491968701418.

17 Elmer Kelton, *The Day the Cowboys Quit* (Fort Worth, TX: Texas Christian University Press, 1986), xi.

18 Robert E. Zeigler, *Cowboy Strike of 1883*, Handbook of Texas Online (Texas State Historical Association, 2020), paragraph 4, https://www.tshaonline.org/handbook/entries/cowboy-strike-of-1883.

19 U.S. Department of Interior, National Parks Service, *National Historical Landmark Nomination Haymarket Martyrs' Monument*, Robin Bachin. OMB no. 1024-0018, Chicago, IL, 1995 4, https://npgallery.nps.gov/NRHP/GetAsset/NHLS/97000343_text.

20 W. F. Strong, "The Historical Accuracy of 'Lonesome Dove,'" *Texas Standard*, August 3, 2023, paragraph 1, https://www.texasstandard.org/stories/lonesome-dove-larry-mcmurtry-historical-accuracy-texas-goodnight-loving-miniseries-call-gus/.

21 Larry McMurtry, *Lonesome Dove* (New York, NY: Simon and Schuster, 2000), 11. "What I suspect this means is that it's hard to go wrong if one writes at length about the Old West, still the phantom leg of the American psyche. I thought I had written about a harsh time and some pretty harsh people, but, to the public at large, I had produced something nearer to an idealization; instead of a poor-man's Inferno, filled with violence, faithlessness, and betrayal, I had actually delivered a kind of Gone With the Wind of the West, a turnabout I'll be mulling over for a long, long time."

22   "About the Intermountain Histories Projects and Team," Intermountain Histories, accessed August 22, 2024, https://www.intermountainhistories.org/about/.

23   Makato Hunter, "Confederate Markers in the Intermountain West," Intermountain Histories, accessed August 22, 2024, paragraph 1, https://www.intermountainhistories.org/tours/show/38.

24   David W. Blight, *Race and Reunion: The Civil War in American Memory* (Cambridge, MA: Harvard University Press, 2002), 99.

25   Blight, *Race and Reunion: The Civil War in American Memory*, 213.

26   "Author Event- *A Matter of Moral Justice: Black Women Laundry Workers & The Fight for Justice*," Illinois Labor History Society, Upcoming Events, May 16, 2022, http://www.illinoislaborhistory.org/upcoming-events.

27   Timothy B. Tyson, "Commemorating North Carolina's Anti-Confederate Heritage, Too," *The News & Observer*, August 17, 2017, paragraph 8, https://www.newsobserver.com/opinion/op-ed/article31123988.html.

28   Marilyn Stasio, "Broadway Review: Oklahoma!," *Variety*, April 7, 2019, paragraphs 1, 4, https://variety.com/2019/music/reviews/oklahoma-review-broadway-1203182746/.

29   Rob Weinert-Kendt, "How Rodgers and Hammerstein Transformed Broadway—and American Culture," *America the Jesuit Review*, June 11, 2018, paragraph 4, https://www.americamagazine.org/arts-culture/2018/06/11/how-rodgers-and-hammerstein-transformed-broadway-and-american-culture.

30   Gary West, "Are the Cowboys Still America's Team?: Are the Cowboys Still America's Team?—The Answer Is Yes. Other Teams May Try to Claim the Title, but There Is Only One America's Team," *Fort Worth Star-Telegram*, January 29, 2012, paragraphs 5, 6, 9.

31   "Malboro Font Download," thefontsmagazine.com, accessed August 24. 2024, https://thefontsmagazine.com/font/marlboro-font/.

32   "Leadership: Keith Burkhart," First Southern Baptist Church, accessed August 24, 2024, https://www.firstsouthern.tv/leadership/keith-burkhart.

33   For one effort in Canada to reach together across the divide of indigenous peoples and descendants of invaders, see "Indigenous Ministries: Standing Stones Sacred Gatherings," Anglican Diocese of Edmonton, accessed August 24, 2024, https://edmonton.anglican.ca/what-we-do/indigenous-ministries/pages/standing-stones-sacred-gatherings.

34   The presenter of this speech and person in front of the film has a current website listed as of 2024: "Host: Brad Clay," Final Descent Outdoors, accessed August 24, 2024, http://www.finaldescentoutdoors.com/host.

35   Chicksaw Cultural Center, accessed August 24, 2024, https://www.chickasawculturalcenter.com/.

36 "Explore Statues & Sculptures, They're Hunting—Owwatta," Chicksaw Cultural Center, accessed August 24, 2024, https://www.chickasawculturalcenter.com/explore/statues-sculptures/.

37 Lew Sterrett's ministry is online: Sermon on the Mount, accessed August 24, 2024, www.sermononthemount.org.

38 Annabeth Poe, "Christianity Plus Cattle: Cowboy Churches Are on the Rise," *Carolina Connection*, Chapel Hill, NC, January 13, 2020, https://carolinaconnection.org/2020/01/13/christianity-plus-cattle-cowboy-churches-on-the-rise.

39 Personal correspondence with Annabeth Poe and The Hussman School of Journalism and Media, "Hussman School of Journalism and Media Wins 2020 Hearst Awards, Five Students Advance to Individual Championships," June 3, 2020, https://www.unc.edu/posts/2020/06/03/hussman-school-of-journalism-and-media-wins-2020-hearst-awards-five-students-advance-to-individual-championships/.

40 Personal correspondence. 2014.

41 Southwestern Baptist Theological Seminary, accessed August 24, 2024, https://swbts.edu/.

42 *Oxford English Dictionary*, s.v. "catholic *(adj.)*, sense I.1.a.i," March 2024.

43 *Oxford English Dictionary*, s.v. "catholic *(adj.)*, sense II.7.a," March 2024.

44 Michael Barnes, "Indian Creek, Rowena and Ballinger: Discovering History Gems in Small West Texas Towns," *USA Today*, November 30, 2021, paragraphs 2, 3, https://www.usatoday.com/story/news/history/2021/11/30/indian-creek-rowena-and-ballinger-history-gems-small-texas-towns/8669849002/.

45 "Saint Joseph: Bulletin Archives," Discover Mass, accessed April 18, 2024, 6, https://bulletins.discovermass.com/download.php?bulletin=43fPSdNnqtvLp8pUsQW1OBiFftYaMHuDyjt8qVoT6pI8hvlokplQ07ghNrLf%2F5S%2B9xJE%2B75%2BtmohmN3hpMvHER9g%2Fciisc%2FMBqyyQPTyKcA%3D.

46 Christopher Hooks, "How the Texas House Could Become More Radical," *Texas Monthly* (Austin, TX), March 2024, paragraph 2.

47 Patrick Svitek, "Texas Republicans Who Defied Gov. Greg Abbott on School Vouchers Face Mounting Primary Attacks," *The Texas Tribune*, January 31, 2024, https://www.texastribune.org/2024/01/31/texas-house-republican-primary-2024-vouchers/.

48 Russell Gold, "A Deposed Texas Republican's Lament About Slander and Corruption," *Texas Monthly* (Austin, TX), March 14, 2024, https://www.texasmonthly.com/news-politics/texas-gop-primary-glenn-rogers/.

49 Dave Lieber, "Defeated Republican Calls Texas State Government the Most Corrupt Ever" *Dallas Morning News*, The (TX), March 14, 2024.

50   "Theaters: Grand Theater," Cinema Treasures, accessed August 24, 2024, https://cinematreasures.org/theaters/21435.

51   "Announcements," Palo Pinto Independent School District, accessed April 19, 2024, https://www.palopintoisd.net/.

52   Gold, "A Deposed Texas Republican's Lament."

53   *High Noon*, Carl Foreman (1952; United Artists).

54   Larry Gelten, "How 'Commie' Writer Turned 'High Noon' into Subversive Hollywood Hit," *New York Post*, final paragraph, https://nypost.com/2017/03/12/commie-writer-turned-high-noon-into-subversive-hollywood-hit/.

55   Glenn Frankel, *High Noon: The Holiday Blacklist and the Making of an American Classic* (New York, NY: Bloomsburg, 2017).

56   "The Billionaire Bully Who Wants to Turn Texas into a Christian Theocracy," *Texas Monthly*, March 2024. See also "Farris Wilks Forbes Profile," *Forbes*, August 25, 2024.

57   Margo Jefferson, Books of the Times; Digging Up a Tale of Terror Among the Osages: [Review], *New York Times*, August 31, 1994, C. 16, paragraph 6. The book she is reviewing is *The Deaths of Sybil Bolton: An American History* by Dennis McAuliffe Jr.

58   "Oklahoma: Oklahoma Lyrics," Rodgers and Hammerstein, accessed August 25, 2024, https://rodgersandhammerstein.com/song/oklahoma/oklahoma/.

59   Rob Weinert-Kendt, "How Rodgers and Hammerstein Transformed Broadway—and American Culture," *America Magazine: The Jesuit Review*, June 11, 2018, paragraph 2, https://www.americamagazine.org/arts-culture/2018/06/11/how-rodgers-and-hammerstein-transformed-broadway-and-american-culture. The book Weinert-Kendt reviews is Todd S. Purdum, *Something Wonderful: Rodgers and Hammerstein's Broadway Revolution* (New York, NY: Henry Holt, 2018). See also "80 Years of Rodgers & Hammerstein," Rogers & Hammerstein, 2024, https://rodgersandhammerstein.com/about/.

60   Darren Dochuk, *Anointed with Oil: How Christianity and Crude Made Modern America* (New York, NY: Basic Books, Hachette Book Group, 2019), 10–11.

61   Essay reprinted in Larry McMurtry, *In a Narrow Grave; Essays on Texas* (Austin, TX: Encino Press, 1968), 110–111.

62   "Home, The Farm & Family," Rhinory, accessed August 25, 2024, https://rhinory.com/.

63   Larry McMurtry, *Duane's Depressed* (New York, NY: Simon and Schuster, 1999), 174–175.

64   "2023 Scorecard on State Health System Performance," The Commonwealth Fund, last modified June 22, 2023, https://www.commonwealthfund.org/publications/scorecard/2023/jun/2023-scorecard-state-health-system-performance.

Chapter 3

1   "Jesus-Modeled Leadership," About Us, Resurgence, accessed September 20, 2024, http://www.thearda.com/Denoms/D_836.asp. Full quotation: "God exists in a perfect community; we call this the Trinity. The three persons of the Godhead are all equal in power, glory, and righteousness, yet each is distinct with different roles. The Son submits to the Father, and the Spirit does the work made possible by the sacrifice of the Son. God calls for this kind of community in church government and Christian households."

2   Scott Marshall, "A Change of Leadership at Acts 29 Network," *Outreach Magazine*, March 28, 2012, https://outreachmagazine.com/in-the-news/4663-acts-29-network-undergoes-leadership-shake-up.html.

3   "Staff, Elders, & Deacons, Tyler Powell," The Village Church, last modified 2022, https://www.thevillagechurch.net/staff-and-elders. Tyler Powell describes his work on the current (2024) Village Church website in this way: "In 2006, I was hired as the church-planting strategist for the Acts 29 Network and moved to Seattle. In the summer of 2012, I moved to Flower Mound, Texas, to continue in my role as assessment director with Acts 29 and then transitioned to The Village staff in the fall of 2015."

4   Barbara Denman, "J.D. Greer Elected SBC President," *Baptist Press*, June 12, 2018, https://www.baptistpress.com/resource-library/news/j-d-greear-elected-sbc-president/.

5   For more background on the term, see Curtis Freeman, "Baptists, United States," in *Encyclopedia of Protestantism*, ed. Hans J. Hillerbrand (New York, NY: Routledge, 2004), 313; Curtis Freeman, *Undomesticated Dissent: Democracy and the Public Virtue of Religious Nonconformity* (Waco, Texas: Baylor University Press, 2017); and Thomas S. Kidd and Barry Hankins, *Baptists in America: A History* (New York, NY: Oxford University Press, 2015).

6   *Oxford English Dictionary*, s.v. "free church *(n.)*, sense 2.a," September 2023.

7   Freeman, *Encyclopedia of Protestantism*, 313.

8   Margaret Atwood, *The Handmaid's Tale* (Boston, MA: Houghton Mifflin Harcourt Publishing, 1986), 82–83.

9   John Bryson et al., "What Preparation Do Ministers Need Today: The Prerequisites of Pastoral Leadership," *Leadership Journal* 34, no. 4 (2013): 69.

10 "Which Grocery Stores Are Union?," Is It Union?, February 27, 2023, https://www.isitunion.com/2023/02/27/grocery-stores-union/. As represented in "Action: Kroger Union," UFCW, last modified 2024, https://www.ufcw.org/actions/campaign/kroger-union/.

11   "Susan C. Faludi of *The Wall Street Journal*," The 1991 Pulitzer Prize Winners in Explanatory Journalism, The Pulitzer Prizes, accessed September 27, 2024, https://www.pulitzer.org/winners/susan-c-faludi.

12   Susan C. Faludi, "The Reckoning: Safeway LBO Yields Vast Profits but Exacts a Heavy Human Toll—The '80s-Style Buy-Out Left Some Employees Jobless, Stress-Ridden, Distraught—Owner KKR Hails Efficiency," *Wall Street Journal* (New York, NY), May 16, 1990.

13   Judith Shulevitz, "The Fall of Man," *New York Times*, October 3, 1999, paragraph 1, https://archive.nytimes.com/www.nytimes.com/books/99/10/03/reviews/991003.03shulevt.html.

14   Susan Faludi, "Heroes—or Victims?," *9/11 Families For a Safe & Strong America*, February 18, 2008, paragraph 4, https://911familiesforamerica.org/reading-room/susan-faludi/.

15   See also Berth Fertig, "9/11 Fire Dept. Dispatch Tapes Released," *NPR*, August 12, 2005, https://www.npr.org/2005/08/12/4798446/9-11-fire-dept-dispatch-tapes-released.

16   Rhaina Cohen, "Why Men Struggle with Friendship," *Time Magazine*, February 16, 2024, https://time.com/6694925/men-friendship-complicated-essay/. See also *American Psychological Association*, "APA Guidelines for Psychological Practice with Boys and Men," August 2018, https://www.apa.org/about/policy/boys-men-practice-guidelines.pdf.

17   "National Institute for Occupational Safety and Health: Understand Noise Exposure," CDC, last modified February 16, 2024, https://www.cdc.gov/niosh/noise/prevent/understand.html.

18   "Andre Mann: Bio," Faith Driven Investor, accessed September 23, 2024, https://www.faithdriveninvestor.org/bios/andre-mann.

19   "Melior Capital Management," accessed September 23, 2024, https://www.meliorcm.com/.

20   For an account of the Moravian history and the Basel Trading Company, see William J. Danker, *Profit for the Lord; Economic Activities in Moravian Missions and the Basel Mission Trading Company* (Grand Rapids, MI: Eerdmans, 1971), 9.

21   Transcript of 2d TV Debate Between Bush, Clinton and Perot: The 1992 Campaign Transcript of 2d Debate Between the Presidential Candidates. 1992. *New York Times*, October 16, 1992, A11, paragraph 6.

22   Andy Greene, "Flashback: Fleetwood Mac Reunite for Bill Clinton Inauguration," *Rolling Stone*, January 22, 2013, https://www.rollingstone.com/music/music-news/flashback-fleetwood-mac-reunite-for-bill-clintons-inauguration-84419/.

23   *Oxford English Dictionary*, s.v. "tent-maker *(n.)*, sense 1," September 2023.

24 Alison Sargent, "Oral Sex, Yoga, and God's Eternal Wrath: Inside the New Hipster Megachurch That Tells Modern Women to Submit," *Bitch Magazine*, October 17, 2012. https://www.alternet.org/2012/10/oral-sex-yoga-and-gods-eternal-wrath-inside-new-hipster-megachurch-tells-modern-women-submit.

25 "2009 RNA Conference," Religion News Association: Friday, September 11, https://rna.org/2009-conference.

26 Video of his talk is available from John Piper's YouTube channel "Desiring God" at John Piper, "John Piper- On the New Calvinists," YouTube, May 22, 2013, video, 12:30, https://www.youtube.com/watch?v=PQHX-7a9MAE.

27 Katherine Weber, "Pastor Larry Osborne Urges Christian Leaders: 'Don't Become Accidental Pharisees,'" *The Christian Post*, March 21, 2013, last paragraph, https://www.christianpost.com/news/pastor-larry-osborne-urges-christian-leaders-dont-become-accidental-pharisees.html.

28 Billy Joel, "Allentown: Live at Yankee Stadium," November 4, 2022, lines 16–18 and 21–22, https://www.billyjoel.com/song/allentown-13/.

29 Billy Joel, "Allentown Is over Its Billy Joel Song," interview by Julian Abraham, *NPR*, March, 27, 2023, https://www.npr.org/2023/03/27/1166340497/allentown-is-over-its-billy-joel-song.

30 Meredith McCarroll, "Hillbillies Need No Elegy," *The Bitter Southerner*, accessed September 27, 2024, https://bittersoutherner.com/hillbillies-need-no-elegy-appalachian-reckoning.

31 McCarroll, "Hillbillies Need No Elegy," paragraph 4.

32 McCarroll, "Hillbillies Need No Elegy," paragraph 5.

33 "2020 Largest Participating Churches," Outreach 100, last modified 2020, https://outreach100.com/largest-churches-in-america/2020.

34 Sarah Edwards, "Ongoing Controversy at Pioneers Church Takes a Turn When the Organization Disaffiliates with Its Denomination," *Indy Week*, June 29, 2022, https://indyweek.com/news/durham/pioneer/.

35 Noah Herrin, "Future Faith- Three Things Gen Z Wants from Your Church," Association of Related Churches, August 14, 2023, https://www.arcchurches.com/future-faith-three-things-gen-z/ and Jamie Schultz, "Pioneers to Prophets: Building a Spiritual Foundation for Numeric Growth," Association of Related Churches, August 14, 2023, https://www.arcchurches.com/pioneers-to-prophets-building-a-spiritual-foundation-for-numeric-growth/.

36 "Our Story," Pioneers Durham, Accessed May 2024, www.pioneersdurham.co/our-story. The website for Pioneers Durham, as of May 2024 reads "Nestled in the historic Old North Durham neighborhood, Pioneers Durham boasts a locally curated retail

store, a cozy coffee and tea shop, a welcoming cafe to study and work in, co-working and classroom space, and a versatile event venue."

37	Sarah Edwards, "After a Controversy-Filled Two Years in an Iconic Geer Street Space, Pioneers Durham Will Close Its Doors," *Indy Week*, paragraph 6, https://indyweek. com/news/pioneers-durham-closing/.

38	Flier shared in personal correspondence.

39	From personal correspondence with one of the signatories of the letter.

40	Sarah Edwards, "North Carolina Conference of the United Methodist Church Issues Letter of Apology for Pioneers Church in Durham," *Indy Week*, paragraph 3, https:// indyweek.com/culture/etc/north-carolina-conference-of-the-united-methodist-church-issues-apology-re-pioneer-durham/.

41	Edwards, "After a Controversy."

42	"It Was Good to Be 'King,' but What Now?," *New York Times*, April 22, 2009, paragraph 5. The full quote reads "It's Richardson, a suburb of Dallas. I actually grew up in Albuquerque, N.M., and had a paper route in a blue-collar neighborhood. West Texas and eastern New Mexico blur a little bit, and I remember my brother and I just noticing that every adult authority figure used to have a Texas accent. There was always someone going [with a twang], 'Excuse me, boys.'"

43	IMBd, "Church Hopping," *King of the Hill*, season 10, episode 11, IMDb.com, directed by Robin Brigstocke and Wesley Archer, written by Mike Judge, Greg Daniels, Jim Dauterive, aired April 9, 2006, https://www.imdb.com/title/tt0790167/.

44	"*King of the Hill* (1997_2010): Season 10, Episode 11- Church Hopping- Full Transcript," Subslikescript, accessed October 4, 2024, https://www.chicago.gov/city/en.html.

45	Towers Watson: United Methodist Church Call to Action: Vital Congregations Research Project, 2010, 43, https://www.umnews.org/-/media/umc-media/2013/12/04/04/10/umc-call-to-action-vital-congregations-research-project.pdf.

46	Heather Hahn, "Keys to Building Vital Congregations," *UM News*, August 26, 2010, paragraph 14, https://www.umnews.org/en/news/keys-to-building-vital-congregations.

47	Hahn, "Cultural Change Seen as Key to Vital Church," *UM News*, April 5, 2012, paragraph 1, https://www.umnews.org/en/news/cultural-change-seen-as-key-to-vital-church.

48	Kansas Area UMC, "Why Should We Participate in Vital Signs?," May 31, 2011, YouTube video, 00:40, https://www.youtube.com/watch?v=DZ5jPWsRAcQ.

49	Hahn, "Keys to Building Vital Congregations," paragraph 26.

50   United Methodist Church, "For the Record- An Increase in the Number of Vital Congregations," The Florida Conference of the United Methodist Church, n.d., 1, http://umccalltoaction.org/files/Increasing-Vital-Congregations-Fact-Sheet.pdf.

51   Hahn, "Keys to Building Vital Congregations," paragraph 14.

52   "U2 Church Service 'Reaches Out,'" *BBC World News*, http://news.bbc.co.uk/2/hi/entertainment/6517449.stm.

53   Steve Albini, "The Problem with Music," *The Baffler*, December 1993, https://thebaffler.com/salvos/the-problem-with-music.

54   Patrick Freyne, Steve Albini Taught Thousands of Musicians that Ethics and Politics are Embedded in Business and Art, *The Irish Times*, May 13, 2024, headline and photo caption, https://www.irishtimes.com/culture/music/2024/05/11/steve-albini-taught-thousands-of-musicians-that-ethics-and-politics-are-embedded-in-business-and-art/.

55   Jim DeRogatis, "Chicago's Leading Alternative," *Chicago Sun-Times*, September 13, 1992. Reprinted in a message to "Sound Opinions" listeners after Albini's death: Jim DeRogatis and Greg Kot, "RIP Steve Albini," *Sound Opinions* (blog), n.d., https://mailchi.mp/soundopinions/newsletter11132020-14182505 in reference to the podcast, Jim DeRogatis and Greg Kot, "RIP Steve Albini," May 10, 2024, in *Sound Opinions*, podcast, https://podcasts.apple.com/us/podcast/rip-steve-albini/id94793843?i=1000655217050.

56   Albini, "The Problem with Music," II.

57   Marjorie Hyer, "Methodist Bishops Blast SDI, A-Arms: Methodist Bishops Approve Letter Condemning SDI, Nuclear Arms Use," *The Washington Post*, April 30, 1986, paragraphs 1–5, 9.

58   United Methodist Church Council of Bishops, *In Defense of Creation: The Nuclear Crisis and a Just Peace: Foundation Document* (Nashville, Tennessee: Graded Press, 1986), https://archive.org/details/indefenseofcreat00unit.

59   Laurie Goodstein and Davis D. Kirkpatrick, "Conservative Group Amplifies Voice of Protestant Orthodoxy," *New York Times*, May 22, 2004.

60   Frank J. Smith, "Henry, Carl F. H.," (1913–2003) in *Religion and Politics in America: An Encyclopedia of Church and State in American Life [2 Volumes]*, 2016, 343–344.

61   See also "Among its board members have been Princeton politics professor Robert George; Fred Barnes, executive editor of The Weekly Standard and Fox News contributor; Janice Shaw Crouse of the Beverly LaHaye Institute; Paul Marshall of the Hudson Institute; and William Saunders of Americans United for Life."

62   Jamie Doward, "US Millionaire Bankrolls Crusade Against Gay Anglican Priests," *The Guardian*, October 11, 2003, paragraph 11, https://www.theguardian.com/world/2003/oct/12/religion.anglicanism.

63 Sarah Hepola, "America's Girls, Episode 7: All-American Sexy Girls," *Texas Monthly*, January 11, 2022, https://www.texasmonthly.com/podcast/americas-girls-episode-7-all-american-sexy-girls/.

64 Barbara G. Wheeler, "Fit for Ministry? A New Profile of Seminarians." *The Christian Century*, April 11, 2001, 16–18.

65 "Dedication of New Addition Highlights 2005 Pastors' School," *Duke Divinity Magazine*, Winter 2006, 3, http://divinityarchive.com/handle/11258/872.

66 Bob Wells, "Resurrecting Excellence," *Duke Divinity Magazine*, Spring 2006, 8, http://divinityarchive.com/handle/11258/865.

67 "Did You Know," *Duke Divinity Magazine*, Winter 2011, 3, http://divinityarchive.com/handle/11258/760.

68 Jon Meacham, "The 2011 TIME 100: Rob Bell Preacher," *Time Magazine*, April 21, 2011.

69 Meredith Bryan, "Heaven Is a Place on Earth: Rob Bell's Revolutionary Mission," *O The Oprah Magazine*, February 2014, paragraphs 2–3, https://www.oprah.com/spirit/rob-bell-finding-deeper-meaning-in-your-life.

70 Daniel Vaca, *Evangelicals Incorporated: Books and the Business of Religion in America* (Cambridge, MA: Harvard University Press, 2019).

71 See Hans Belting, *Likeness and Presence: A History of the Image Before the Era of Art* (Chicago, Illinois: University of Chicago Press, 1996).

72 Church Soundguy, "CONTEMPORVANT," YouTube, November 16, 2011, video, 03:09, https://www.youtube.com/watch?v=giM04ESUiGw.

73 Shama Mrema, "The Worship Song Song by Random Action Verb Worship," YouTube, March 15, 2020, video, 03:39, https://www.youtube.com/watch?v=fWicNLXxtj4&t=12s.

74 "I designed the font when I was 23 years old. I was right out of college. I was kind of just struggling with some different life issues, I was studying the Bible, looking for God and this font came to mind, this idea of, thinking about the biblical times and Egypt and the Middle East," From Justin Bey, "Papyrus Font Creator Reacts to Viral 'Avatar' Skit from 'Saturday Night Live,'" *CBS News*, October 1, 2017, paragraph 7, https://www.cbsnews.com/news/papyrus-font-avatar-saturday-night-live-chris-costello-ryan-gosling-viral-video/.

75 Cast: Lead Vocalist/Acoustic: Shama Mrema, Female Vocalist: Abby Gilbert, Vocalist/Electric: PD Bachmann, Vocalist/Keys: Andrew Simmons, Bass: Chris Freeland, Lead Guitar: Mason Bayne, Drums: Allen Ellis, Tambourine: Robert Therrell; Production Crew: Executive Producer: Dan Patton, Producer: Shama, Director/DP: Robert Therrell, Cam Ops: Robert Therrell & Tony Palacino Gaffer: Matthew Seest;

Post-Production Crew: Editors: Shama & Mason Bayne; Colorist: Robert; Lyrics: Shama Mrema, PD Bachmann, & Robert Therrell; Vocals: Shama, Abby Gilbert, PD, & Andrew; Produced/Mixed by Andrew "dru" Simmons; Engineered by Shane Nelson & Jay Arrington; Guitars, Keys, Bass, by Andrew; Lead Guitar by Mason Bayne; Drums by Shane Nelson (Asaph Studios); Recorded and filmed at Greenbriar Studios; Mastered by Chas Tackett at The Audio Planet.

76   Wikipedia, s.v. "The Night Shift (*Poker Face*)," last modified September 7, 2024, https://en.wikipedia.org/wiki/The_Night_Shift_(Poker_Face).

77   Susan Faludi, *Stiffed: The Betrayal of the American Man* (New York, NY: Perennial, 2000), 33.

78   Richard (Rick) J. Goossen, "Scott Beck, Rick Rusaw & Gloo: Building a Global Faith Ecosystem (Part III)," *ELO Network*, March 29, 2022, paragraph 2, https://www.entrepreneurialleaders.com/blog/355/Scott-Beck-Rick-Rusaw–Gloo-An-Opportunity-Part-I.

79   "Film & Television—Metrotone Media," accessed October 13, 2024, https://metrotonemedia.com/category/film_television/; "The People You May Know Files—Metrotone Media," n.d., https://metrotonemedia.com/category/the-people-you-may-know-files/.

80   Kristen Thomason, "'He Gets Us' Is Feeding Information to Data Analysts and, Ultimately, Conservative Political Groups," *Baptists News Global*, March 24, 2023, https://baptistnews.com/article/he-gets-us-is-feeding-massive-amounts-of-data-to-cambridge-analytica-and-conservative-political-groups/.

81   "Local News Landscape," Texas, Northwestern Local News Initiative, last modified 2020, https://localnewsinitiative.northwestern.edu/projects/state-of-local-news/explore/#/state-localnewslandscape?state=TX&stateCode=48.

82   David Bauder, "Gannett, McClatchy News Chains Say They Will Stop Using Associated Press Content,"*Associated Press*, March 19, 2024, https://apnews.com/article/gannett-associated-press-contract-97405e4715c9a25d21477b992028db2a.

83   Read more at: Andrew Carter, "ACC Tournament the Biggest Story in Greensboro. There's Barely a Hometown Paper Left to Cover It," *News & Observer*, March 11, 2023, https://www.newsobserver.com/sports/college/acc/article273004255.html.

84   "The Summit Church," accessed May 29, 2024, video included in documentation. https://summitchurch.com and "Photos: Remembering Adam Yauch of the Beastie Boys," *CNN*, May 4, 2012, https://www.cnn.com/2012/05/04/showbiz/gallery/adam-yauch-obit/.

85   "Our History: Theater History," Carolina Theatre, accessed September 29, 2024, paragraph 11, https://carolinatheatre.org/about/venue/history/.

86   "Who We Are: History," Durham Arts Council, last modified 2022, https://durhamarts.org/who-we-are/#history.

87   "About Hayti: Our History," Hayti, accessed September 29, 2024, paragraph 2, https://
     hayti.org/our-organization/.

88   "First Time DPAC Visitor Is 3 millionth Guest," *WRAL News*, August 16, 2016,
     https://www.wral.com/first-time-dpac-visitor-is-3-millionth-guest-/15932546/.

89   Erin Williams, "A Half-Century Ago, Durham Separated Hayti from Downtown.
     Now, the Neighborhood's Leaders Want to Reconnect It to the City's Core," *Indy
     Week*, April 17, 2019, paragraph 6, https://indyweek.com/news/durham/durham-
     separated-hayti-from-downtown-reconnect-black-wall-street/. The plan was funded
     in part by the Safe Routes to Parks program: https://www.saferoutespartnership.org/
     healthy-communities/saferoutestoparks/2019 a national non-profit.

90   "About US," American Tabacco Campus, https://americantobacco.co/about-our-
     campus/.

91   "Tim Keller to Speak Next Week at DPAC," *Durham Herald-Sun*, April 28, 2011,
     paragraphs 1–4.

92   Heather Jones, "Celebrate Durham at an Evening with Time Keller in a Benefit
     Fundraiser for the DurhamCares Partners!," DurhamCares, March 31, 2011,
     paragraph 1, https://web.archive.org/web/20110507040918/http://www.durhamcares.
     org/blog/comments/tim_keller/.

93   DurhamCares, "Love Your Neighbor Film," YouTube, October 6, 2010, video, 03:48,
     https://youtu.be/8yDgn6iQzu4?si=Pb12_a9NX49gsNbp.

94   Flashy714, "In Memory of David McKnight," YouTube, June 20, 2019, video, 01:11,
     https://www.youtube.com/watch?v=xt3DZe9QLtQ. There are other tributes online,
     including: William Erwin, "Memories of David McKnight on Ninth St., Durham,
     and 'Mecklenburg Waltz,'" Vimeo, January 17, 2017, video, 07:54, https://vimeo.
     com/199855940; Ken Fine, "A Requiem for David McKnight: Prodigy, Journalist,
     Politician, Homeless Street Musician," *Indy Week*, January 18, 2017, https://indyweek.
     com/music/requiem-david-mcknight-prodigy-journalist-politician-homeless-street-
     musician/.

95   Jim Morrill, "David McKnight, Street Fiddler Who Walked Across NC in Political
     Bid, Dies of Brain Tumor," *The Charlotte Observer*, January 18, 2017, paragraph 1,
     https://www.charlotteobserver.com/news/politics-government/article127107154.
     html#storylink=cpy.

96   Tim Keller's speech is linked here: DurhamCares, "An Evening with Tim Keller to
     Benefit DurhamCares Partners," YouTube, June 6, 2011, video, 01:00:17, https://
     youtu.be/9jCfJH7V_C8?si=akZn1FS8DqmpPsZx.

97   "Best of the Triangle," *Indy Week*, 2018, 3, 7, https://issuu.com/indyweeknc/
     docs/606_flipbook.

98   Amanda Abrams, "Summit Church's JD Greear Wants to Take the Southern Baptist
     Convention into the Twenty-First Century. The Old Guard Would Rather He Not,"
     Indy Week, June 6, 2018, https://indyweek.com/news/northcarolina/summit-church-

s-jd-greear-wants-take-southern-baptist-convention-twenty-first-century-old-guard-rather-not/.

99 *Independent Weekly Records*, 1982–2004, 05319, Southern Historical Collection, Wilson Special Collections Library, University of North Carolina at Chapel Hill, abstract, https://finding-aids.lib.unc.edu/05319/.

100 Amanda Abrams, Journalism: Faith in Action, last modified 2016, http://www.amandaannabrams.com/new-journalism-page/.

101 "About Southeastern," Academic Catalog, Southeastern Baptist Theological Seminary, accessed October 13, 2024, https://catalog.sebts.edu/content.php?catoid=12&navoid=1033#Affirmed_Statements. See for example: "The Baptist Faith and Message," The Baptist Faith and Message, Southeastern Baptist Theological, accessed October 13, 2024, https://catalog.sebts.edu/content.php?catoid=12&navoid=949#Baptist_Faith_and_Message.

102 "The Danvers Statement," Academic Catalog, Southeastern Baptist Theological accessed October 13, 2024, https://catalog.sebts.edu/content.php?catoid=12&navoid=951.

103 *Indy Week: Best of the Triangle,* June 6, 2018, 2, https://issuu.com/indyweeknc/docs/606_flipbook.

104 See, for one example: Nick Bryant, "Donald Trump's History Book," *Foreign Policy*, April 3, 2022, paragraph 6, https://foreignpolicy.com/2022/04/03/trump-presidency-history-journalism-legacy-zelizer/.

105 *Oxford English Dictionary*, s.v. "Overton window *(n.)*," July 2023.

106 Chandra Childers, "Rooted in Racism and Economic Exploitation," *Economic Policy Institute*, October 11, 2023, https://www.epi.org/publication/rooted-in-racism/.

107 Mick LaSalle, "Workers' Souls Lost in 'Space,'" *San Francisco Chronicle*, February 19, 1999, paragraph 5, https://www.sfgate.com/movies/article/Workers-Souls-Lost-In-Space-2946061.php.

108 Susan Wloszczyna, "No-frills 'Office' Party," *USA Today*, February 19, 1999, paragraph 4.

Chapter 4

1 Available archived here: William J. Ghent, *Our Benevolent Feudalism* (New York, NY: Macmillan, 1902), https://archive.org/details/ourbenevolentfeu00ghenrich/page/28/mode/2up.; Richard Hofstadter, *Social Darwinism in American Thought*

(Boston, MA: Beacon Press, 1955), 45 footnote 48 https://archive.org/details/ socialdarwinismi00rich/page/222/mode/2up.

2   "Oral Roberts Clarifies 'Vision' of Jesus," *United Press International*, May 7, 1982, https://www.upi.com/Archives/1982/05/07/Oral-Roberts-clarifies-vision-of-Jesus/1739389592000/.

3   "About the Chapel," Duke University Chapel, accessed March 8, 2022, pull quote from James Buchanan Duke, https://chapel.duke.edu/about-chapel/history-architecture/.

4   "Wikipedia: John Crichton-Stuart, 3rd Marquess of Bute," Wikimedia Foundation, last modified September 6, 2024, 11:05 (UTC), paragraph 8, https://en.wikipedia.org/ wiki/John_Crichton-Stuart,_3rd_Marquess_of_Bute.

5   *Oxford English Dictionary*, s.v. "folly *(n.1)*, sense 5.b," March 2024.

6   From Liston Pope, *Millhands and Preachers*, page 308, footnote 4. The note reads: Gastonia Gazette, p. 12-C (September 30, 1930).

7   From Liston Pope, *Millhands and Preachers*, page 321, footnote 34. The note reads: Gastonia, North Carolina, "The South's City of Spindles" (Three Radio Talks Made Over Station WBT, Charlotte, N.C., May 14, 1930, printed in a leaflet distributed by the Gastonia Chamber of Commerce).

8   "North Carolina, Gaston County, Historic Districts: Loray Mill Historic District," National Register of Historic Places, accessed September 30, 2024, https:// nationalregisterofhistoricplaces.com/NC/Gaston/districts.html.

9   "Preserving Our Past for the Future," National Park Service, accessed October 1, 2024, headline, paragraph 1, https://www.nps.gov/subjects/ncptt/index.htm.

10 Karin Larkin and Fawn-Amber Montoya, *Communities of Ludlow: Collaborative Stewardship and the Ludlow Centennial Commemoration Commission* (Denver, Colorado: University Press of Colorado, 2022), muse.jhu.edu/book/94548.

11 Larkin and Montoya, *Communities of Ludlow,* 3–4.

12 Vesna Jaksic Lowe, "Public Broadcasting Turns 50," Carnegie Corporation of New York, November 3, 2017, https://www.carnegie.org/news/articles/public-broadcasting-turns-50/.

13 Mark Bittman, "Appreciation: The Thing (or Things) About Wendell Berry," National Endowment for the Humanities, paragraphs 5–7, https://www.neh.gov/about/ awards/jefferson-lecture/wendell-e-berry-biography. Wendell Berry, "Interview," interview by Jim Leach, *National Endowment of the Humanities,* 2012, https://www. neh.gov/about/awards/jefferson-lecture/wendell-e-berry-biography.

14 Lecture included under heading "Lecture Text," https://www.neh.gov/about/awards/ jefferson-lecture/wendell-e-berry-biography.

15   https://billmoyers.com/series/a-walk-through-the-twentieth-century/.

16   A Walk Through the 20th Century Episode: "The Image Makers," April 14, 1983, https://www.youtube.com/watch?v=iBEclayBCdc, https://billmoyers.com/content/image-makers/.

17   https://billmoyers.com/content/image-makers/.

18   Committee of Coal Mine Managers and Colorado Fuel and Iron Company, *Facts Concerning the Struggle in Colorado for Industrial Freedom* (Denver, Colorado: Denver, 1914), https://archive.org/details/factsconcernings00commrich. The preface reads: "The facts have been beclouded with unusual venom. The position and the activities of the coal mine managers have been most seriously misrepresented."

19   https://billmoyers.com/content/image-makers/.

20   Charles Silver, *Charles Chaplin: An Appreciation* (New York, NY: MOMA, 1989), https://www.moma.org/documents/moma_catalogue_2136_300062892.pdf. The Museum of Modern Art, New York published in conjunction with the exhibit "Chaplin: A Centennial Celebration" at the Museum of Modern Art.

21   Museum of Modern Art, "The Museum of Modern Art Honors Charles Chaplin's Contributors to Cinema," press release, March 1989, 1, https://assets.moma.org/documents/moma_press-release_327525.pdf.

22   Duke University Chapel, "History & Architecture," accessed October 1, 2024, paragraph 1, https://chapel.duke.edu/about-chapel/history-architecture.

23   Oxford English Dictionary, s.v. "folly *(n.1)*, sense 1.c," September 2024.

24   Joan Mellen, "Toward Modern Times." in *Modern Times*, BFI Film Classics (London: British Film Institute, 2006), 22–37, accessed November 28, 2024.

25   Silver, *Charles Chaplin*, 9.

26   Joan Mellen, "The Little Fellow," in *Modern Times*, BFI Film Classics. (London: British Film Institute, 2006), 6–22, accessed November 28, 2024.

27   Lily E. Kay, *The Molecular Vision of Life: Caltech, The Rockefeller Foundation, and The Rise of the New Biology* (New York, NY: Oxford University Press, 1993), 10.

28   Kay, *The Molecular Vision of Life*, 8.

29   Kay, *The Molecular Vision of Life*, 3.

30   Kay, *The Molecular Vision of Life*, 6.

31   Harry E. Fosdick, "Shall the Fundamentalists Win?" *The Christian Century* 39 (1922): 713–717; "Shall the Fundamentalists Win?" *The Christian Work* 102 (1922): 716–722.

32 "Archive for Category: Religion & Morality in Public Life," Voices of Democracy: The U.S. Oratory Project, accessed October 6, 2024, https://voicesofdemocracy.umd.edu/category/topics/religion-morality-in-public-life/.

33 "Harry Emerson Fosdick, 'Shall the Fundamentalist Win?' New York City, NY," Voices of Democracy: The U.S. Oratory Project, accessed October 6, 2024, Classroom activities 6, 8, Student Research 3, https://voicesofdemocracy.umd.edu/category/topics/religion-morality-in-public-life/.

34 Eric C. Miller, "Dr. Harry Emerson Fosdick, 'Shall Fundamentalists Win?' New York City, NY (May 21, 1922)," *Voices of Democracy* 14 (2019): 29, https://voicesofdemocracy.umd.edu/wp-content/uploads/2019/06/VOD-Miller_Essay-10.9.19.pdf.

35 B. C. Forbes, "OWEN D. YOUNG A Revolutionary Capitalist: The Chairman of the Board of Directors of the General Electric Company Advocates, Among Other Things, That Labor Should Hire Capital," *McClure's* 60, no. 6 (1928): 2.

36 Bruce Barton, *The Man Nobody Knows* (New York, NY: Grosset & Dunlap, 1925), 162, https://archive.org/details/mannobodyknows00bart_0/page/162/mode/2up?q=wist.

37 Raymond B. Fosdick, *The Old Savage in the New Civilization* (Garden City, New York: Doran, Inc., 1928), 32, https://archive.org/details/oldsavageinnewci0000fosd/page/32/mode/2up.

38 Fosdick, *The Old Savage in the New Civilization*, 64.

39 Fosdick, *The Old Savage in the New Civilization*, 7.

40 Fosdick, *The Old Savage in the New Civilization*, 49.

41 Fosdick, *The Old Savage in the New Civilization*, 11

42 Fosdick, *The Old Savage in the New Civilization*, 18.

43 Fosdick, *The Old Savage in the New Civilization*, 31.

44 Fosdick, *The Old Savage in the New Civilization*, 50.

45 Fosdick, *The Old Savage in the New Civilization*, 46.

46 Fosdick, *The Old Savage in the New Civilization*, 86.

47 Fosdick, *The Old Savage in the New Civilization*, 184.

48 Fosdick, *The Old Savage in the New Civilization*, 198.

49 Raymond B. Fosdick, *The Rockefeller Annual Report* (New York, NY: The Rockefeller Foundation, 1936): 8, https://www.rockefellerfoundation.org/wp-content/uploads/Annual-Report-1936-1.pdf.

50   Accessed through Duke Rubenstein Library archives. Title: Tobacco Road. Author: Duke University.—Duke University. Volume/Box: 1978–1985—v.1:no.1(1978:Mar.)-no.3(1985:Apr.19): Includes October 5, 1983–April 11, 1984 when published as Chronicle supplement.

51   https://archives.lib.duke.edu/catalog/uapub_aspace_ref118_bj4.

52   Robert J. Bliwise, "The Nixon Library That Wasn't," *Duke Magazine*, June 1, 2022, paragraphs 1–3, https://alumni.duke.edu/magazine/articles/nixon-library-wasnt.

53   Ben Dixon MacNeill, "Duke," *The American Mercury*, 1929, https://www.unz.com/print/AmMercury-1929aug-00430/Contents/.

54   Dixon MacNeill, "Duke."

55   https://finding-aids.lib.unc.edu/03617/; https://www.ncpedia.org/biography/macneill-ben-dixon; *The American Mercury*, August 1929, 430–438.

56   "About the Chapel," Duke University Chapel, accessed March 8, 2022, pull quote from James Buchanan Duke, https://chapel.duke.edu/about-chapel/history-architecture/.

Chapter 5

1   *Oxford English Dictionary*, s.v. "cowboy *(n.)*, sense C.2.a," September 2024.

2   Albin Krebs, "Slim Pickens, Known for Cowboy Roles, *New York Times*, December 10, 1983, 28, https://www.nytimes.com/1983/12/10/obituaries/slim-pickens-known-for-cowboy-roles-dies.html.

3   Norman Grubb, *Modern Viking: The Story of Abraham Vereide, Pioneer in Christian Leadership* (Grand Rapids, Michigan: Zondervan Publishing House, 1961).

4   Grubb, *Modern Viking*, 12.

5   Diane Winston, "National Prayer Breakfast: What Does Its History Reveal?," *The Conversation*, February 1, 2017, paragraphs 1, 3, https://theconversation.com/national-prayer-breakfast-what-does-its-history-reveal-71978?xid=PS_smithsonian.

6   *Oxford English Dictionary*, s.v. "'to break bread' in bread *(n.)*, sense P.1.b," September 2024.

7   Jeff Sharlet, "The Secret Political Reach of 'The Family,'" November 24, 2009, in *Fresh Air*, produced directed by NPR, https://www.npr.org/2009/11/24/120746516/the-secret-political-reach-of-the-family.

8   "Excerpt: 'The Family,'" NPR, November 24, 2009, chapter 1, paragraph 4, https://www.npr.org/120746584.

9   Jeff Sharlet, "Jesus Plus Nothing: Undercover Among America's Secret Theocrats," *Harper's Magazine*, March 2003, 53-64, https://harpers.org/archive/2003/03/jesus-plus-nothing/.

10   Sharlet, "Jesus Plus Nothing," paragraphs 4–5.

11   James Guth, review of *The Family: The Secret Fundamentalism at The Heart of American Power* by Jeff Sharlet, *The Christian Century*, October 21, 2008, 45-46, https://www.christiancentury.org/reviews/2008-10/family-secret-fundamentalism-heart-american-power.

12   Lucy Bryan Green, "A Friend of the Family," *Sojourners Magazine*, June 2011, 32-35. For background, see Jeff Sharlet, "Straight man's burden: the American roots of Uganda's anti-gay persecutions," *Harper's Magazine*, September 2010, 36-48. Sharlet won the 2011 MOLLY National Journalism Prize for this piece. The award was named after journalist Molly Ivins. https://home.dartmouth.edu/news/2011/06/english-professor-wins-journalism-prize-harpers-magazine-article.

13   "Great Lakes Initiative in Africa," Center for Reconciliation, Duke Divinity School accessed July 27, 2024, paragraph 1, https://divinity.duke.edu/initiatives/cfr/gli. "The mission of the Great Lakes Initiative (GLI) is to mobilize restless Christian leaders from across the Great Lakes region of Africa, create a space for their transformation, and empower them to participate in God's mission of reconciliation in their own communities, organizations, and nations."

14   https://www.amnesty.org/en/documents/ior40/008/2002/en/.

15   See Emma Madden, "'Kony 2012,' 10 Years Later," *New York Times*, March 8, 2022, https://www.nytimes.com/2022/03/08/style/kony-2012-invisible-children.html.

16   I am grateful to journalist Chris Gehrz for reminding me of the exact timing on these publications and the history. Chris Gehrz, "Jesus Is Not a Republican or a Democrat: A History," last updated February 8, 2021, https://www.patheos.com/blogs/anxiousbench/2021/02/jesus-republican-democrat-history/.

17   See Tony Campolo, "My Response to Sojourner's Article About 'The Family,'" *Sojourners*, June 10, 2011, https://sojo.net/articles/my-response-sojourners-article-about-family.

18   Kathryn Joyce and Jeff Sharlet, "Hillary's prayer: for 15 years, Hillary Clinton has been part of a secretive religious group that seeks to bring Jesus back to Capitol Hill. Is she triangulating—or living her faith?" *Mother Jones*, September-October 2007, https://www.motherjones.com/politics/2007/09/hillarys-prayer-hillary-clintons-religion-and-politics/.

19   "Remembering Alonzo McDonald, Dean's Council Member," News Archive, Harvard Divinity School, November 26, 2019, https://news-archive.hds.harvard.edu/news/2019/11/26/remembering-alonzo-mcdonald-deans-council-member.

20   Indrani G. Das, "Former Divinity School Dean Ronald F. Thiemann Dead at 66," *The Crimson*, December 3, 2012. https://www.thecrimson.com/article/2012/12/3/ronald-thiemann-obituary/.

21   "Hempton Named First McDonald Family Professor," *The Harvard Gazette*, August 24, 2006, paragraph 2, https://news.harvard.edu/gazette/story/2006/08/hempton-named-first-mcdonald-family-professor/.

22   "David H. Hempton," Directory, Harvard Divinity School, https://hds.harvard.edu/people/david-n-hempton.

23   Mark Oppenheimer, "From One Benefactor, Diverse Seeds in Theology: [National Desk]," *New York Times*, July 17, 2010, paragraphs 9–11.

24   "Faculty of Theology and Religion Announces New Regius Professors," Faculty of Religion and Theology, University of Oxford, June 13, 2024, Date of copyright or modification or access, https://www.theology.ox.ac.uk/article/faculty-theology-and-religion-announces-new-regius-professors.

25   Stephen Bates, "Unholy Row at Oxford's College for Clergy Staff Exodus and Claims of Bullying," *The Guardian*, May 16, 2007, paragraphs 1–3, https://www.theguardian.com/uk/2007/may/16/topstories3.religion.

26   William Crawley, "Wycliffe Hall: Evangelicalism's Internecine War," *BBC*, September 29, 2007, paragraph 1, https://www.bbc.co.uk/blogs/ni/2007/09/wycliffe_hall_evangelicalisms.html.

27   Bill Bowder, "Wycliffe Hall Admits Breach of Law over Sacked Lecturer," *Church Times*, January 2008, https://www.churchtimes.co.uk/articles/2008/11-january/news/uk/wycliffe-hall-admits-breach-of-law-over-sacked-lecturer.

28   Sam Hailes, "Elaine Storkey: 'Most People Do Not Understand Academic Christians,'" *Premier Christianity*, paragraph 2, https://www.premierchristianity.com/interviews/elaine-storkey-most-people-do-not-understand-academic-christians/2670.article.

29   David Lilff, "Ethics and Empire: An Open Letter from Oxford Scholars," *The Conversation*, paragraph 2, https://theconversation.com/ethics-and-empire-an-open-letter-from-oxford-scholars-89333.

30   Eleanor Harding, "After Warning Students That Shame over the Part Has Gone Too Far …," *Daily Mail* (London), December 15, 2017, paragraphs 6–8.

31   "'Ian Jack' Journalist Who Edited Granta and The Independent on Sunday and Has Few Peers as a Long-Form Writer," *Daily Telegraph* (London), November 7, 2022, paragraphs 3, 10. Ian Jack, "The sun may never set on British misconceptions about our empire," *The Guardian*, January 6, 2018.

32   Nigel Biggar, "Don't feel guilty about our colonial history," *The Times*, November 29, 2017. https://www.thetimes.com/comment/article/don-t-feel-guilty-about-our-colonial-history-ghvstdhmj.

33   Sherryl Kleinman, Professor Emeritus Department of Sociology University of North Carolina, personal correspondence, 2023. The documercial is *Doing Virtuous Business*, WFYI Public Media, April 4, 2011, https://www.wfyi.org/programs/doing-virtuous-business/television/doing-virtuous-business.

34   *Oxford English Dictionary*, s.v. "infomercial (n.)," July 2023.

35 Sarah Ginolfi, "16 Reasons to Celebrate: New Titles by YDS Faculty," News, *Yale Divinity School*, May 4, 2013, paragraph 15, https://divinity.yale.edu/news/16-reasons-celebrate-new-titles-yds-faculty.

36 Theodore Roosevelt Malloch, "About the Author," in *Practical Wisdom in Management* (New York, NY: Routledge, 2015), abstract, https://www.taylorfrancis.com/chapters/mono/10.4324/9781351286329-10/author-theodore-roosevelt-malloch; Theodore Roosevelt Malloch, *Doing Virtuous Business: The Remarkable Success of Spiritual Enterprise* (Nashville, Tennessee: Thomas Nelson, 2011), https://archive.org/details/doingvirtuousbus0000mall.

37 Henry Mance, "Oxford Distances Itself from Trump Favourite Ted Malloch," *Financial Times*, February 23, 2017, 2. Originally published February 11, 2017; article updated February 22, 2017 with a footnote responding to statements by Ted Malloch. The updated version concludes, "The FT stands by its reporting and will continue to set the record straight in the face of any further false claims."

38 Mance, "Oxford Distances Itself," 2.

39 *Doing Virtuous Business*, PBS, aired April 3, 2011, video, 56:57, https://www.pbs.org/video/doing-virtuous-business/.

40 "At the Divinity School: The Upside of 'Doing Virtuous Business,'" *Yale News*, October 19, 2010, paragraph 2, https://news.yale.edu/2010/10/19/divinity-school-upside-doing-virtuous-business.

41 Roger L. Martin, "The Virtue Matrix: Calculating the Return on Corporate Responsibility," *Harvard Business Review*, March 2002, paragraph 1, https://hbr.org/2002/03/the-virtue-matrix-calculating-the-return-on-corporate-responsibility.

42 Colette Shade, "25 Years Ago, the Battle of Seattle Showed Us What Democracy Looks Like," *The Nation*, November 29, 2024.

43 *The Corporation*, Joel Bakan, Harold Crooks, and Mark Achbar (2003; Big Picture Media).

44 "Parents' Guide to The Corporation," Common Sense Media, last modified October 1, 2025, https://www.commonsensemedia.org/movie-reviews/the-corporation.

45 "Wendell Ray, M.B.A.," Radio TV Film, University of Wisconsin Oshkosh, accessed October 7, 2024, https://www.uwosh.edu/rtf/wendell-ray/.

46 Barbara G. Wheeler, "Fit for Ministry? A New Profile of Seminarians," *The Christian Century* (April 11, 2002) 16-18. https://www.christiancentury.org/article/fit-ministry.

47 Sasha Rogelberg, "Eli Lilly," *Fortune*, December 17, 2023, https://web.archive.org/web/20240616224442/https://fortune.com/company/eli-lilly/.

48 "Doing Virtuous Business," WFYI Public Media, April 4, 2011, https://www.wfyi.org/programs/doing-virtuous-business/television/doing-virtuous-business.

49 "John E. Hare," YDS Faculty, Yale Divinity School, accessed October 7, 2024, biography, https://divinity.yale.edu/faculty-and-research/yds-faculty/john-e-hare.

50 Hayley Peterson, "Amazon-Owned Whole Foods Is Quietly Tracking Its Employees with a Heat Map Tool That Ranks Which Stores Are Most at Risk of Unionizing," *Business Insider*, April 20, 2020, paragraphs 1–6.

51 Grace Kay, "Whole Foods CEO Says 'Socialists Are Taking Over' in the US and Young People in Liberal Cities 'Don't Seem Like They Want to Work'," *Business Insider*, August 12, 2022.

52 Nick Gillespie, "Whole Foods' John Mackey: 'I Feel Like Socialists Are Taking Over'," *The Reason*, August 10, 2022, paragraph 1, https://reason.com/podcast/2022/08/10/whole-foods-john-mackey-i-feel-like-socialists-are-taking-over/.

53 Grace Kim, "Whole Foods CEO Says 'Socialists Are Taking Over' in the US and Young People in Liberal Cities 'Don't Seem Like They Want to Work'," *Business Insider*, August 12, 2022, paragraphs 13–14.

54 John Mackey, "The Whole Foods Alternative to ObamaCare," *Wall Street Journal*, August 12, 2009.

55 Mackey, "The Whole Foods Alternative to ObamaCare," opening quote, paragraphs 12–13, 17–19.

56 "About TomDispatch," TomDispatch, last modified 2024, https://tomdispatch.com/about/; "Thomas M. Engelhardt," Fellows, John Simon Guggenheim Memorial Foundation, awarded 1991, https://www.gf.org/fellows/thomas-m-engelhardt/.

57 "Wallace Shawn, Are You Smarter Than Thomas Jefferson?," TomDispatch, February 3, 2011, https://tomdispatch.com/wallace-shawn-are-you-smarter-than-thomas-jefferson/; The essay was reprinted in *The Nation*, Wallace Shawn, "Why I Call Myself a Socialist," *The Nation*, February 3, 2011, https://www.thenation.com/article/culture/why-i-call-myself-socialist/.

58 Wallace Shawn, "Aunt Dan and Lemon," Details/The Company, Royal Court, last modified May 20, 2009, https://royalcourttheatre.com/whats-on/aunt-dan-and-lemon/?tab=0.

59 "The Princess Bride (1987)—IMDb," IMDb, accessed October 11, 2024, https://www.imdb.com/title/tt0093779/fullcredits.

60 Shawn, "Why I Call Myself a Socialist."

61 Nicole Daniels, "Lesson of the Day: 'Gaps in Amazon's Response as Virus Spreads to More Than 50 Warehouses'," *New York Times*, May 8, 2020, paragraph 3, https://www.nytimes.com/2020/05/08/learning/lesson-of-the-day-gaps-in-amazons-response-as-virus-spreads-to-more-than-50-warehouses.html.

62   Daniels, "Lesson of the Day."

63   The full quotation from their website as of August 14, 2024: "About the New Canaan Society. NCS is a National Movement of over 24,000 men who gather together to encourage each other in friendship and faith and to support each other to be better husbands, fathers and leaders in the marketplace and in our communities. NCS is often described as Young Life for marketplace men, where we focus on being open, honest, and vulnerable to grow in friendship with Jesus and each other. Our 65 chapters meet weekly or bi-weekly around the country in 26 states." "What Is NCS," New Canaan Society, accessed October 13, 2024, https://newcanaansociety. org/about/. See also https://www.nytimes.com/2006/12/24/nyregion/ nyregionspecial2/24ctcanaan.html.

64   Zach Montague, "Doug Coe, Influential Evangelical Leader, Dies at 88," *New York Times*, February 22, 2017, https://www.nytimes.com/2017/02/22/us/obituary-doug-coe-fellowship-foundation.html.https://newcanaansociety.org/new-canaan/team-member/douglas-coe/.

65   https://newcanaansociety.org/new-canaan/team-member/james-davison-hunter/.

66   Joe Loconte, "The Case for Converting Kings: Os Guinness on how to prevent the American experiment from flopping," *Christianity Today*, September 4, 2000, 182-183.

67   Jason Willick, "The Man Who Discovered 'Culture Wars,'" *Wall Street Journal*, May 25, 2018, https://www.wsj.com/articles/the-man-who-discovered-culture-wars-1527286035.

68   Jeff Sharlet, "Jesus Plus Nothing: Undercover among America's secret theocrats" *Harper's Magazine*, March, 2003, 53-64. https://harpers.org/archive/2003/03/jesus-plus-nothing/.

69   Psychvideos, "Doug Coe Speaks to Navigators-1989, Part 1," Youtube, March 2, 2010, https://www.youtube.com/watch?v=zn098XYE7pk.

70   "Honorary Co-Chairs," National Prayer Breakfast Foundation, accessed October 12, 2024, https://npbfoundation.com/honorary-co-chairs/.

71   Clifford Green, "Hijacking Bonhoeffer," *Christian Century*, October 19, 2010, 34-35,37-39. https://www.christiancentury.org/reviews/2010-09/hijacking-bonhoeffer.

72   Motoko Rich, "Christian Novel Is Surprise Best Seller," *New York Times*, June 24, 2008.

73   "The Story Behind William Paul Young's Best-Seller, the Shack," Super Souls Sunday, Video, July 6, 2017, https://www.oprah.com/own-super-soul-sunday/the-story-behind-william-paul-youngs-best-seller-the-shack-video.

74   See Richard Rohr, "God Is a Dance," Wm. Paul Young, blog post, accessed October 12, 2024, https://wmpaulyoung.com/god-is-a-dance/.

75   Sonja Livingston, "Richard Rohr's Living School Is No Utopia. But It Taught Me to Love Our Imperfect World," *America Magazine*, August 20, 2021, https://www.

americamagazine.org/faith/2021/08/20/richard-rohr-living-school-imperfection-blessings-241253.

76 Todd Brewer, "The Apocryphal Imagination of Richard Rohr," Theology, *Mockingbird*, February 11, 2021, https://mbird.com/theology/the-apocryphal-imagination-of-richard-rohr/.

77 Peggy McGlone, "Hobby Lobby's Illicit Artifacts Are Returned to Their Iraqi Homeland," *Washington Post*, May 2, 2018, https://www.washingtonpost.com/entertainment/museums/hobby-lobbys-illicit-artifacts-are-returned-to-their-iraqi-homeland/2018/05/02/3f59842a-4e44-11e8-84a0-458a1aa9ac0a_story.html.

78 See "Transcript of Dr. Martin Luther King's Speech at SMU on March 17, 1966," *SMU News*, January 10, 2014, https://www.smu.edu/news/archives/2014/mlk-at-smu-transcript-17march1966.

79 Abraham Joshua Heschel, *The Prophets: Two Volumes in One* (Carol Stream, Illinois: Hendrickson Publishers, 2007).

80 For an alternative to Dr. Carson's prescription, I recommend this resource: "Just Action: How to Challenge Segregation Enacted Under the Color of Law," Just Action, accessed October 13, 2024, https://justactionbook.org/.

81 Gustav Niebuhr, "Abortion, Contraception Condemned," *Washington Post*, February 4, 1994, https://www.washingtonpost.com/wp-srv/inatl/longterm/teresa/stories/dc94.htm.

82 Bill Frist, "How a Rock Star, a Physician-Legislator, and an Evangelical Senator Bonded to Help End the Global AIDS Pandemic: A Backstory," *Forbes*, December 2, 2022, https://www.forbes.com/sites/billfrist/2022/12/01/how-a-rock-star-a-physician-legislator-and-an-evangelical-senator-bonded-to-help-end-the-global-aids-pandemic-a-backstory/. The text of the 2006 speech is available online at: "Online Speech Bank: Bono—2006 National Prayer Breakfast Keynote Address," American Rhetoric (Text-audio-video) delivered February 5, 2006, https://www.americanrhetoric.com/speeches/bononationalprayerbreakfast.htm.

83 For Bono's description of the campaign in 2018, see Althea Legaspi, "Bono Wants His Charity to Be 'the NRA for the World's Poor'," *Rolling Stone*, December 9, 2018, https://www.rollingstone.com/music/music-news/bono-one-campaign-economic-club-chicago-dinner-766263/.

84 Peter Boyer, "Frat House for Jesus," *The New Yorker*, 13 September 2010: 52.

85 341.5 All clergy of The United Methodist Church are charged to maintain all confidences inviolate, including confessional confidences, except in the cases of suspected child abuse or neglect or in cases where mandatory reporting is required by civil law.

86 "Concerning the Rite: Reconciliation of a Penitent," *The Online Book of Common Prayer* (The Church Hymnal Corporation), https://www.bcponline.org/PastoralOffices/concernreconciliation.html.

87 Joanna Cattanach, "The Wright Process: Pulitzer Prize Winner Lawrence Wright on Writing, Donkeys, and his 4x6 Approach to Research," *The Mayborn*, 2014, 61–67.

88 Alec Baldwin, "Lawrence Wright on Religion, ISIS, and Scientology," April 14, 2015, in *Here's the Thing*, podcast. https://www.wnycstudios.org/podcasts/heresthething/episodes/lawrence-wright.

89 C.S. Lewis, "The 1944 Memorial Lecture at King's College, University of London." Quotation from page 3. https://archive.org/details/1944-the-inner-ring/page/2/mode/2up page 3.

90 The Family, "The Wolf King," *Netflix* video, August 9, 2019.

91 See related to Ayric Peyton, and media coverage in Portland: Megan Allison, "March Against Murder Organizer Reflects on Portland Gun Violence Challenges," KATU, January 23, 2022, https://katu.com/news/local/march-against-murder-organizer-reflects-on-portland-gun-violence-challenges.

92 Paul Vitello, "Ray Anderson, a Carpet Innovator, Dies at 77," *New York Times*, Aug 11, 2011. https://www.nytimes.com/2011/08/11/business/ray-anderson-a-carpet-innovator-dies-at-77.html.

Conclusion

1 Nadia Lee Cohen, "Losing My Religion," *Autre Magazine*, Fall/Winter 2022.

2 Mattel, "Thomas & Friends Toys," last modified 2024, https://shop.mattel.com/collections/thomas-friends.

3 Shauna Wilton, "A Very Useful Engine: The Politics of Thomas and Friends," in *The Politics of Popular Culture: Negotiating Power, Identity, and Place*, ed. Tim Nieguth (Montreal, Quebec: McGill-Queen's University Press, 2015), 19–27.

4 The longer quotations from each of Sotomayor's dissent available: KENNEDY v. BREMERTON SCHOOL DISTRICT No. 21–418. Argued April 25, 2022—Decided June 27, 2022.

5 Wayne Besen, "The Gathering: The Religious Right's Cash Cow, *Two Care*," April 30, 2014, https://twocare.org/the-gathering-the-religious-rights-cash-cow/. See "Raising Up a New Generation from the 4/14 Window to Transform the World," Luis Bush Papers, September 9, 2009, https://luisbushpapers.com/414window/2009/09/09/raising-up-a-new-generation-from-the-4-14-window-to-transform-the-world/.

6 David Carson v. A. Pender Makin, 20-1088 U.S (2021), https://www.supremecourt.gov/DocketPDF/20/20-1088/192044/20210910125550095_Carson%20v%20Makin%20merits.pdf.

7 James Davison Hunter, *Culture Wars: The Struggle to Define America* (New York, NY: Basic Books, 1991), xii. See also James Davison Hunter, *The Death of Character: Moral Education in an Age Without Good or Evil* (New York, NY: Basic Books, 2000) and *To Change the World: The Irony, Tragedy, and Possibility of Christianity in the Late Modern World* (New York, NY: Oxford University Press, 2010).

8 Bethany Moreton, "Jesus Saves: Christians in the Age of Debt" (unpublished manuscript).

9 Ronit Y. Stahl, "The Supreme Court Is Decimating Public Education as a Common Good," *Arc Magazine*, July 7, 2022. https://arcmag.org/the-supreme-court-is-decimating-public-education-as-a-common-good.

10 *Spotlight*, Tom McCarthy and Josh Singer (2015; Universal Studios).

Select Bibliography

Albini, Steven. "The Problem with Music." *The Baffler* 5 (December 1993), II. Available online: https://thebaffler.com/salvos/the-problem-with-music.

American Social Health Association. "What Kind of Children?" 1922. Poster. University of Minnesota Libraries. Available online: https://gallery.lib.umn.edu/exhibits/show/youth_and_life/item/56.

Berry, Wendell. "Jefferson Lecture in the Humanities." In *Wendell E. Berry*, by David Skinner. National Endowment for the Humanities, 2012. Available online: https://www.neh.gov/about/awards/jefferson-lecture/wendell-e-berry-biography.

Bowder, Bill. "Wycliffe Hall Admits Breach of Law over Sacked Lecturer." *Church Times*, January 11, 2008, 5.

Boyer, Peter J. "Frat House for Jesus." *New Yorker*, September 13, 2010.

Campolo, Tony. "My Response to Sojourners' Article About 'The Family.'" *Sojourners*, June 10, 2011. Available online: https://sojo.net/articles/my-response-sojourners-article-about-family.

Coffman, Elesha. "A Long Ride on the Mainline: 100 Years of the Christian Century." *Christianity Today*, November/December 2008. Available online: https://www.booksandculture.com/articles/2008/novdec/12.20.html.

Darwin, Charles. *On the Origin of Species by Means of Natural Selection*. London: Watts, 1903.

Dochuk, Darren. *Anointed with Oil: How Christianity and Crude Made Modern America*. New York, NY: Basic Books, 2019.

"Doing Virtuous Business." Video. WFYI public media, April 4, 2011. Available online: https://www.wfyi.org/programs/doing-virtuous-business/television/doing-virtuous-business.

Edwards, Sarah. "North Carolina Conference of the United Methodist Church Issues Letter of Apology for Pioneers Church in Durham." *Indy Week*, December 9, 2022.

Faludi, Susan C. "The Reckoning: Safeway LBO Yields Vast Profits but Exacts a Heavy Human Toll." *Wall Street Journal*, May 16, 1990, A1.

Faludi, Susan C. *The Terror Dream: Myth and Misogyny in an Insecure America*. New York, NY: Picador, 2007.

Forbes, B. C. "Owen D. Young—A Revolutionary Capitalist: The Chairman of the Board of Directors of the General Electric Company Advocates, Among Other Things, That Labor Should Hire Capital." *McClure's* 60, no. 6 (June 1928): 46.

Fosdick, Harry Emerson. "Shall the Fundamentalists Win?" *The Christian Century* 39 (1922): 713–717.

Freeman, Curtis. "Baptists, United States." In *Encyclopedia of Protestantism*, edited by Hans J. Hillerbrand, 313. New York, NY: Routledge, 2004.

Freeman, Curtis. *Undomesticated Dissent: Democracy and the Public Virtue of Religious Nonconformity*. Waco, TX: Baylor University Press, 2017.

Ghent, William J. *Our Benevolent Feudalism*. New York, NY: Macmillan, 1902.

Gloege, Timothy E. W. "The Name You Can Trust." In *Guaranteed Pure: The Moody Bible Institute, Business, and the Making of Modern Evangelicalism*, 219. Chapel Hill, NC: University of North Carolina Press, 2015.

Gold, Russell. "A Deposed Texas Republican's Lament About Slander and Corruption." *Texas Monthly*, March 14, 2024. Available online: https://www.texasmonthly.com/news-politics/texas-gop-primary-glenn-rogers.

Goodwyn, Lawrence. *The Populist Moment: A Short History of the Agrarian Revolt in America*. New York, NY: Oxford University Press, 1978.

Goossen, Richard (Rick) J. "Scott Beck, Rick Rusaw & Gloo: Building a Global Faith Ecosystem (Part III)." *ELO Network*, March 29, 2022. Available online: https://www.entrepreneurialleaders.com/blog/355/Scott-Beck-Rick-Rusaw–Gloo-An-Opportunity-Part-I.

Grem, Darren E. "*Christianity Today*, J. Howard Pew, and the Business of Conservative Evangelicalism." *Enterprise & Society* 15, no. 2 (2014): 337.

Grubb, Norman. *Modern Viking: The Story of Abraham Vereide, Pioneer in Christian Leadership*. Grand Rapids, MI: Zondervan, 1961.

Handley-Cousins, Sarah, and Elizabeth Garner Masarik. "National Parks in America: Health, Manhood, and Wilderness." *Dig: A History Podcast*, May 16, 2018. Available online: https://digpodcast.org/2018/05/06/national-parks-america-manhood.

Harrison, Jim. "Geopiety." In *West of 98: Living and Writing the New American West*, edited by Lynn Stegner and Russell Rowland, 71. Austin, TX: University of Texas Press, 2011.

Heschel, Abraham Joshua. *The Prophets: Two Volumes in One*. Carol Stream, IL: Hendrickson, 2007.

Hofstadter, Richard. *Social Darwinism in American Thought*. Boston, MA: Beacon Press, 1955.

Kay, Lily E. *The Molecular Vision of Life: Caltech, the Rockefeller Foundation, and the Rise of the New Biology*. New York, NY: Oxford University Press, 1993.

Kelton, Elmer. *The Day the Cowboys Quit*. Fort Worth, TX: Texas Christian University Press, 1986.

Kidd, Thomas S., and Barry Hankins. *Baptists in America: A History*. New York, NY: Oxford University Press, 2015.

Kingsley, Charles. *The Water-Babies: Fairy Tale for a Land-Baby*. London: Macmillan, 1863.

Lamont, Victoria. *Westerns: A Women's History*. Lincoln, NE: University of Nebraska Press, 2016.

LaSalle, Mick. "Workers' Souls Lost in 'Space.'" *San Francisco Chronicle*, February 19, 1999.

Mackey, John. "The Whole Foods Alternative to ObamaCare." *Wall Street Journal*, August 12, 2009.

MacNeill, Ben Dixon. "Duke." *The American Mercury*, August 1929, 430–438.

Martin, Roger L. "The Virtue Matrix: Calculating the Return on Corporate Responsibility." *Harvard Business Review*, March 2002.

McCarroll, Meredith. "Hillbillies Need No Elegy." *The Bitter Southerner*. Available online: https://bittersoutherner.com/hillbillies-need-no-elegy-appalachian-reckoning (accessed September 27, 2024).

McMurtry, Larry. *In a Narrow Grave; Essays on Texas*. Austin, TX: Encino Press, 1968.

McMurtry, Larry. *Duane's Depressed*. New York, NY: Simon and Schuster, 1999.

Mellen, Joan. "The Little Fellow." In *Modern Times*, 6–22. London: British Film Institute, 2006.

Miller, Eric C. "Dr. Harry Emerson Fosdick, 'Shall Fundamentalists Win?'" New York City, NY (May 21, 1922). *Voices of Democracy* 14 (2019): 18–31.

Montague, Zach. "Doug Coe, Influential Evangelical Leader, Dies at 88." *New York Times*, February 22, 2017.

Moreton, Bethany. "Jesus Saves: Christians in the Age of Debt." Unpublished manuscript.

Moss, Jesse, dir. *The Family*. Season 1, episode 5, "Wolf King." Aired August 9, 2019, on Netflix.

Moyers, Bill. "The Image Makers." *A Walk Through the 20th Century*. Transcript. April 14, 1983. Available online: https://billmoyers.com/content/image-makers.

"Mr. Kingsley's Water-Babies." *London Times*, January 26, 1864, 6.

Mrema, Shama. "The Worship Song Song by Random Action Verb Worship." Video. March 15, 2020. Available online: https://www.youtube.com/watch?v=fWicNLXxtj4&t=12s.

National Parks Service, U.S. Department of Interior. "Haymarket Martyrs' Monument." National Historical Landmark Nomination. OMB no. 1024-0018, 1995.

Oppenheimer, Mark. "From One Benefactor, Diverse Seeds in Theology." *New York Times*, July 17, 2010.

Oppenheimer, Mark. "A Muckraking Magazine Creates a Stir Among Evangelical Christians." *New York Times*, November 8, 2014.

Poe, Annabeth. "Christianity Plus Cattle: Cowboy Churches Are on the Rise." *Carolina Connection*, January 13, 2020. Available online: https://carolinaconnection.org/2020/01/13/christianity-plus-cattle-cowboy-churches-on-the-rise.

Pope, Liston. *Millhands and Preachers: A Study of Gastonia*. New Haven, CT: Yale University Press, 1942.

Proulx, Annie, Larry McMurtry, and Diana Ossana. *Brokeback Mountain: Story to Screenplay*. New York, NY: Scribner, 2005.

Rogers, Glenn. "I'll Wear No Man's Collar." Guest column. *Reporter-Statesman*, March 7, 2024.

Roosevelt, Theodore. "The Strenuous Life" (speech). April 10, 1899. Transcript edited by Leroy G. Dorsey, Voices of Democracy. Available online: https://voicesofdemocracy.umd.edu/roosevelt-strenuous-life-1899-speech-text.

Rothstein, Richard, and Leah Rothstein. *Just Action: How to Challenge Segregation Enacted Under the Color of Law*. New York, NY: Liveright, 2023.

Sager, Mike. "The Devil and John Holmes." *Rolling Stone*, June 15, 1989.

Seidman, Rachel F. "This Little House of Mine." *Common-Place: The Journal of Early American Life* 3.3 (April 2003). Available online: https://commonplace.online/article/little-house-mine.

Sharlet, Jeff. "Jesus Plus Nothing: Undercover Among America's Secret Theocrats." *Harper's Magazine*, March 2003.

Shawn, Wallace. "Are You Smarter than Thomas Jefferson? Why I Call Myself a Socialist." *TomDispatch*, February 3, 2011. Available online: https://tomdispatch.com/wallace-shawn-are-you-smarter-than-thomas-jefferson.

Silliman, Daniel. "An Evangelical Is Anyone Who Likes Billy Graham: Defining Evangelicalism with Carl Henry and Networks of Trust." *Church History* 90, no. 3 (December 17, 2021): 621–643.

Silver, Charles. *Charles Chaplin: An Appreciation*. New York, NY: Museum of Modern Art, 1989.

Slotkin, Richard. *Gunfighter Nation: The Myth of the Frontier in Twentieth Century America*. Norman, OK: University of Oklahoma Press, 1998.

Smith, Lillian. *Killers of the Dream*. New York, NY: W. W. Norton, 1961.

Thomason, Kristen. "'He Gets Us' Is Feeding Information to Data Analysts and, Ultimately, Conservative Political Groups." *Baptists News Global*, March 24, 2023. Available online: https://baptistnews.com/article/he-gets-us-is-feeding-massive-amounts-of-data-to-cambridge-analytica-and-conservative-political-groups.

Tyson, Timothy B. "Commemorating North Carolina's Anti-Confederate Heritage, Too." *News & Observer*, August 17, 2017.

United Methodist Church Council of Bishops. *In Defense of Creation: The Nuclear Crisis and a Just Peace: Foundation Document*. Nashville, TN: Graded Press, 1986.

Vaca, Daniel. *Evangelicals Incorporated: Books and the Business of Religion in America*. Cambridge, MA: Harvard University Press, 2019.

Van West, Carroll. *Capitalism on the Frontier: Billings and the Yellowstone Valley in the Nineteenth Century*. Lincoln, NE: University of Nebraska Press, 1993.

Wheeler, Barbara G. "Fit for Ministry? A New Profile of Seminarians." *The Christian Century* 118, no. 12 (April 11, 2001): 16–18.

White, John. *Westerns*. New York, NY: Routledge, 2011.

White, W. Thomas. "Boycott: The Pullman Strike in Montana." *Montana: The Magazine of Western History* 29, no. 4 (October 1979): 4–5.

Will, Barbara. "The Nervous Origins of the American Western." *American Literature* 70, no. 2 (June 1998): 293–316.

Willick, Jason. "The Man Who Discovered 'Culture Wars.'" *Wall Street Journal*, May 25, 2018.

Wright, Lawrence. "The Future Is Texas." *New Yorker*, July 10 & 17, 2017.

Index

Index